Fundamentals of Public Credit Analysis

CONTEMPORARY STUDIES IN ECONOMIC AND FINANCIAL ANALYSIS, VOLUME 65

Editors: Professors Robert J. Thornton and J. Richard Aronson,
Lehigh University

CONTEMPORARY STUDIES IN ECONOMIC AND FINANCIAL ANALYSIS

An International Seires of Monographs

Series Editors: **Robert J. Thornton** and **J. Richard Aronson**

Lehigh University

Fundamentals of
Public Credit Analysis

by   ARTHUR J. HAUSKER
President
Dealer & Bondholder Services, Inc.
Summit, New Jersey

 **JAI PRESS INC.**

Greenwich, Connecticut   *London, England*

Library of Congress Cataloging-in-Publication Data

Hausker, Arthur J.
   Fundamentals of public credit analysis
  by Arthur J. Hausker.
      p.   cm. — (Contemporary studies in economic and financial
analysis ; v. 65)
   Includes index.
   ISBN 1-55938-152-3
   1. Debts, Public—United States—Accounting. 2. State bonds—
United States—Ratings. 3. Municipal bonds—United States—
Ratings. 4. Credit ratings—United States. I. Title.
II. Series.
HJ8119.H35   1991
657′.835048—dc20   90-26913

Dedicated to
T. G. Evensen and Richard C. Lonergan

CONTENTS

CONTENTS

PART II.   CREDIT RATING PERSPECTIVES

PART IV. APPENDICES

Preface

This book is intended for the use of entry level professionals in the area of public finance, and for students of government whose interests or academic requirements involve a knowledge of public credit analysis.

The author believes that in the area of credit analysis references to actual financings and credit reports (in Part II and the Appendix) referred to in the main text will make many points clearer than the use of words alone. Part II includes perspectives on specific credit rating issues, contributed by various experts in the field. Some of these materials, particularly some of the credit rating worksheets included in Part III, may seem dated. They have been included because they provide classic illustrations of many of the central problems that will continue to confront credit analysis into the 1990s.

Special thanks are due to reviewers of the text material, including James Cusser, Kidder Peabody; Claire Cohen, Fitch Investors Service; Hyman Grossman, Standard & Poor's; William McCarthy, Fitch Investors Service; Joan Perry, formerly with the American Municipal Bond Assurance Corporation (AMBAC); Robert Riehle, Wainwright and Ramsey, Inc.; Freda S. Johnson (Freda S. Ackerman), formerly with Moody's Investors Service; and Joseph Mysak, Editor—The Bond Buyer. I am particularly indebted to Dr. James Leigland, of the University of Kentucky, for his inspiring me to write the book, his contribution to text material and for many other personal contributions too numerous to mention. I am also indebted to Moody's Investors Service; Standard & Poor's; The Bond Buyer (and Credit Markets); California Municipal Statistics; and Mr. James Spiotto, of Chapman and Cutler, for their contributions to the book.

Introduction

A few years back I had an experience that shattered my smug feeling about how important it was to be a municipal credit analyst. During one particular week of commuting to New York a young lady just out of grad school happened to be riding to the City and shared the four seat configuration with me and two other regulars. We began sharing ideas and discovering who the other persons were.

On Friday, the young lady decided it was time to find out about me. She asked, "What do you do?" I proudly replied, "I'm a municipal bond analyst." She had me pegged as a college professor due to the fact that I wore a beard. Her response was, "Oh, I'm disappointed!"

Can you image that? Here, at a time just after the New York City fiasco, was a real live person who was unimpressed with meeting a municipal analyst. I just don't get no respect!

*   *   *

The practice of municipal credit analysis is not a new phenomenon. The first recorded analytical endeavor took place not in this century, nor in the last, nor even in the post Renaissance period. The first analyst of record was Pliny (the younger), who in 111 AD was sent by the emperor Trajan to the provinces of Bethynia and Pontus to "inspect the cities and help them with their financial woes."

Mr. Robert Wilken, writing in *The Christians as the Romans Saw Them*, further states that:

> the cities in the area were prospering, but some had misused their resources. Overly enthused about outdoing their neighbors with a new amphitheater or a more spacious gymnasium some cities simply lacked the funds to carry out their construction projects.

Was this written about cities in the first century in the Christian era, or does it have a ring of familiarity that sounds like some situations we know today?

Wilken states further that in one of Pliny's letters to Trajan he wrote, "I am now examining the finances of the town of Prusa, expenditures, revenues, and sums owing, and finding the inspection increasingly necessary the more I look into the accounts."

In my own experience, which dates back to 1955, I first became aware of credit analysis and credit reporting with my exposure to John Nuveen & Co., who I rightfully or wrongfully credit with having invented municipal credit research as we know it today. One of Nuveen's foremost contributions to credit reporting was to furnish to portfolio managers annual reports and credit updates on bonds that Nuveen had underwritten and sold to them.

When I first joined a Wall Street firm (Halsey Stuart & Co.) in a credit analyst role I told them my goal was to establish a research service that would make Nuveen jealous. I knew that the goal was an ambitious one, but one I would bend every effort to reach. The leg up that I had in my endeavor was that I had just completed five years of credit analysis in my work with the portfolio of one of the nation's largest casualty insurance firms.

In Part I of this book, I attempt to sketch the fundamentals of credit analysis. I have included credit analysis worksheets and other analytical aids developed over 30 years in nearly every aspect of public finance. Subsequent Parts provide what I consider to be a unique and innovative learning approach to this field, with classic aspects of the subject from highly respected Wall Street professionals.

The writing in this book is meant to be simple and straightforward— the book's purpose is to aid the reader to understand the fundamentals of both public credit analysis and financial analysis partly by dispelling some of the myths and cutting through some of the complexities often incorrectly associated with these subjects.

About the Author

Arthur J. Hausker is president and co-founder of Dealer & Bondholder Services, Inc. and is retired from Wall Street after 34 years of service in all aspects of municipal finance and the municipal bond business. He began his working career as a Bank Examiner with the State of Minnesota, then moved into municipal finance with T.G. Evensen & Associates (now Evensen Dodge Inc.), in Minneapolis. After 5 years there he moved to the deal side of the bond business, and was active in underwriting, trading and sales. Subsequently he moved to Allstate Insurance Company for 5 years portfolio work.

After Allstate Hausker started a Municipal Research Department for Halsey Stuart & Co. (which was later acquired by Bache & Co.), and other Wall Street firms. His experience also includes supervising the Debt Management Assistance Program for local government units at the State of New Jersey.

Hausker's final role before retiring was to assist in forming the Municipal Division of Fitch Investors Service rating agency.

Hausker holds a Bachelor of Science of Science degree in Economics and Business Administration and is a Senior Fellow with the Institute of Public Administration in New York. He is a member of the GFOA, Municipal Analysts Group of New York and the Municipal Forum of New York.

Part I

CREDIT ANALYSIS

Chapter I

The Practice of Credit Analysis

An important distinction should be made between Credit Analysis and Financial Analysis. The two functions serve different kinds of users. Financial Analysis is very broad in scope, although, depending on the user, it may focus on a very narrow range of financial activity of the subject under study.

Credit Analysis, on the other hand, is narrower in scope, and the users are generally limited to those involved, one way or another, in the borrowing activities of the subject under consideration. Credit analysis can have two facets, descriptive or evaluative. The descriptive analysis is just that, it describes the pledge securing debt, describes the borrower, and describes the aspects of the pledge that the investor ought to be concerned about. Objectivity is more or less assured in accurate descriptive credit analysis in that opinions should not enter into description.

Evaluation in credit analysis is of two types, quantitative and qualitative. The quantitative side is similar to descriptive analysis, but seeks to do more than describe. It measures. The qualitative analysis evaluates; it assigns values to the quantitative measurements.

ABILITY TO PAY

Qualitative analysis aims at determining the ability of a borrower to meet, on a timely basis, interest and principal payments on debt, or debt substitute obligations such as leases or other contracts. All three "nationally recognized statistical rating organizations" operating in the realm of government finance (Fitch, Moody's and Standard & Poor's) are primarily engaged in ascertaining ability to pay.

An important qualitative judgment in the analysis of credit of state and local government is that the ability to pay is almost inherent in the existence of a governmental unit that has the powers of taxation. Therefore, a judgment may really be made as to the likelihood that the borrower may NOT be able to meet its obligations. This is true especially for general obligation bonds. A similar judgment could be made if the debt is secured by payments from a governmental unit that has the power to fix "rates, fees and charges" for providing broad based essential services.

Ability to pay, and the quality of the ability, are not best measured by comparison to some other borrower. This method can end up with results as fallacious as those resulting from "grading on the curve" at some educational institutions. If all the test takers are at an average ability level, the highest scores may not be "high" in an absolute sense.

This is not to say that comparisons have no validity in the process of evaluation, but great care must be used in determining the standard utilized. The credit of the United States government is assumed by all to be of the highest grade. But if the commonly used yardsticks of credit worthiness were applied to this credit it would fail the test. Only two things give the United States the claim to high credit, the unlimited power to tax and the printing press. Other borrowers with poor financial practices and management, and who never repay debt (just roll it over), find it difficult to enjoy a credit rating equivalent to "investment grade."

Not all borrowers have access to the lender of last resort, the Federal Reserve System, for the purposes of rolling over debt if the market is closed. New York State's Urban Development Corporation and the City of New York learned the hard way that closed access to markets can force an unwilling default.

Ability to pay may be altered by drastic increases in taxes or charges for a service, or in the case of an enterprise, a competing facility. An example of what competition can do to a revenue bond is the Chicago Calumet Skyway's bonds. A partially elevated toll road from Chicago's south side to the Indiana Turnpike in the vicinity of Calumet, Indiana, the Skyway was financed by bonds secured by the toll charges, after payment of operating and maintenance expenses. The Skyway provided a time and distance saving, which at the time was well worth the toll charge. This arrangement should have led to a successful bond issue. What happened?

The State Highway Department, in conjunction with the Federal Highway Administrator, constructed a free interstate highway (I-94, the Dan Ryan Expressway, or as Mayor Daley often called it, the GREAT Dan Ryan Expressway), connecting an existing expressway to I-80, which subsequently incorporated the Indiana Turnpike into its route. The Skyway could not stand the competition of a free route and, as traffic dwindled, the bonds went into default.

The Skyway Authority had, of course, covenanted to increase the toll charges if necessary, but as can happen with the price of any commodity or service, increases in the price reach a point of diminishing returns. The bonds are still in default, not paying all the interest due. The principal on the bonds was set into a single maturity (a "balloon" payment) due in 1995.

Needless to say, the bondholders will not be paid at maturity unless the debt is refinanced. That is not likely for a bond that cannot currently pay its way. The bonds could end up as "perpetual bonds," like those of the Canadian National Railway.

Tax increases can reach the point of being so onerous as to cause taxpayers to "vote with their feet," and leave town or the state, thus diminishing the tax base and further increasing taxes on those remaining. New York City and State have experienced this particular phenomenon.

WILLINGNESS TO PAY

Willingness to pay has two aspects. The first is the express (or implied, in the case of tax supported bonds) covenant to impose taxes or charges on a constituency at a level that will produce revenues sufficient for payment of principal and interest on debt. In some states the issuer has the power to levy taxes for debt, but does not necessarily covenant to do so.

The second aspect of willingness involves those taxes and/or charges and the willingness of the taxpayer/user to pay them. In some individual instances the willingness of the payer might be based on his or her personal ability to pay. The best example of the unwillingness to pay soaring taxes occurred in California and caused passage in 1978 of the infamous Proposition 13—with subsequent after shocks in many other states. Fortunately the taxpayer revolt did not result in non-payment of debt. In the Golden State, not all taxpayers can afford prosperity, or at least not the prosperity of the real estate market.

Most states have some kind of law requiring property to be assessed at some level relative to the value of property in the market. Many things contributed to the inflation of real estate values in California as well as the entire nation in the late 1970s. Among the contributing factors were the soundness of real estate as an investment during and after the stock market "crash" of 1969-70, the favorable federal income tax treatment of mortgage interest and property taxes, the pressure from the extraordinary rate of formation of households occasioned by a high divorce rate and the desire of single persons to want their own residences. In California these factors were reinforced by a tremendous in-migration during the 1970s.

The Peter Principle of government expenditures always rising to the level of the amount of income received seemed to find its greatest expression at the local level in California. It appears that California municipalities were ready and willing to avail themselves of the windfall resulting from higher property values.

If a government budget is relatively constant in terms of dollars, an increase in assessment of property should result in a lowering of tax rates, in that tax rates are a function of application of the dollar amount of taxes against the assessment roll. Property tax rates are expressed in "cents per $100" value of property, or "mills per thousand" value. In too many areas the tax rates did not go down.

As if the local tax burden growth was not enough, Californians watched the state accumulate unconscionable surpluses, riding the tide of a high level of economic activity against which state taxes were based. A surplus of approximately $5 billion (high at the time) was more than voters in the state could take. Messrs. Jarvis and Gann, the instigators of the constitutional referendum, found more than sufficient taxpayers (and non-taxpayers) to pass the question. The result of the amendment was to roll back tax assessments and to severely limit future tax increases and assessment increases. In many ways, the medicine had foreseeable and unforseeable side effects, but the forseeable is not always evident if one is looking in another direction.

Fortunately the tax rate limits did not apply to taxes levied for outstanding general obligation bonds, for which unlimited taxes were pledged in referendums authorizing the bonds. Stresses were put on many "tax allocation" or "tax increment" bonds which are often highly dependent on rising assessments and tax rates. Many "near miss" defaults occurred, as well as some temporary defaults, before a slower rate of growth caught up with debt service requirements. As a result of Proposition 13 the new issue market of general obligation bonds in California all but disappeared (although it was already weak due to the fact that a two-thirds majority was required to pass a bond issue referendum).

An unwillingness to pay that "will live in infamy" is the revolt of electric ratepayers in the State of Washington that culminated in 1983 in the largest default on state and local bonds in history. The event being, of course, the default of the Washington Public Power Supply System (WPPSS, pronounced in the bond business, "Wups," not "Whoops," as the media erroneously refer to it—the bond business simply applied an acronym to WPPSS whereas the press apparently thinks that the name came from the default event).

Uncontrollable construction costs, poor management practices, and borrowing at the highest interest rates in history led to power costs that were, to Washingtonians, as intolerable as California's surpluses were to property owners in that state in 1978. This default will be discussed in more detail below.

UNWILLINGNESS—NEAR MISS

One way for an entity, public or private, to avoid contractual obligations such as debt (a bond is a debt contract) is to file bankruptcy. Basically there are two kinds of bankruptcy, voluntary and involuntary (forced by creditors). Chapter 9 of the Federal Bankruptcy Code (as amended) provides that governmental units may not be forced into bankruptcy, they may file only on a voluntary basis. Whether bankruptcy is voluntary or otherwise there are two classes of creditors—secured and unsecured. A secured creditor has his advance of credit secured by a pledge of specific assets, e.g., a mortgage on property or a pledge of accounts receivable. These assets may be sold to satisfy the claim of the creditor, to whom they are pledged if there are liquidation proceedings ordered by the court.

In the late 1970s, the San Jose, California, School District, like many other local governments in the state, found itself severely crimped by the limitations imposed by Proposition 13. The District could not raise taxes enough to make pay raises to teachers, which had been contracted for. The teachers union threatened to strike, so the District filed bankruptcy. This kind of action would normally not be expected from a debtor who wanted to protect his credit.

Fortunately for investors the bonds were secured by unlimited taxes, collected by the county treasurer and held for the bondholders. If the bonds were not secured by a specific tax the bondholders could have been left with an obligation paying less than the contacted-for interest rate, or, even worse, being paid at maturity at less than the stated amount of principal.

As mentioned above, the best (or perhaps the worst) illustration of the results of unwillingness to pay on the part of a constituency is the WPPSS default in 1983. WPPSS contracted for nearly simultaneous construction of five nuclear power plants, numbered 1-5, inclusive. The projects were separated into two groups, projects 1, 2, and 3, and projects 4 and 5. Projects 1, 2 and 3 were first initiated, and through a complex contractual arrangement the power to be generated was sold to participating public owned utilities (municipal systems and power districts), REA systems and investor-owned utilities, and resold by them to a federal agency, the Bonneville Power Administration (BPA). The Grand Coulee Dam in Washington State is owned and operated by BPA, along with the hydro-electric generating facilities constructed at the dam site, and more importantly to WPPSS, power transmission lines.

Under a so-called "net billing agreement" between the participants, WPPSS and BPA, the power from the nuclear generating plants would be blended with that from BPA's hydro-electric plants and sold to the participants (already customers of BPA) and delivered on BPA's transmission lines, which were already in place.

Under these agreements, BPA contracted to be responsible for debt service payments on bonds issued for projects 1, 2 and 3, and its purchase of nuclear power from WPPSS was to be treated as an operating expense of BPA, ranking ahead of its payments on debt to the U.S. Treasury. Subsequent Congressional action formalized the arrangement, and with the broad rate base of BPA to support them, the bonds were rated Aaa by Moody's and by Standard & Poor's.

Due to later limitations imposed on BPA by the federal government, projects 4 and 5 could not benefit from the same billing agreements, and the aggregate power demands of the participants in those projects formed a source of revenue to finance the debt incurred for the two projects.

The WPPSS 4 and 5 bond default resulted in part from the use of a "take or pay contract," also called a "hell or high water contract," between WPPSS and the 4 and 5 participants. These contractual arrangements were later declared invalid by the Washington State Supreme Court. In essence the contract, widely used across the country, provided that the participants, up to the extent of their participation, pay all of the costs to WPPSS resultant from construction and operation of the projects, including the debt service on the bonds. The contract also provided that "come hell or high water" (phrase not in the contract), i.e., even if the projects were never completed, any costs associated with projects, "mothballing," debt service, etc., would be paid by the participants. The State Supreme Court later ruled that this contractual arrangement illegally put the "dry hole risk" on the participants, not on WPPSS.

A series of events, exacerbated by poor management on the part of WPPSS officials, together with rapidly increasing power rates through BPA to finance a similar obligation for projects 1, 2 and 3, resulted in ratepayer disgruntlement. Revised power need estimates—unexpectedly low—led to cancellation of projects 4 and 5. This left the participants and their customers responsible for total costs involved in halting construction and for debt outstanding totaling $2.25 billion. Principal and interest over the life of the bonds total about $7.5 billion—all for nothing. Through the take or pay contracts the participants had guaranteed repayment of that debt.

The uproar led to a case before the State Supreme Court regarding the enforceability of the contracts. The appeal was made to an elected court. The Court examined state laws to determine if the contracts were signed for purposes authorized by statutes. One of the key purposes outlined in the contracts involved the purchase by the participants of the "capability" of the two generating plants. In what most observers consider to have been a political decision, the Court ruled that municipalities and public utility districts in the State were authorized to purchase electricity from, or ownership in, generating facilities. There was no authorization to purchase capability, which in the Court's judgment was neither electricity nor ownership. The contracts, by their nature, resulted in the guarantee of debt, which was not authorized. Therefore the contracts were deemed to be unenforceable.

Power rates in the Pacific Northwest are among the lowest in the nation. Some experts have argued that after paying $7.5 billion for project 4 and 5 debt, and paying for completion of project 2, and the debt for the incomplete projects 1 and 3 (completion of project 3 has been delayed and project 1 is all but terminated), average user rates would still be low compared to the national average. This is scant comfort to a user who has electric heat and sees his bill increase by tenfold, nor is the argument necessarily valid in all cases. For example, rural electric co-ops have a low user base and the cost per user would be much higher than in a densely populated area. Moreover, the willingness to pay in the WPPSS case would not be assessed on the basis of a comparison of user rates to those, say, of Con Edison customers (much higher rates). Much more important would be the exceptionally low rates in place before the nuclear construction program was begun. Unwillingness to pay was reflected in the State's highest court.

Not challenged in the Court, and perhaps pointedly unaddressed by the Court, was the nature of the contracts securing payment for bonds issued for projects 1, 2 and 3, wherein some of the same participants purchased the capability of those projects and resold it to BPA. Could they sell what they could not purchase? If not, is BPA obligated to make payment?

TAXES SECURING GENERAL OBLIGATION BONDS

As mentioned earlier, general obligation bonds secured by taxes usually involve ad valorem taxes on property, i.e., taxes based on the value of the property. In most states the taxable property includes real estate, some kinds of tangible personal property such as automobiles, household goods, business machinery and equipment, and business inventories. Intangible personal property includes such things as bank accounts and stocks and bonds (the principal amount, rather than the interest income). However, most states have dropped taxes on "intangibles" due to collection difficulties and the fact that the cost of collection often exceeded revenues. Some states have bowed to political pressures and reduced or dropped the personal property tax, at least on business inventories.

Wherever there is a tax there will be efforts to either avoid the tax (legal act), or to evade it (illegal). Annual "spring inventory" sales by merchants are often due not to the generosity of the merchant, but are well calculated to avoid the annual "spring roundup" of inventories by the assessor. Reno and other cities situated on or near the California state line have been the locations of gigantic warehouses in which merchandise enroute to California is stored temporarily at the "wrong" time of the year. Such arrangements are attractive to shippers as long as Nevada does not impose a tax on goods in those warehouses.

Of course, states and their local government units can impose only those taxes authorized by their constitutions or tax laws. Some states, although authorized to levy property taxes, do not make such a levy for state purposes, but vacate the privilege in favor of local government units.

The tax base, the aggregate value of all taxable property in the taxing jurisdiction, is represented as the Assessed Value of Taxable Property in a financial statement, implying that the value has been determined by the local/state assessor. The method that the assessor uses to make this determination will vary at least from state to state, depending on each state's laws regarding the procedure of assessment.

Not all property within the bounds of the taxing unit is subject to taxation. Among the types of property exempt from the collection are the land that streets are located on (including the sidewalks, if any), church property (except in some states, income producing property), state and local government owned land and buildings, and, in some states, property of nonprofit organizations. Property owned by the federal government is also exempt from taxation.

Within a state the laws will determine whether or not procedures for determining value are uniform throughout the state. One kind of procedure would be to measure the number of square feet in a parcel of ground and assign value per square foot. The same procedure could be used with buildings. This base value could be adjusted by style and quality of construction. For residences, adjustments could be based on number of baths, fireplaces, attached or detached garage, etc. This method of valuation may or may not have any relationship to market value.

A broad based awareness of the inequities of real estate assessments, and particularly the problems associated with systematic underassessments, brought about laws in many states during the late 1970s requiring regular and more frequent assessments. As mentioned earlier, homeowners in California were victimized by the re-assessments and people on fixed or low incomes were literally taxed out of their homes while tax rates stayed constant.

Tax assessors were not always simply inept in assessing property at levels far below market value, nor were they just being generous or protective to homeowners and senior citizens. In some cases they were practicing an art called "shift the tax burden."

Counties include cities, villages and townships within their bounds. Rural consolidated school districts usually include several townships and perhaps a village within their perimeters, as do some suburban districts. The tax levy for the larger taxing unit is distributed over the smaller ones on the basis of proportional assessed value. If the assessor of a given village wants to ease the tax burden of his constituency he can use assessment standards that he thinks are lower than those of his neighbors.

In Minnesota, several years ago, the ratio between assessed value of property and the estimated market value was 30 percent. On the Iron Range area of the state the ratio was 10-12 percent. This was to elude a portion of a small state property tax levy and the levy of St. Louis County, which included the City of Duluth. Homeowners on the "Range" lived in the best of all possible worlds. Taxes on mined iron ore, levied by the state, were returned to the local municipalities, and during the heydays of the iron ore industry their taxes were very low. Palatial schools were built and were the envy of the rest of the state. When the prices of iron ore, and even taconite, dropped precipitously, the schools were nearly abandoned.

Most states have taken steps to ensure uniform assessments, usually through a state assessor office. Re-assessments may be required, for example, every five years, with 20 percent of the properties being re-assessed each year. Some states require that property be assessed at 100 percent of market value, with some acquiescing at 80 percent in order to insure against over-zealous appraisers.

Some municipalities in New Jersey have provided good examples of the need for such insurance. Commercial and high-rise apartment properties felt that they were the targets of over-appraisal and over-collection of taxes. Successful law suits were brought in several cases and the tax refunds were so large that bonds had to be issued to raise the funds for the rebates.

A similar phenomenon in New Jersey involved complaints by large apartment complex owners, especially in rent controlled or rent leveling communities. The owners went to court in hopes of a finding that rental income was more a determinant of value than an appraisal based on the usual factors of land, buildings, etc. This successful plea won some re-assessments. In some townships and boroughs the taxpayers gained tax refund judgments from courts, and the taxing jurisdictions had to issue bonds to pay the judgments when they were sizable. Budgets of the townships and boroughs were also affected by the re-assessments.

Reference was made earlier (under Willingness to Pay) to tax rates. Some analysts, and others, wanting to compare tax burdens in different municipalities, compare tax rates. This can be an inaccurate measure, given that assessment standards may never be fully uniform even within as small a jurisdiction as a county. The best method of comparison is to look at actual tax bills for similar parcels of property. Admittedly this can be difficult due to the fact such comparisons are seldom reported.

Tax rates are simply a derivation from the application of an amount to be taxed as spread against the tax base, unless a rate for a special purpose is arbitrarily fixed. Tax rates are usually expressed in terms of either "mills" (or "millage") per $1,000 of of assessed value, or dollars per $100 of value. One mill produces $1.00 against $1,000 of tax base, as does a $1.00 rate against $100 of tax base.

To establish a mill rate needed to raise a given amount of tax revenue move the decimal point three places to the left on the amount of total tax base then, divide that amount by the amount of revenue desired. To establish a dollar tax rate move the decimal point two places to the left, and divide as with the mill rate formula.

Taxpayers can be confused or intimidated by their tax bills, as happened to a lady taxpayer in Minneapolis (as reported in a local newspaper). The city had done some resurfacing of the street on which she lived, and her property was one of many to be specially assessed for the benefit. When the tax bill arrived, it included an item of "Sealcoat..... $....." The woman called city hall to complain. "I don't even own a fur coat," she pleaded, "but you should go after my neighbor. She has a *mink* coat!"

TAX COLLECTING

A key factor in the appraisal of credit is to ascertain who collects the taxes for a municipality, who holds the taxes after collection, when taxes are levied, and what, if any, are the provisions for delinquent taxes. The ratio of collections to levies is very important.

In many states taxes are levied and collected by the county auditor, who sends the tax bills out for payment. Payments are made to the county treasurer. If any funds are to be disbursed, for example, to the paying agent for bonds, the treasurer makes the disbursement.

The tax bill received by a property owner reflects an aggregate of all the taxes levied by any taxing political subdivision authorized to tax his property. The county auditor receives certification from each authorized taxing unit as to the amount of money that the unit has decided to raise via the property tax. When the county's own tax amount is added to all other amounts the auditor is prepared to "spread the levy."

Some taxing units may be authorized to levy only a specific amount of taxes, measured in either mill rates of taxes or dollar/cent tax rates. These are very special instances, however, and generally the taxing units are not limited in that fashion except for upper limits of tax rates that fall on property.

When the auditor is ready to make the levies he ascertains from the tax roll aggregates how much of the county assessed value lies in each underlying taxing subdivision (taxing unit) and assigns a portion of the county levy to each unit. He then makes the same determination for taxing units which overlap one another, e.g., school districts, municipalities, etc.

In states where the county auditor does not actually levy the tax, or where the county treasurer does not collect the tax, the local city, village or township will do those jobs. State laws may prescribe that the local unit remit the full amount of the county and school district levies back to those units at the end of the collection year and then absorb the delinquencies in that they are the only collecting mechanism for collecting current or delinquent taxes.

In Wisconsin, counties are not required to remit in full, but in practice they do. Statutes require tax liens to be put up for sale by the counties. When publishing a sale notice, counties usually provide that the county "shall be the sole bidder," thus fully absorbing delinquencies.

Tax collecting periods vary from state to state, as do tax due dates. Most states will allow splitting the tax bill into at least semi-annual payments. Some will have quarterly payments, and may even allow a discount on full payment made on the first due date. This encouragement provides taxing units with better cash flows and may preclude the necessity of short term borrowing (if allowed in the state).

In Texas even school districts may collect their own taxes, or as is more often the case, they and municipalities may hire a tax collector from the private sector and compensate him on the basis of performance. The costs of collection in this manner are, of course, added into the tax levy, as are any discounts granted.

In Minnesota, a rather unique levying device is used to protect bondholders. Tax levies for debt service are set at the time of bond sale award for the life of the bonds. Bond attorneys add a 5 percent excess levy to protect against delinquencies.

As noted above, an important aspect of credit analysis involves determining which office is responsible for tax collections. In some cases, the individual may be more important than the office, as illustrated by the tenure of the late Paul Powell, an elected Illinois Secretary of State. Mr. Powell did not collect any property taxes but he did collect motor vehicle license fees for the state. He had a disdain for anything except cash for payment of fees, and it was said that truckers were required to pay cash. People other than truckers (who traversed the state anyway and could go through Springfield) were given special dispensation and could pay by check. The instructions accompanying the registration forms were, however, very specific, stating that checks were to be payable to "Paul Powell," not to "Paul Powell Secretary of State," nor to "Secretary of State."

Mr. Powell died unexpectedly in office, and when the usual inventory of records was made approximately $800,000 was discovered in shoe boxes in his office. Fortunately no bonds were secured by motor vehicle registration fees.

There is, of course, no guaranty that tax collections will go to bondholders, or even that a debt service levy will be deposited to a debt service fund or credited to a debt service fund on the books of an issuer. Again, state laws will prevail. In the case of the San Jose School District, mentioned above, taxes were collected by the county auditor and held by him for bondholders.

Perhaps the best structural protection in the entire budgeting and tax collection procedures for state and local governments is that afforded by appropriations. Money appropriated for one purpose cannot be used for another. The collections of taxes must generally be allocated among the several purposes for which the tax levies were made. The first period tax collections may be half of the total annual levy; if so, each fund, including the debt service fund, is credited with half of its appropriated money.

If the money in the debt service fund is inadequate for meeting a payment due, the issuer may be able to temporarily transfer free balances from other funds, to be repaid before the end of the fiscal year, perhaps at the next collection period. The timing of debt service payments may cause special problems however. Principal is normally paid once a year, and interest paid semi-annually. As a result, one debt service payment is larger than the other.

There are two ways to avoid this potential problem. The first is to set principal payments just after the largest collection period. The other is to make semi-annual principal payments in a way that takes collection periods into account. One other pitfall an issuer may stumble into has to do with setting the first principal payment of a bond issue. Depending on what time of year the bonds are sold, there may not be time to include the first debt service payment in the new tax levy. Sometimes this trap is built into the statutes governing the issuance of debt.

In New Jersey, the first principal payment may not be longer than one year after the date of issue. Cash poor governments may have problems unless there are some escape clauses in the statutes.

Chapter II

Credit Characteristics of Issuers

STATES

Under the principles that established the nation, states were recognized as sovereign governments, yielding any of their powers only to the federal government, and only as prescribed under the federal constitution. About the only limits on the activities of states which are subject to federal jurisdiction are those dealing with trade between the states.

States can pass laws that are enforceable only within their boundaries. Laws of other states have no effect. Persons accused of crime, or those convicted, may find haven in a neighboring state, unless the states have extradition laws providing for their return to any or all states.

For the greater part, states are limited as to their total sovereignty only by their own constitutions. Subsequent to the many defaults by states after the civil war, many states changed their constitutions insofar as debt was concerned. Limits were set at (what even 50 years ago were very small) amounts of $100,000 or $200,000, except to raise funds with which "to suppress insurrection," or to march off to war.

Not many states have limits of amounts of taxes or tax rates, except for income taxes or sales taxes. Legislators can, and do, pass a large variety of so called "nuisance taxes." Taxes on alcoholic beverages, cigarettes, real estate transactions, utility bills are not onerous enough to engender tax revolts. Taxes that hit everybody's pocketbook are the kind that are generally limited by constitutions.

Rising expectations of what states should provide for their residents, prompted many new or revised constitutions after World War II. What some states had been unable to do with borrowed money, they could now do with a referendum. Today, with most borrowing still limited by referenda, purposes allowable include just about anything a legislature can convince the public of the necessity.

The debt authorized by the electorate usually pledges the "faith and credit" or "full faith and credit" of the state (FFC in bond market notation). In most cases, FFC also means full taxing power, but this does not necessarily mean "unlimited taxing power." The taxes a state may impose may also be limited by a constitution. The limit may be an amount or rate, rather than kind. Some states that do not levy a real estate tax covenant in a bond resolution that they will levy "ad valorem taxes without limit as to rate or amount" if necessary to provide monies with which to retire debt.

What FFC can mean is demonstrated by an issue of industrial development bonds that came to market from the State of Mississippi. This state has a degree of notoriety for issuing industrial development bonds backed by the general obligation of the state or its political subdivisions. The particular issue was one financing a shipbuilding yard, and the official statement recited that the bonds were backed by the full faith and credit of the State of Mississippi. On that basis one of the rating agencies assigned a rating that was the lowest investment grade level. Upon appeal of the rating, the state's attorney general was advised that the rating officer did not think that FFC included full taxing power. Upon being convinced that taxing power was included in the security, the rating was upgraded two steps.

As discussed below under Overlapping Debt in the section on general obligation bond analysis, some states have resorted to debt schemes other than direct debt to finance their purposes, when it is apparent that a referendum will not authorize borrowing.

If a bond issue is supported by a special limited tax, for example, a gasoline tax or a sales tax, the state should covenant to impose the tax as long as any bonds are outstanding, and not to reduce the tax. Such a pledge makes a revenue bond, and it should be analyzed as to coverage of debt service, etc.

MUNICIPALITIES

This category is all-encompassing in that it includes counties, cities, villages, boroughs, towns, townships, and school districts. School districts are included here because typically they issue general obligation bonds almost exclusively, and because of their close ties to the other kinds of "municipalities" mentioned.

Municipalities are creatures of the states in which they are located. In general, unless they are home rule charter cities, they are limited by statutes as to what their functions are, how they may raise revenue, and for what purposes they may borrow money. A local finance law, or a counterpart, dictates the time period during which debt may be outstanding, debt limits, in some states the maximum interest rate that may be paid, whether or not the bonds must be retired in installments, and the proportionate size between the largest and smallest installments.

Except for enterprise financing, i.e., water, sewer electric systems, most municipalities in most states issue general obligation bonds, FFC, with a pledge of "unlimited ad valorem taxes levied against all taxable property located within" the issuer's boundaries. An unlimited tax (UT) bond does not necessarily mean that only the property tax is pledged. The bonds are payable, in most instances from any legally available funds, but with a tax pledge the source of funds is defined and is broad based, and the taxes are levied for the particular purpose and should not be used for any other purpose.

Municipalities in most states may also, under statutes, issue "special obligation" bonds (or revenue bonds). The pledges may be in the form of user charges, as with a utility system, or a sales tax at the local level. The sales tax pledge may also be an allocation of a sales tax imposed by the state and shared with local governing units. Similarly, a city may pledge an allocation of state highway user taxes (gasoline, vehicle registration, etc.) shared with local units.

A local sales tax is usually voted, and as with a state, the issuer should covenant not to lower the tax and to continue to impose it as long as the bonds are outstanding. At the local level the tax is usually voted at a fixed rate and the referendum may, if the tax is to support a bond issue, pledge it over the life of the bonds. If the pledged tax is an allocation of a state tax there is no assurance of continuation or non-dimunition. Arizona protects cities and bondholders by continuing gas tax allocations to cities that have pledged the tax allocation to support debt.

School district bonds generally find favor with many investors and analysts because of the high degree of budget funding provided by most states. Tax collections at the local level are not as serious a consideration as with other municipalities. Additionally, some states give direct capital contribution funds to their school systems, and the funds at least should find their way to the Debt Service Fund of the school district. Among the states giving strongest support to schools are New York, Pennsylvania, California, Michigan, and Minnesota. School districts sometimes circumvent debt limits, and like other municipalities, or even states, are forced to do so in order to provide adequate facilities. Pennsylvania, Indiana and Kentucky have, or in the case of Pennsylvania did have, extremely tight constitutional debt limits that affected schools as well as all government units (including the states themselves). To accommodate the borrowing needs of school districts, laws were passed enabling the creation of school building authorities or non-profit corporations to borrow money to build schools for lease to school districts. All three states required the school districts to budget the lease rentals annually. Pennsylvania went so far as to provide that if a school district failed to budget the amount, the state Department of Education would withhold that amount from state-aid payments to the district and remit the money directly to the pay agent for the bonds. The State of New Jersey provided a similar arrangement under its Qualified Bond Act (for municipalities with poor market acceptance), except that payments are made to the pay agent without regard for budgeting.

California schools faced not a debt limit problem, but the problem of needing a two-thirds approval of a referendum to authorize a bond issue. That, coupled with the tax rate limits imposed by the Jarvis-Gann amendment (Proposition 13), resulted in special legislation.

SPECIAL DISTRICTS

As noted above in connection with Overlapping Debt, special districts can overlay one, or some, of a municipality, a school district or another special district. This type of quasi-governmental subdivision can provide almost any kind of service or facility that a municipality can, and some that a municipality cannot. Special districts have been created for mosquito abatement, fire protection, drainage, water, sewer, electric power supply and/or distribution, ports for air and/or water, education (e.g., junior colleges), parks, roads, hospitals, etc.

In most cases, special districts cannot levy unlimited ad valorem taxes for debt. Nor can they typically levy unlimited taxes or ad valorem taxes for any purpose. They tend generally to be small in area served, provide a special service in a special area such as drainage, and can levy taxes limited by rate if they tax at all. Some may impose a user charge, and perhaps issue a revenue bond payable from gross revenues of the user charge, levying a tax for operating expenses. Some may incur debt secured by a tax levy, again, limited by rate. With such a pledge the tax collection experience is a vital element in credit analysis. There are no possibilities of an overlevy to allow for delinquent tax payments, and a coverage factor of at least 1.25 times is desirable, perhaps even higher if no bond reserve is provided. If there are no other uses for the excess revenues, such as for expenses, the surplus would be used to call or purchase bonds, and the levy would cease after debt retirement.

An exception to the non-levy of unlimited ad valorem taxes for debt or operating expenses is the Texas based Municipal Utility District. In the past it has been possible for a real estate developer and members of his family to form a district in a developing, or hoped for developing area, near a large city. The developer and his family are the residents and taxpayers of such a district. The developer can install water and sewer systems at borrowed money cost of tax exempt bonds. As with an Industrial Development Bond, the borrower can borrow 100 percent of the costs of the project, in spite of a poor credit line.

These taxpayers could, for example, vote $5,000,000 in general obligation bonds (against $1,000,000 in assessed value) to finance water and sewer lines and systems to serve the homes, etc., to be constructed in the district. Perhaps only $1,000,000 would initially be issued, but the authorization would exist for the total. In such a situation, taxpayers who move into the new homes would not have any say about additional debt. Of course, the developer and his family pay taxes on their holdings too, and pay most of those taxes for some time.

The bonds would be paid in the first instance from net revenues of the water and sewer systems, and from taxes if the revenues were insufficient. The trouble for the analyst in this kind of financing is that the creditworthiness, or possible lack of it, of the developers is seldom disclosed.

Other states have had similar problems with so-called "development" districts. In California for example, a farmer decided to subdivide his land so as to enjoy the benefits of residential development of raw land. A district was formed which sold unlimited tax bonds to finance water and sewer. The hoped for real estate sales never occurred, so there never was an enlarged tax base to support the debt, and the bonds did default.

AUTHORITIES

Most authorities in most states are formed by the states to accomplish a purpose for which tax moneys cannot or should not be used. Sometimes the authority is titled "agency," as in the case of a Housing Finance Agency. Authorities seldom have any taxing power, an exception being The Metropolitan Airport Authority in Minnesota, which can levy a limited ad valorem tax in a several county area.

Some authorities are formed by bi-state compacts to serve two states with a commonality of interest. One of the outstanding examples of this kind of bond issuer is The Port Authority of New York and New Jersey, which has control over all of the underwater and overwater accesses to Manhattan Island from New Jersey, as well as all air access routes to the greater New York metropolitan area. The Authority was originally named the Port Authority of New York. New Jersey residents, who pay most for using the bridges and tunnels pressured for the change of name. Other bi-state agency/ authorities are primarily interstate toll bridge operators.

Most authorities are formed to borrow money for purposes that voters would not authorize via a referendum. Through leases to regular government entities citizens pay for the debt anyway. Sometimes the debt is paid through user charges rather than lease payments. Authorities in Pennsylvania were formed at the local level to provide water and sewer service to municipalities who could not legally borrow money to provide the necessary facilities. The authorities were classified as operating authorities, or as lease-back authorities. The operating authority operates the facility and either bills each user for the service, or sends a master billing to the municipality for the amount of operating expense and debt service, with the municipality making payment from any available funds. With the lease-back, the authority simply borrows, constructs, and then leases the facility to the municipality, which operates it, and sends its billings if a user charge is in effect. The lease payment is in an amount sufficient to pay debt service on the authority's debt.

California has a large number of special leasing arrangements because of the difficulty of obtaining voter approval of general obligation bonds. One method is the "joint powers authority (or agency)." Two or more governmental units will create the authority to provide a facility that both will have some use for, perhaps one more than the other. Los Angeles County rents a room in many city hall buildings.

Many state authorities, such as the Power Authority of the State of New York (PASNY), are not vote dodgers, but are created to provide a service that a state cannot provide under its constitution or statutes. An authority that can render an economic good or service can pay its way without resort to hidden tax money. The intent of the creator is usually evident in names such as Building Commission, or Leasing Authority. Authorities that utilize the so-called "moral obligation" pledge are discussed further under Overlapping Debt. The potential complexity of public finance is demonstrated in the Appendix, "New York State Constitutional and Statutory Provisions Regarding the Contracting of Debt."

Since the advent of industrial development financing and later, housing financing, by state and local government, a large number of authorities have been formed which do not provide a facility or service for government (in the generally accepted sense). They fill a role only as financing vehicles in order to pass on to a non tax exempt borrower the lower costs of borrowing at tax exempt bond rates. These third party beneficiaries are numerous in character, and include:

1. Private Industry (industrial and pollution control facilities)
2. Private Colleges
3. Private Hospitals (proprietary and non-profit)
4. Tax-Shelter Limited Partnerships
5. Private Real Estate Developers
   - Multifamily Housing
   - Single family Housing
6. Tenants or Mortgagors of Housing
7. Professional Athletic Team Owners and Players
8. Private Convention Operators and Attendees

The pledge securing bonds of this nature depends generally on the creditworthiness of the beneficiary of the financing, with the issuer playing only a passive role, and having no resources of its own to pledge. The bonds are secured by payments received by the issuer from the beneficiary, and passed on (usually) to a trustee for the benefit of the bondholders. The third party payment may be lease rentals, if the facility financed is leased to the third party, payments under an installment purchase contract or lease purchase contract, or simply loan payments made under a loan agreement with the third party. A security interest in the "demised property" should be established in favor of the bondholders so that there is, in case of a default which cannot be cured so as to make the bondholder "whole," the market value of the property offers some security other than the promise to make payments.

A mortgage on a hospital, though, does not make very good collateral for a loan, due to the limited use that a hospital building has in unaltered form, but it does prevent the borrower from incurring other debt pledging the real estate to a loan. If a hospital operator has an existing mortgage loan at the time of seeking tax exempt financing, the laws permitting the tax exempt loan allow for the prior loan to be refunded under the same loan as is used for new financing. This ties up the total hospital debt into a single package. The loan agreement should then restrict the ability of the hospital to undertake any loan obligation that would be on parity with the tax exempt loan.

In the case of any loan to a third party beneficiary, the bondholder should have the same protection against excessive additional debt incursion by the beneficiary. In case of a public utility or large industrial borrower with existing debt, the tax exempt loan may be secured by so called "mirror bonds." These bonds are issued not to the market but to the trustee (usually involved and always should be), and the payment on those bonds are the security for the tax exempt issue. The mirror bonds are issued on parity, or should be, with the senior secured debt of the borrower. That way there is no doubt as to the standing of the tax exempt bondholder in the event of bankruptcy of the borrower.

Individual investors may not be in a position to examine all the security intricacies involved in loans to third parties, and then may be better off investing in "common garden variety" tax exempts.

A device used to protect both the individual and professional investor from the possible credit weakness of a third party borrower is what the trade calls "credit enhancements." Enhancements may take the form of a Letter of Credit from a bank, or a surety bond from an insurance company. Here again, though, the credit standing of the enhancement provider must be ascertained. A credit rating from one of the full service nationally recognized rating agencies indicates that the credit standing has been checked.

In the case of tax exempt bonds for industry, it usually is a wasted effort to seek the opinion of a common stock analyst. Upon being queried as to the quality of a long term lease with an industrial company, the stock analyst is likely to provide a guess as to the next quarter's earnings. One can probably derive comfort from the old market adage that "if you like the common you have to love the bonds."

Industrial development bonds for a start-up operation should be avoided unless a guarantee or enhancement from a substantial provider is present. Insurance of the bond issue by one of the well known, and regarded, providers of insurance is not likely to be forthcoming, in that unlike almost all other kinds of insurance, the insurers of municipal bonds do not want to insure an issue where there is patently a loss possibility.

COLLEGE FINANCING

During the 1960s and early 1970s college financings were numerous, consisting primarily of two types—dormitories and educational facilities. Occasionally an issue would come along for a student union, or perhaps a field house or stadium. With at least a temporary lull in the baby boom, college bonds are seldom seen in the market in the 1980s, but older issues may turn up in the secondary market. Basic considerations for revenue bonds generally apply to these bonds, but in addition there are special characteristics that must be considered. Unless the school is very prestigious, a small school presents risk when the source of funds for bonds depends on enrollment. So called "parietal rules" were important considerations for dorms. These rules dictated that students were required to live in school furnished housing to the extent that such rules were necessary to keep dorms occupied, and thus paying debt service. Court rulings left some question as to the enforceability of the rules.

Educational and other facility bonds were usually paid from special fees charged to all students enrolled, so a covenant to raise the fee if necessary was looked for in the authorizing resolution. Overall cost of attending a particular school was measured against costs at schools deemed to be possibly competitive. The broadness of the geographical area represented by the student body was important, along with the number and kinds of degrees conferred, and whether or not graduate degrees were also conferred.

Chapter III

General Obligation Bond Analysis

As mentioned before, there are two aspects to credit analysis—quantitative and qualitative. The first deals with review of numbers, the second with verbal descriptions and evaluations of the nature of an issuer.

Quantitative analysis examines the so-called Financial Statement (not to be confused with a Financial Report), usually the one that appears in the document by which the bonds are offered for sale. In today's parlance this document is called an official statement, or O.S. It used to be called many other things, but mainly a Prospectus (as is used with a corporate offering) or Offering Circular.

GENERAL OBLIGATION BOND WORKSHEET

Probably the most effective tool in the credit analysis is a worksheet, like the one illustrated in Table 1 for use with general obligation bonds. Perhaps not all analysts would agree that this particular version is the best, but it is a very useful list and has served the writer well for many years.

A careful review of this form reveals a number of credit issues of special interest to the analyst. The first point of real analytical interest is Purpose. What are the bonds being sold for? A school, a water system, street improvements—or perhaps a purpose of somewhat more questionable value, such as a professional sports stadium or a convention center (the so-called "edifice complex").

The next item of interest is Authorization. How was the sale of bonds authorized? Was the bond issue subject to a referendum, whereby the voters had a say in the purpose of borrowing? This is an important consideration in Willingness to Pay. If a vote was required by law, what plurality of affirmative votes was required by law for the vote to pass? What was the

Table 1. General Obligation Bond—Check List

Name: _____ Amount: _____
Purpose: _____
Authorization: _____
_____

Financial Statement   As of: ___/___/___

Full Valuation (or Market Value): $ _____
Assessed Valuation (% of Full): $ _____
Direct Net Debt* (Inc. this issue): $ _____
Chargeable Overlapping Debt: $ _____
Direct and Overlapping Net Debt: $ _____
Ration Direct Debt/Full Value: $ _____
Overall Net Debt/Full Value: $ _____
Population—1970: _____ 1980: _____ Current: _____
Per Capita Direct Debt: $ _____
Per Capita Overall Net Debt: $ _____

*Amount excluded short term debt discussed later. Reflects deductions for self-supporting debt.

Tax Collections
    Tax Year: 19___   19___   19___
Amount Levied: $ $ $
% Collected Year of Levy   _____   _____   _____
% Collected Total   _____   _____   _____

Short Term Debt
Total Outstanding: $ _____
Type—BAN:* _____ TAN**: _____ RAN***: _____

In case of TAN or RAN when must they be paid?: _____
In case of BAN—Legal Term Limit: _____
How many times can BANs roll over?: _____
S.T.D. as Percent of Last Year's General Fund receipts: _____
*BAN-Bond Anticipation **TAN-Tax Anticipation ***RAN-Revenue Anticipation Notes

Overlapping Debt	Total Outstanding	% Applicable	Chargeable Amt.
County:	$_____	_____	_____
School District:	$_____	_____	_____
City G.O.:	$_____	_____	_____
City Revenue:	$_____	_____	_____
Other:	$_____	_____	_____
Total:	$_____	_____	_____

Future Financing

Subject Issuer: _____
Overlapping Tax Bodies: _____

(continued)

Table 1. *(continued)*

Receipts and Expenditures—General Fund

Fiscal Year Ending:	19____	19____	19____	19____
Begin Cash:	$_____	_____	_____	_____
Receipts:	$_____	_____	_____	_____
Transfers in:	$_____	_____	_____	_____
Total:	$_____	_____	_____	_____
Less Expenditures:	$_____	_____	_____	_____
Transfers out:	$_____	_____	_____	_____
Ending Cash:	$_____	_____	_____	_____
Less Encumbrances:	$_____	_____	_____	_____
Unencumbered Cash:	$_____	_____	_____	_____
Direct Net Debt Service as				
% of Revenue	$_____	_____	_____	_____
Highest Year Projected	$_____	_____	_____	_____

Pension Plan:

Contributory: _____ Non Contributory: _____ Part Contributory: _____

Unfunded Liability: _____

Amount: _____ % of Receipts: _____

Source of Revenues of General Fund (% in last fiscal year)

Property Taxes: _____ State: _____

Income Taxes: _____ Federal: _____

Sales Tax: _____ Other: _____

Community Profile:

Type—Rural: _____ County Seat/Capital: _____

Urban: _____ Blue Collar: _____

Suburban: _____ White Collar: _____

Agriculture: _____ Manuf.: _____ Other: _____

Distribution of Employment:

Manufacturing: _____ % Service: _____ %

Retail/Wholesale: _____ % Government: _____ %

Unemployment: _____ % U.S.: _____ %

Per Capita Income:		Issues	State
Median Family Income:		$_____	$_____
Median Home Value:		$_____	$_____
% Owner Occupied:		_____ %	_____ %

Distribution of Taxable Property:

Residential: _____ % Industrial: _____ %

Commercial: _____ % RR/Utility: _____ %

Major Taxpayers:

Taxpayers	Assessed Value	Number of Employees
_____	_____	_____
_____	_____	_____
_____	_____	_____

Other Comments: _____

vote count? What kind of voter turnout was there at the election? In some states either the state or its municipalities are authorized to sell bonds without a referendum. A resolution to sell bonds may be subject to petition and referendum, but the electorate must be aware of, or alerted about, the need for such action.

The worksheet's sections covering purpose and authorization constitute an initial step in the qualitative analytical process. Subsequent sections of the worksheet shift to a quantitative orientation, focusing on finances. The first item is the date. This should be no older than the last fiscal year end of the issuer. Sometimes what is called a "stub period" is shown—that is, a date more recent that can show perhaps a sale of bonds after fiscal year end, or perhaps a current tax collection amount. Ordinarily, year end figures will do, unless a dramatic event has occurred in the stub period that drastically alters the normal pattern.

Full Valuation and Assessed Valuation were discussed before. Full value is the more important of the two, but both should be shown. In seeing both, assessment standards become obvious and tax rates can be compared. Taxes are levied against the assessed value, and if tax rates appear high it may be that the reason is low assessments. Somewhere later in the worksheet a history of either, or both, of the valuations should be shown. An examination of valuations ten years ago and five years ago will indicate whether or not the tax base is growing, and if the municipality currently enjoys fiscal health.

The purpose in showing valuations on a financial statement are numerous. The most important are as follows:

1. To appraise the amount of debt against a measure of value or worth;
2. To compare the debt/value ratio of one municipality against another;
3. Where debt incursion is limited by constitution or statute it is usually expressed as a percent of value (usually "assessed" value). The investor or investment banker can know how close the borrower is to its debt limit;
4. If debt repayment is from taxes limited by fixed rates it can be determined whether or not the debt service can be levied within the limits permitted;
5. In states where the determination of taxable, or assessed, value is a local function, but with an upper limit of "full value," it can be determined if a limited tax can produce more revenue by writing up the taxable value of property;
6. Where any degree of reliability of full value is established, the assessment standards of local government can be appraised and/or compared with other municipalities.

DEBT

This part of the financial statement should be subject to very close scrutiny. Direct Net Debt in this kind of worksheet should always include the bond issue currently being offered, simply because if it is always shown, we know that the amount is accurate. Debt statements in an official statement are not always shown in a manner that is easy to understand. New Jersey debt statements indicate how difficulty can be encountered. The debt statements used are those required by the Local Finance Board to determine whether or not the statutory debt limit is being exceeded, and the presentation is convoluted. It is also important to note that a statement like the one discussed here may have to be constructed by the analyst from information presented in another fashion. For 100 percent accuracy in showing debt, the so called "sinking funds" should not be deducted from the amount of bonds outstanding (including the current offering). The reason for this is that sinking funds are sometimes defined in different ways.

In corporate or municipal finance, a sinking fund is normally used to accumulate amounts of money for use in paying principal, sometime in the future, for what is called a "term bond," or "term maturity," if the entire issue is not due at a single date in the future. Normally, "mandatory sinking fund payments" are required in order to ensure that funds will be available for principal payment on the future due date. Most state bond laws require that the state and its municipalities pay debt in annual installments. In this case a so-called sinking fund is really only a debt service fund out of which current payments are made, and a great many financial reports show the fund as a debt service fund. In fact, where a financing allows for a term bond or a term maturity, and if funds are required to be set aside for that payment, both a sinking fund and a debt service fund are created under the bond resolution or ordinance in order to differentiate between purposes.

Where a sinking fund or a debt service fund is used for current payment of principal and interest, the amount of money in the fund at a given time may be only that amount, or a portion thereof, that will meet the next interest payment if the time period is such that principal has been paid within the last six months. Deducting sinking funds might then lead to an inaccurate statement of debt.

Another way that net debt can, and should be shown, if a debt description is not shown later, is to show gross debt first, then deductions, then net debt. Sinking funds should not be deducted if they are only debt service funds. There are two principal kinds of deductions. The first kind is debt that is legally outstanding, but for which adequate funds have been set aside to pay principal and interest either to maturity date or an optional redemption date on which all of the particular bond issue may be retired (call date).

This usually occurs when bonds are "advance refunded," or "pre-refunded," i.e., a sale of bonds occurs for a refunding purpose in advance of the date on which the bonds in question are subject to the optional redemption. Sometimes funds for this purpose come from a windfall of some kind rather than from a refunding sale.

The second kind of deduction is that of self-supporting debt. The self-supporting aspect must be carefully ascertained. In some states certain kinds of debt may be deducted from a debt statement for purposes of determining if the issuer is within statutory debt limits. However, such deductions may or may not be valid. For example, in Minnesota, debt to finance a purpose for which a user charge *may* be imposed is deductible. Thus general obligation bonds issued for water, sewer, electric system and other kinds of enterprises are not chargeable to debt limit. In New Jersey, this deductibility is determined each time a new offering of bonds is made by a municipality. In New Jersey, revenue bonds may not be issued by municipalities, so water and sewer bonds, etc., are always general obligations. If the municipality has created a utility system of some kind, it may impose a user charge to pay operating costs and debt service on the bonds that financed the utility. The issuer is not, however, required to impose the charge. If the bonds are self supporting in one year they may be deducted from gross debt for ascertaining borrowing margin under legal limits. If the same bonds are not self supporting in the following year, they are added back into the debt statement either in whole or proportionately to the extent not self supporting. It is entirely possible for a debt limit to be exceeded via this route.

Ideally, a definitive statement should be included in the official statement of the bond offering as to the self supporting nature of the bonds deducted. That statement should indicate that the system financed by the bonds supports the bonds from gross or net revenues, whether or not the system also supports the operating expenses of the system, whether or not the bonds have been self supporting since issuance, or how many successive years prior to the debt statement the bonds have been self supporting. From the analyst's point of view, it would also be ideal for the issuer to covenant at the time of issuance to impose charges for system use that would pay all expenses including debt service.

Where such a covenant exists, general obligation bonds are said to be "double-barreled," implying two separate sources of payment, one backstopping the other. The phrase can be somewhat misleading, however. If, for example, a water system serving the entire municipality is financed, water bonds said to be "double-barreled" really do not have two sources of payment—taxes and watercharges. There is only one source—whoever is connected to that system.

When a city (village, township, etc.) and a school district occupy the identical area, they are said to be "coterminous."

In rural or suburban areas, the overlap may look like this:

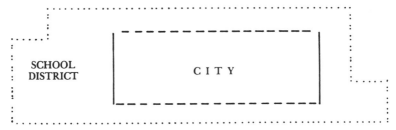

Or even like this:

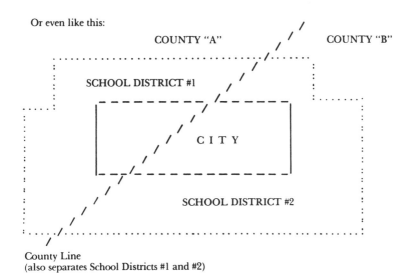

County Line
(also separates School Districts #1 and #2)

Figure 1.   Coterminous Jurisdictions

Chargeable Overlapping Debt is an item on the worksheet that can cause confusion. Generically the term means the debt of subdivisions (municipalities or units of local government) with taxing powers, whose area overlaps the subject municipality, and who have debt that is payable in whole or in part from taxable property in the subject issuer's area. It is easy, but often incorrect, to conclude that the only overlapping debt may be that of the school district with which the subject municipality shares tax base, or conversely, the municipality with which the school shares base.

In New England and other northeastern states, the township was originally the basic unit of local government, and the township issued school bonds as well as bonds for other purposes. In the generic sense, school bonds were not overlapping debt. This arrangement still holds true in some areas, and is carried over into cities. Most large cities in the country are not in school districts. The education system is run by a schoolboard that may be appointed and is responsible to the appointing officials rather than to an electorate. If the schools need capital funds, the city or township provides what is needed at the request of the schoolboard.

Figure 1 illustrates the kinds of complexities presented by overlapping debt in other kinds of situations. If a city straddling a river and lying in two counties and two school districts does not present problems enough (the second illustration in Figure 1), imagine overlaying a Mosquito Abatement District in part of the city that is in County B, and a Drainage District that takes in all of the city that is in County A and part of the city that is in County B.

The State of California probably possesses the most complicated local debt structures in the country. Table 2 is a debt statement summarized from material published by by California Municipal Statistics Inc., of San Francisco, acknowledged to be the most reliable source of accurate debt statements in the state.

Simply showing the debt of an overlapping issuer does not adequately present the nature of the overlapping debt burden. On the basis of proportional assessed value, the portion of the overlapping issuer's debt that is chargeable against the subject issuer must be shown if the statement is to be accurate.

Of course, states do not have any overlapping debt, at least any that is apportioned against a property tax base. The enormous and fast growing debt of the Federal Treasury overlaps, and with no specific taxes to pay even the interest, there is no way to accurately measure how much may be paid from each state. Perhaps the only measure would be how much of all federal revenue comes from any state. This probably changes little from year to year, but over a period of several years much more is coming from the Sunbelt.

Some states and counties report, where ascertainable, the debt of all of the various taxing subdivisions within their bounds. This debt has come to be called "underlying debt." The failure of this measure is that all of the debt of each issuer in a state or county is not chargeable against the entire tax base, and in measuring Per Capita Debt, all of the taxpayers are not paying all of the debt. It would be a gross injustice to imply that the huge debt of New York City is an underlying debt of New York State and is therefore payable by all the state's taxpayers.

Table 2. Overlapping Debt: City of Fairfield, California, 1983-84

1983-84 Assessed Valuation:	$1,216,350,901 (after deducting $207,435,600 redevelopment tax allocation increment)	

Direct and Overlapping Debt:	% Applicable	Debt 10/1/84
Solano County	18.366	899,934
Solano Cty Community College Dist.	19.970	1,027,837
Fairfield-Suisun Jt. Unified Sch. Dist.	68.560	1,927,758
Fairfield-Suisun Jt. Unified Sch. Dist. Certificates of Participation	68.560	647,381
Travis Unified School District	50.332	62,915
Solano County Library Authority	68.196	1,288,904
Bay Area Pollution Control Authority	0.686	5,968
Solano Irrigation District	27,168	497,174
Fairfield-Suisun Sewer District	83.119	1,147,042*
City of Fairfield	100.	1,350,000
City of Fairfield General Fund Obligations	100.	25,275,000
City of Fairfield Facilities District, ID #1	100.	27,940,000
City of Fairfield 1915 Act Bonds (est.)	100.	34,657,104
TOTAL GROSS DEBT & OVERLAPPING BONDED DEBT		$96,727,101**
LESS: City of Fairfield Water Bonds (100% self-supporting)		300,000
Fairfield Public Improvement Corp. (36.782% self-supporting from water revenue)		6,105,812
City of Fairfield Facilities District (100% self-supporting)		27,940,000
City of Fairfield 1915 Act Bonds		34,657,104
TOTAL NET DIRECT AND OVERLAPPING BONDED DEBT		$27,724,101**

* Excludes water revenue bonds to be sold.
** Excludes revenue, mortgage revenue and tax allocation bonds.
Source: California Municipal Statistics Inc., San Francisco, CA

Conventional analytical wisdom adds the direct debt and the overlapping debt to produce Total Debt. This total may indeed include all tax supported debt, but it may not include water and sewer, or electric, revenue bonds, or sales tax revenue bonds. It is much easier to identify total debt of a city, village, etc., than of a school district. If the direct debt is for a village, the revenue debt (where it is paid by the entire village) can simply be added to the tax debt for an accurate accounting of the total debt owed. But if the school district is one that includes more than one municipality, the analyst faces a problem similar to that of overlapping tax debt. If all of the municipalities have some revenue debt, it could all be added in, but as with overlapping tax debt it must be remembered that not all of the taxpayers are paying all of the debt.

Every analyst next wants fundamental information concerning ratios of debt to the value of the source of payment. Some analytical worksheets still include an item designated ratio of debt to assessed value, and will show the ratio of total debt to assessed value. Measuring the ratio of either debt amount to assessed value is of little value unless the assessed value and "market," or "full" value are the same or nearly so, indicating an assessment standard of approximately 100 percent. Similarly, measuring only direct debt to full value does not always serve a useful purpose. Total debt vis-à-vis the source of payment is what really matters, and measuring against full value is the only valid method of comparison of one municipality to another.

Another measurement that is typically included on analytical worksheets is ascertainment of per capita debt (total debt per capita). A history of at least three census counts should be shown in the financial statement, and if three or four years have passed since the last U.S. census, an estimate should be given for the current period if, and only if, the estimate is from a state agency that is in the business of doing so, or if the subject issuer is equipped to do so.

Population is an analytical category that is useful, but one that can be misused. A growing city (if not too fast) can generally be assumed to be fiscally healthy and fully able to pay its debts. Conversely, a city that is not growing in population, or worse yet, losing population, is more likely to default on debt, according to conventional wisdom.

Population is a quantitative measure, the qualitative tool is demographics. Who are all the taxpayers, why are their numbers changing? In-migration of persons can mean that the city is a desirable place to live, for whatever reasons. But will this necessitate incurring of debt to provide water, sewer, streets, schools, etc.? Will the debt grow faster than the taxbase ("ratables") that supports it?

Population has two primary uses in analysis. It can be used as a measure of a city's success or failure, or it can be used to measure debt per capita, which may or may not be a fruitful endeavor. The important aspect of population change is the cause and effect relationship between the change and possible result.

If there is a loss, who is moving out? Is it the well-to-do, or the middle class, or is it the working poor and/or welfare recipients? Experience indicates that in our industrial, older central cities, the middle class is the group most likely to "vote with their feet." The well-to-do seem to manage to insulate themselves from the problems of street crime and inadequate schools. The working and nonworking poor, if in family status, probably cannot incur the expense of moving.

Population and debt paying ability may not have a great deal to do with each other, depending on the variety of revenues a city has from which debt charges as well as other expenses are paid. A heavy dependence on property taxes, as was the case in Massachusetts before the recently passed "proposition 2 1/2," can mean a decline in revenues if there is a mass exodus by home owners and business establishments. Many properties can simply disappear from the tax rolls.

Per capita debt is a valuable tool for the comparative analysis of one municipality with another. What is equally important, but not always shown or easy to ascertain, is per capita ability to pay. The best indicator of this crucial credit aspect is per capita personal income. Does the trend line exceed the rate of inflation, or does it track inflation, or worse yet, does it not keep up with inflation? If the latter is so, and if per capita debt is growing, serious fiscal problems may result.

Fashionable suburban areas with high per capita income catch the eye of a lot of analysts. It is too easy to think that only blue collar workers lose their jobs, but the severe economic slump of 1981-83 showed how, particularly in the auto industry, white collar workers, including the high echelons of management, can be seen as superfluous to the productive efforts of industry. The auto industry was not alone, by any means, in drastic cutbacks in overhead employment. The farm implement and high technology industries had their unemployment horror stories, and some jobs simply disappeared—with no subsequent call backs, as with the production line people.

The most valuable use of analytical ratios comes when all other considerations about an issue show it to be very similar to another one under consideration. The ratios can then be used to fine tune a credit comparison. Some times the results can be surprising. North Slope Borough, Alaska, is a good case in point. In the Borough, oil drilling and exploration companies and the Alaska oil pipeline make up over 95 percent of the tax base. Three companies, Arco, Sohio, and Alaska Pipeline Company (a consortium) account for 90 percent of the tax base. Per capita debt and per capita full valuation are both extremely high, but the ratio of debt to valuation and per capita debt to per capita valuation are only a little higher than those of "lower 48" municipalities. The Borough functions as does a county in the "lower 48," and provides many municipal functions, as well as school district functions, on a borough-wide basis. There are separate municipalities in the borough, but for all practical purposes it serves as a single unit of government. The Borough borrows money for capital needs for county, municipal and school district purposes, and its ratio of debt to full valuation is just under 10 percent. Many municipalities have direct and overlapping debt totals that approach 10 percent of full value, but in North

Slope Borough the single entity has no overlapping debt, and the direct debt is as mentioned.

Because there are so many ways to show a record of tax collections this quantitative measure needs an amount of qualitative analysis, and perhaps some question asking. A format for this record should show the following:

> Year of levy
> Gross tax levy
> Abatements, etc.
> Net tax levy
> Amount collected in current year
> Amount collected to date
> Amount of current and delinquent collections each year

A typical format would look like this:

Table 3. Tax Collections (in $000s)

Year of levy	Gross levy	Abate-ments	Net levy	(1) Current collect	(2) Collected to date	(3) Total coll.	(1) %	(2) %
1990								
1989	10,000	120	9,880	9,500	(in process)	. . . .		
1988	9,990	118	9,772	9,450	9,650	9,700	97	99
1987	9,900	115	9,785	9,400	9,700	9,675	96	99
1986	9,885	112	9,773	9,375	9,773	9,665	96	100

If special assessments enjoy the same lien status as taxes, the levy and collection patterns will generally track those of taxes.

The qualitative analysis of Table 3 provides a number of items of information:

1. The current year's collection of tax levies is high (95 percent or better is considered a strong performance);
2. Subsequent years' collections of levies are such that total delinquency is low;
3. In each year the collection of current and delinquent taxes is such that the taxing agency receives 99 percent of its current tax levy.

Additional qualitative analysis consists of investigating the tax levy and collection procedures in the subject municipality. When are taxes levied and bills sent out? When are the taxes due? Are they payable in installments, and if so when are the installments due? Is a discount given for full payment on the first due date? What are the penalties for delinquencies? If taxes are due on January 1, the chances of full payment on top of Christmas bills is slight. Experience has shown that historical tax payment patterns are difficult to break without a substantial incentive. So if, for many years running, the current collections are only 90 percent, but if the collections in the following year of the prior levy are very high, and if the collections in a given year of current and delinquent taxes are 97-98 percent of the current levy, the pattern should not cause concern on the part of the analyst.

Analytical warning signals include slower collections, with increases in the amount of outstanding uncollected taxes and tax foreclosures on property. In the past, the City of Chicago's collection record has been abysmal at times. The reason was that the tax levies included personal property taxes, and the city simply did not have an adequate method of enforcement of these taxes, and did not bother to press collections. The collections of real estate taxes was, however, quite adequate, and sufficiently supported the city's budget.

Personal property taxes, except on automobiles, trucks etc., or on business equipment and inventory, often do not bring enough to pay the cost of enforcement, and as indicated earlier there are many ways to dodge business taxes. Many states have abolished the tax on household goods, and some have greatly diminished or abolished the business tax as being burdensome on the means of production.

SHORT TERM DEBT

Short term debt is among the greatest fiscal dangers facing states and municipalities. The best, recent example of the result of unrestrained short term borrowing involves the State of New York's Urban Development Corporation (UDC). Critics often contend that New York State is not content to let one agency do all of any one kind of work—not enough political appointments can be made that way. If a new project is deemed necessary, the State too often seems to create a new agency (or public corporation) to do it. As an example, three different New York State agencies are involved in health care financing, each one with a slightly different policy posture toward hospitals and/or nursing homes.

UDC was created primarily to build housing and undertake urban redevelopment. Very recently it was assigned to build prisons to lease to the state. UDC did not identify projects with bonds issued for the purpose, and did not assign revenues from each project to a bond issue or series of bond issues, as is the custom in enterprise financing. Instead, UDC pledged its "full faith and credit." The corporation started construction on project after project, with no project revenues to make debt payment with. Critics joked that UDC issued "vagrant bonds"—debt with no visible means of support.

UDC quickly began paying its debts with borrowed money. Part of each series of bonds after the first issuance was used to pay principal and interest on outstanding bonds. Underwriters showed little concern, probably because the bonds were thought to be protected by the so called "moral obligation" of the State of New York.

Outstanding short term debt quickly multiplied in the form of Bond Anticipation Notes (BANs). In February 1975, the market began to recognize that a huge risk was developing in the form of a large amount of unsupported debt accumulating, which would be paid only if the market continued to respond favorably to new offerings. UDC official statements did indeed disclose its worsening financial position. When a manager of the one of the lead group of underwriters was asked, "When did anyone last read the official statement?" the response was, "The first issue."

Eventually, when the maturing notes could not be "rolled over," a default occurred that sent shock waves through the entire tax exempt bond market. Although the "moral obligation" did not apply to notes of UDC, the State legislature did make an appropriation to pay the maturing notes and interest. That episode was the last one involving a UDC sale of its "full faith and credit" in the municipal market place.

The market quickly recognized that New York City was in the same posture in the accumulation of massive short term debt. As with UDC, the market was the only source of payment. The basic difference between the two issuers was that UDC had BANs outstanding while the city had Tax Anticipation Notes (TANs) and Revenue Anticipation Notes (RANs) outstanding. In 1975, the city did not receive a bid for its roll over sale of notes, and consequently could not make payment on outstanding debt.

New York City's rescue was engineered by the Municipal Assistance Corporation (MAC), or as the market affectionately called it "Big Mac." A "moratorium" on payment of the notes was called, and MAC became the borrower to raise funds to lend to the City in order to make delayed payment on the notes.

Was there reason to believe that if New York City defaulted no municipal credits were safe investments? Not really. The City was an aberration—its financial practices were such as no other city would dream of. Among the oddities of its system was the long practice of including uncollected taxes in its receipts budget and by that method balancing expenditures against its receipts. Unfortunately, the large bulk of the uncollected taxes were in reality uncollectible. This situation led to a series of year end revenue shortfalls that were solved by short term borrowings, and the borrowings grew larger each year.

Another device the City used, one that is forbidden in many state's local finance laws, was to hide some operating expenses in its capital budgets. The result was more needless borrowing for budgetary purposes. Among the things most often hidden in debt were payments to retirement funds. Such a practice was legal only for five years. The pattern of bond issue structures for many years involved the scheduling of the bulk of the bond issue for payment within 5 years and the rest out to 30 years. This resulted in budget increases, with insufficient revenues, and the short term debt continued to grow.

Of course, it is not always possible or even advisable to avoid short term borrowing. The timing of tax collections is usually set by state laws, and these and other receipts may not be in any way synchronized with the expenditure patterns of the governmental unit, state or local. Temporary revenue shortfalls can easily occur, and often will, particularly if there is no ongoing sizable surplus of cash with which to make expenditures. Several Rhode Island municipalities have issued Tax Synchronization Bonds in order to bring tax years and fiscal years into alignment. This results in part of a budget being funded by long term debt, but on a short term basis. Historical patterns of short term borrowing should concern the analyst when they suddenly increase or, if it can be determined, when the maturity of the debt suddenly and significantly lengthens.

Bond Anticipation Notes (BANs) generally are not a serious problem unless they are allowed to be rolled over and accumulated, as often happens in a state such as New Jersey. The danger of this practice, as was the case with UDC, is the possible evaporation of market access. If the size of the BANs is large, the municipality usually cannot, for political reasons more than any other, make a tax levy to retire the debt, although BANs are in most cases full faith and credit obligations (as are the anticipated bonds) and payable (if the bonds are) from unlimited taxes.

In New Jersey and in some other states, BANs may be "rolled over" on their due date and retired from a new issue. In New Jersey, after two years, the outstanding amount of BANs must be reduced on each rollover as if bonds were being retired, although the statute that spells this out is somewhat vague. In New York State, BANs may be rolled over once and the final maturity must be no longer than two years after the original date of issuance. Exceptions to the rollover provisions are made in the case of BANs issued to finance access improvements such as curbs, gutters and sidewalks. There is no limit to the number of renewals, but the maturity date of the last renewal must be no longer than the period of probable usefulness of the project, computed from the date of completion. New York State does not require any reduction of principal at the time of rollover. Rhode Island municipalities may issue BANs, and may roll them over for five years without any reduction in the principal amount. Some states however do not authorize the sale of BANs.

Although New York City operates under a City Charter, that charter does not make possible home rule. In the recent past, whenever local finance laws were too restrictive to accommodate what were deemed to be the finance requirements of the city, the city's legislative delegation to the state capital would introduce a bill to either change the local finance laws or to pass special legislation to legalize whatever the city wanted to do. Occasionally, action was taken to legalize what has already been done. Municipalities in New Jersey and other states have used similar strategies.

In New York State Tax Anticipation Notes (TANs) may be issued in anticipation of the collection of taxes or assignments levied for any of the four preceding fiscal years. TANS may be renewed for one year periods, which in total cannot exceed five years after the close of the fiscal year for which the taxes and assessments were anticipated.

A serious structural defect exists in paragraph (e), Section 24.00 of the New York State Local Finance Law regarding TANs. If a municipality, or district does not make a budgetary appropriation for redemption of the notes, it is required to set aside the collections of the anticipated taxes or assessments to be used only for the payment of the notes. If an appropriation is made, payment into a special account is not required, and the collections may be used in the manner provided by the law. In the absence of any provision of the law the proceeds shall be treated as surplus monies for the fiscal year. In other words, the proceeds of collections are not restricted solely for payment of the notes under all circumstances. Under the State Finance Law the collections of anticipated taxes and revenues for which TANs and RANs are issued are pledged to the respective notes issued by the state.

Municipalities other than New York City may issue RANs in anticipation of a specific kind of revenue. The city may issue RANs against aggregate revenues (in this sense, revenues are receipts other than taxes). The proceeds of RANs must be used for meeting expenditures payable from the anticipated revenue(s), or for redemption of notes to be renewed. The final maturity of RANs must be no longer than the end of the second year after the year of issue.

Although a single RAN issue may combine all or some revenues, the note resolution must specify the amount chargeable against each specific type of revenue. This does not constitute a pledge of the revenues for payment to the noteholders, nor is there a lien against the revenue receipts.

With this loose structure and rather minimal restrictions on the use of RANs and TANs, there is little wonder that New York City exhibited such poor financial management and eventually defaulted on its notes in 1975. The legal structure and lien, if any, associated with short term debt must be closely scrutinized and understood when an investor is considering investing in short term debt. In most states which allow tax anticipation notes, they must be retired within the budget year in which they are issued. A limit of 75 percent of the taxes in process of collection can be borrowed against them and collections of the taxes are pledged for payment.

Short term debt can be an early warning signal concerning fiscal health when it increases in size and when factors such as economic conditions affecting tax collections do not indicate that the situation is cyclical. One of the prime reasons that New York State has not received high grade credit ratings in the past is that deficits accumulated via the short term debt route to the point where $4.3 billion had to be rolled over two years in a row in years of economic recovery.

A rule of thumb in municipal finance is that government expenditures always rise to the level of funds available (a variation of the "Peter Principle"). The notion that it is better to spend surpluses than to reduce deficits, or taxes, has become an unfortunate attitude shared by too many politicians. Public employee unions sometimes support this attitude. They often contend that if a dollar of surplus exists at the end of the fiscal year it should be added to payroll.

State and local governments cannot, or at least should not, use short term, or long term, debt as simply another way of raising funds with which to meet budget expenditures. Sovereign governments may escape the consequences of this kind of action when they borrow domestically because they may print money. However even the printing press may not solve all problems. The federal government came close to a default in November, 1985, when the Congress could not come to an agreement on increasing the limit of the federal debt. The U.S. Treasury was out of money and could not borrow any without an increase in the debt limit.

The Treasury had already borrowed up to its limit. Congress finally gave in with a short term increase, and no default occurred. A long term increase was subsequently enacted. (The "printing press" in this context really means financing through the banking system, which creates bank deposits that are as spendable as paper money.) This situation continued into December, when on December 6, the Treasury announced that sales of Series E Savings Bonds were being discontinued because the short term increase had run out. Similarly the sale of State and Local Government series of Treasury bonds (the so called SLUGS issued to accommodate refundings without running afoul of arbitration restrictions) was also stopped.

This sort of financial mismanagement earns severe criticism when it is done by the heavily indebted Latin American nations or "third world" nations.

FUTURE FINANCING

A small amount of debt outstanding can be misleading, in that a potentially large amount may exist in the form of Debt Authorized but Unissued. This indicates that debt is forthcoming. The official statement should also indicate any debt contemplated for authorization, usually by referendum, at the next election. Seldom are authorizations ever cancelled. An accurate statement as to this kind of potential debt should also indicate the same information about overlapping taxing jurisdictions. Non-tax supported debt that will affect all taxpayers, i.e., water or sewer revenue bonds or sales tax revenue bonds, deserve the same treatment that they get in the financial statement.

OVERLAPPING DEBT AND MORAL (?) OBLIGATIONS AND LEASES

A class of debt that too frequently is listed as Overlapping Debt is that consisting of so called Moral Obligation Debt. This really a ruse of sorts. There is no obligation identified with this sort of debt, if by obligation one means something that is binding and enforceable. This type of debt is issued when an agency, usually of a state, issues bonds that may not have a sound pledge of funds for payment. Such a bond cannot be marketed, so the bond resolution creates a Debt Service Reserve (bond reserve) and funds it initially from proceeds of the bond sale. If the pledged funds are inadequate for payment of principal and interest, a transfer is made from the reserve to the debt service fund, putting the reserve balance below its required level. At this point the executive director is required to notify the governor that the deficiency exists, the governor is required to ask the legislature to appropriate the amount of the deficiency, and the state treasurer pays the amount to the agency.

A drawback of this arrangement is that the legislature is not legally obligated to make the appropriation. The so called "moral" aspect of the scheme arises from the notion that in creating the particular agency, allowing it to incur debt and creating the "reserve makeup" mechanism the legislature is "morally" obligated to make the requested appropriation.

New York State has made an art form of this technique in the past by allowing 10 state agencies to issue "moral obligations." The state has fulfilled that obligation for three agencies, including the Urban Development Corporation (UDC) discussed above. Similarly, Pennsylvania fulfilled its "obligation" to its Housing Finance Agency by appropriating funds to avoid a default on HFA notes.

Unfortunately, this kind of financing is too often a way of circumventing voter approval that may be required for a particular kind of debt. Sometimes it is used after a referendum for a bond issue has failed. In recent years, voters in New York State have voted down general obligation bonds issues to finance jails. The state in turn has authorized UDC to borrow money for jailbuilding, and to lease the facilities to the state. Although UDC issues the bonds, they are actually secured by the lease to the state. The state's obligation under the lease is the security that must be evaluated.

Lease financing can be effected in two ways. As mentioned above, bonds may be secured by lease payments, and customarily the lease payments are minimally sufficient in amount so as to equal the principal and interest payments on the bonds. A second method involves, as security offered to investors, the cash flow generated by the lease. The investor "participates" in the cash flow through a "Certificate of Participation."

Leases, in general, have two fundamental structural weaknesses. The first is that under all state laws except Illinois they are not debt and have no continuing pledge, nor legal requirement, to provide monies for their payment over the period of the lease. Lease payments can be made from "any funds legally available." There is no requirement to levy taxes for payment of rentals, nor to provide payment from any other specific source of funds. If a payment is missed, the lessee can not be forced to make good the missed payment in a succeeding year.

The second weakness of a lease is the fact that a lease is binding, under its terms, only for the year in which an appropriation is made. In some states the appropriation period may be for two years if the state is on a biennial budgetary basis.

As with all other "rules of thumb" referred to here, there are exceptions to these generalities about leases. For example, in Illinois the State Supreme Court has ruled that leases are debt and payable from taxes, and that the entire amount of the lease, i.e., the aggregate amount of the lease payments, is debt and as such chargeable against statutory debt limit. In other words, bonds secured by leases have principal and interest payments, and with lease payments set so as to equal annual bond debt service, that part of a lease payment representing interest is also debt and chargeable to debt limit. Needless to say, leases are not a popular method of financing in Illinois.

In California, the State Supreme Court has ruled that although leases are not debt, they are binding over their stated periods, and that the lessee is obligated to budget the lease payments annually, and to appropriate the funds.

In most leases the lessee covenants to budget the rental payments annually (or bi-annually as the case may be) and to appropriate necessary funds. The weakness of the lease is that the investor does not have the legal remedies in most states that a holder of the bond of a state or municipality has. The remedies are those spelled out in the lease, the strongest of which is to terminate the lease and evict the tenant.

Budgets are usually subject to veto by a governor in the case of a state, by a mayor in some cities (depending on statutory or charter powers of a mayor), or even by the voters if a state's laws give the taxpayers this option, either by budget approval or by initiative and referendum. The budgetary process is an important part of lease analysis, particularly the question of whether a lease payment is subject to line item veto.

Ideally, leases should be for facilities that are necessary for the function of government. Municipal offices cannot be held on the village commons, nor a courthouse maintained in a tent. Where possible a "no substitution clause" should be sought in a lease. This provides that the lessor will not lease any other facility so long as the subject facility meets the needs and purpose of the lessee.

In the absence of a dedicated source of funds with which to pay lease rentals, the ability of the general fund to handle an increase in budget expense is usually the first step in determining where monies might come from for the lease. This is particularly important in a state where tax rate limits are imposed, as in California. If the general fund cannot handle an increase, water utility surpluses often become a target. In a resolution authorizing a lease, a "probable" source may be indicated.

Nor can money not available be appropriated. For example, a California community college district financed a co-generation project and training facility through participation certificates. It was anticipated that payment funds would be derived from the sale of excess energy to Pacific Gas and Electric Co. (PG&E). For whatever reasons the plant was not completed and unable to generate power to PG&E. The college had no other funds with which to make payment, in that a large portion of its budget came from state appropriations. In order to protect its educational function, the district filed for bankruptcy, and the certificates went into default.

Until quite recently bonds secured by lease payments financed buildings and similar facilities. An important aspect of lease financings backing investment securities is that the useful life of the demised property must be at least as long as the last maturity of the security. Of course, a lease could be for land only, and useful life is not a consideration unless the land is subject to some sort of deterioration. As with "moral obligations," the reason issuers have used this technique in Kentucky, Indiana and Pennsylvania (before a recent change in the constitution) is to escape very restrictive limits in the constitutions of those states regarding the issuance of debt. California does not have the tight debt limit, but requires a two thirds majority at a referendum to carry an election to authorize general obligation bonds. Lease obligations are often made use of because they do not require voter authorizations.

"Moral obligations" are contingent liabilities, and like obligations of agencies (usually of states) that are guaranteed by the state's credit, they are not provided for in conventional financial statements used in the trade. The analytical worksheet illustrated in Table 1, follows convention and omits categories for "moral obligations," guaranteed debt of agencies (or others) and lease obligations.

What constitutes a "moral obligation" and what does not, became a bone of contention recently in the State of Minnesota. The State authorized its State Zoological Board to enter into an installment purchase contract to acquire a monorail system for the Board's new zoo. The transaction was financed by certificates of participation in the installment purchase payments. The enabling statute also provided that the contract could provide for the payment of money from any funds of the Board not pledged or appropriated for another purpose.

The Board had no funds of its own, in that all receipts from the operation of the zoo were required to be paid to the State's general fund. The Board covenanted to include the payments in its annual budget and to seek approval of its budget and appropriations sufficient to make such installment payments. According to the State Attorney General's Office, in the absence of an appropriation the Board had no obligation or authority to make the payments. The legislature refused to appropriate funds for the payment due 30 months after the transaction, and the certificates went into default. The legislature may not have obligated itself in any way to appropriate the funds for the installment payments, but critics contend that the state also acted in bad faith. In effect, the state refused to back the debt of its own operating agency.

RECEIPTS AND EXPENDITURES

If the analyst is interested in the managerial aspects of state and local government, the Receipts and Expenditures, along with the Balance Sheet, are as useful as they are to the corporate analyst. Where does the government unit get its money and what does it do with the funds? Does it have cash balances at fiscal year end? Does it use one fund, or more than one? Are some revenues (especially taxes) dedicated revenues or are all receipts available for all purposes?

What kind of reporting do governmental units use—cash accounting, accrual accounting, modified accrual, modified cash? There is a wide diversity of opinion as to the best method. Analysts with an accounting

Table 4. Reporting Format:
General Government Funds Receipts and Disbursements

Receipts shown are only as actually received.
Expenditures are those for which a liability has been incurred.

| | | All Governmental Funds | | FY ended — / — / — | | |
Receipts	Fund	Trust Funds	— Fund	— Fund	Capital Fund	Total
Beginning Cash						
(& equivalent)	$					
Major Taxes (list)						
Other Nondedicated						
Taxes (total)						
Other Major Rec. (list)						
User Charges						
Other Misc. Rec. (total)						
Federal Grants						
State Grants						
Inter Fund Transfers						
Permanent (1)						
Temporary (2)						
Long-term Borrowing						
Short-term Borrowing						

Total Cash Receipts $

(1) May include trasfers from enterprise funds.
(2) Should be equal to temporary Expenditure transfers and would be only within the reporting year unless footnoted explained.

Note: Any item usually large or small or new should be footnoted and explained.

Expenditures (including carry forward expenditures)

General Expenses
Police & Fire
Public Assistance
Social Services
Streets
Other Transportation
Recreation
Education (1)
Capital Outlay (2)
Other Capital Outlay
Debt Service (Bonds)
  Principal
  Interest
Short-term Debt Repaid
Transfers
  Permanent (3)
  Temporary

(continued)

Table 4. (*continued*)

Total Expenditures
Ending Cash (4)
Less Encumbrances (5)
Free Cash

   (1)   Other than School Board.
   (2)   From Capital Fund.
   (3)   Can Include School Board if School Funds are Accounted for Separately.
   (4)   Carry Forward Balances.
   (5)   Carry Forward Appropriations.

background may want to look at government books from a corporate perspective and consequently possess a strong bent for accrual, or modified accrual, systems. Some analysts (including the author) prefer a cash based system with accrual of expenditures. Cash receipts and accrued expenses prevent the counting of cash that has not been received. Debt service is paid from money in the bank, not from taxes in process of collection. Accrual of expenses tends to prevent the misleading process of putting expenditures in one year's outlay in order to look good in another year. The worksheet illustrated in Table 1 is admittedly an oversimplification, but it works well as a rendering down to basics of the much larger reporting form. Only the General Fund is shown because most municipalities pay debt service from the General Fund, and other funds are for special purposes.

General Accepted Accounting Principles (GAAP) are recommended by professional accounting standard setting groups, but what GAAP appears to overlook is the fact that debt service is paid from cash, not the accountants' Fund Balances. It is easy to be fooled by a GAAP statement of Receipts and Expenditures. The statement always ends with Fund Balances. These are not the cash balances in any funds. They represent a cumulative excess or deficit position of receipts over/under expenditures over whatever period the records have been kept in such fashion.

There are those who argue that the GAAP method more accurately represents the "position" of the reporting entity as of a point in time. What is important for credit analysis purposes is to accurately report the amount of cash receipts that have been taken in, what cash expenditures have been paid out, and if appropriations have been authorized for which no cash outlays have been made. It bears repeating that debt service is paid from cash.

Table 4 illustrates a reporting format that can be utilized by governmental units (other than agencies) and can bridge the seemingly insurmountable gulf between GAAP accounting and the 50 different (if only slightly so) methods required by and for the states and their municipalities.

SOCIO-ECONOMIC CONSIDERATIONS

The remainder of the worksheet illustrated in Table 1 is self-explanatory. Suffice it to say that the most important factor in the financial well being of a municipality is its economic health. A diverse tax base, well balanced between residential, commercial and industrial properties, amenities that make the community an attractive place in which people like to live and in which business wants to locate or remain located—all of these factors eventually show up in the financial reports.

Chapter IV

Revenue Bond Analysis

As mentioned earlier, bond issues secured by anything other than the full faith and credit of an issuer with taxing power is a "revenue bond," or in legal terms, a "special obligation" rather than a "general obligation."

Revenue bonds may or may not be secured by revenues of the issuer identified with the purpose of the bond issue. "Revenues" pledged may be payments from a third party, as with industrial development bonds or most pollution control bonds (although these financings are much less common after the Tax Reform Act of 1986). Some revenue bonds may be secured only from the flow of funds generated under a lease contract or an installment payment contract. This type of investment security is not a bond, but rather a "certificate of participation" (these are discussed in more detail below).

The pledge aspects of the credit behind tax-supported bonds are written into laws dealing with the issuance of such bonds. With revenue bonds, the pledge or pledges are provided in the resolution authorizing the issuance of the bonds or, as applicable, the trust indenture securing the bonds.

A revenue bond resolution or a trust indenture is in effect a contract between the issuer and the bondholder. A great many details in the resolution/indenture are the same as those that appear in a general obligation bond resolution—things that come to be known as "boilerplate." Boilerplate sections make similar financings somewhat easier to deal with, and reassure lawyers, investment bankers, financial consultants—and investors—who prefer to know that a given kind of financing is similar to a financing with which they are already familiar.

Perhaps what should receive the most attention in a bond resolution (resolution and indenture will be used synonymously) is the section titled "particular covenants." Here the issuer explains to the bondholder what he promises to do. Also important is the "additional bonds clause." The "ABC" can prevent a dilution of the initial security of a financing. Without

Table 5. Revenue Bond—Check List

NAME: _____   SELLING: ___ / ___ / ___

MATURITIES 19___ thru ___   Callable ___ / ___ / ___ at ___

LEGAL OPINION (Law Firm) _____

PURPOSE _____

CAPITALIZED FUNDS—INTEREST $ _____ for _____ months. Bond Reserve $ _____

SECURITY _____

DEBT	Prior Lien Bonds	$ _____	Connections	_____
	Parity Lien	_____	Total Debt	_____
	This Issue	_____	Per Conn. $	_____
	Total	$ _____		

COVERAGE   Historical (Years Ending)   Pro forma or
                                                             Projected

___ / ___ / ___   ___ / ___ / ___   ___ / ___ / ___

Operating Revenue   _____   _____   _____
Operating Expense**   _____   _____   _____
Net Op. Rev.   _____   _____   _____
Net Other Revenue   _____   _____   _____
Net Avail for d/s   _____   _____   _____
Annual d/s ($ ___)   Cover ___ x   ___ x   ___ x
Est Max d/s ($ ___)   Cover ___ x   ___ x   ___ x
**Before interest and depreciation

BOND RESERVE(S)

Prior Lien Required $ _____ On Hand $ _____ Pmts Current _____

Parity Bonds—Single Reserve _____ Special for Each Issue _____

   Required $ _____ On Hand $ _____ Pmts Current _____

   If not filled, balance to accrue from (surpluses)

   (fixed pmts _____ yrs)

DEPRECIATION RESERVE (Or Similar)   Available for d/s _____

   Required $ _____ On Hand $ _____ Pmts Current _____

   Balance to accumulate from (fixed payments over _____ years) (surpluses)

OTHER REQUIRED RESERVES _____

ADDITIONAL PARITY BONDS TEST _____

COVENANTS

Rates—to Produce _____ Revenues Sufficient to Cover _____ d/s _____ x Insurance _____

Audits and Books _____ Proper Operation _____ No Free Service _____

No Competing Service _____ No Prior Lien _____

(continued)

Table 5. (continued)

FLOW OF FUNDS
O & M
P & I (prior lien)
Bond Res (prior lien)
P & I (parity)
Bond Reserve
Depreciation
Other
Surplus   (Any lawful purpose)
          (____ % locked in)

WATER AND/OR SEWER

RATE STRUCTURE (Residential)

Present Rates in Effect Since ____ / ____ / ____ Single Billing for W&S ____

WATER	SEWER

First ____ gal/cu. ft. $ ____ per ____
Next ____ gal/cu. ft. $ ____ per ____
Next ____ gal/cu. ft. $ ____ per ____
Monthly 5M gal or equiv. water and/or sewer $ _____

Proposed Rates   Effective ____ / ____ / ____

First ____ gal/cu. ft. $ ____ per ____
Next ____ gal/cu. ft. $ ____ per ____
Next ____ gal/cu. ft. $ ____ per ____
Monthly 5M gal or equiv. water and/or sewer $ _____

Any Special Customers _____

Provision for Delinquent Collections _____

Water System—Reflecting Improvements

Supply _____
Adequacy _____
Design Capacity—adequate for ____ Population or Till Year ____
    (pumps & storage, treatment)

Max. use—historical _____ gpd   Treatment capacity _____ gpd
Max. use—anticipated (19   ) _____ gpd   Storage capacity _____ gal
Aver. use—historical _____ gpd   Pumping capacity _____ gpd
Aver. use—anticipated (19   ) _____ gpd

Sewage Treatment—Reflecting Improvements

Primary _____   Treatment capacity _____ gpd
Secondary _____   Current load _____ gpd
Tertiary _____   Project load (19   ) _____ gpd
Design capacity _____   Population _____

(continued)

Table 5. *(continued)*

Construction

Are Bids let _____

Performance Bonds _____

Contracts for turnkey job _____ or can costs escalate _____

Comments—Additional Financing and/or improvements

_____

_____

_____

_____

ELECTRIC UTILITY
(for System with generating capacity)

Energy Available:

Unit Description	Year Installed	Capacity
_____	_____	_____
_____	_____	_____
_____	_____	_____
_____	_____	_____
_____	_____	_____
_____	_____	_____
_____	_____	_____
_____	_____	_____
_____	_____	_____

Total current capacity	_____
Less largest unit	_____
Firm Gen. Capacity	_____
Plus unit to be financed	_____
Total firm gen. Capacity	_____
Firm intertie capacity	_____
Total Available Energy	_____

System History:	KWH Sales	Peak Daily Demand (KW)	No. of Customers***
1970	_____	_____	_____
1975	_____	_____	_____
1980	_____	_____	_____
1981	_____	_____	_____
1982	_____	_____	_____
1983	_____	_____	_____
1984	_____	_____	_____
1985	_____	_____	_____
1986	_____	_____	_____
____			
____			
____*			
____**			

*5 year proj.   **10 year proj.

***or meters inn use.

(continued)

Table 5. (*continued*)

Current Year:
1. Residential equiv. customers _____
(Equate non res. to res. on basis of equiv. annual revenue)

2. Sales Mix	Current Year	5 Years Ago
Res.	$	$
Com'l	$	$
Ind'l	$	$
Other	$	$

Community Profile:

Type:	Rural _____	County Seat/Capital _____
	Urban _____	Blue Collar _____
	Suburban _____	White Collar _____
	Agriculture _____	Manuf. _____ Other _____

Distribution of Employment:

Manufacturing _____	%	Services _____	%
Retail/Wholesale _____	%	Government _____	%
Unemployment _____	%	U.S. _____	%

Per Capita Income:
Median Family Income $ _____ State _____
Median Home Value $ _____
% Owner Occupied _____ %

Distribution of Taxable Property:

Residential _____	%	Industrial _____	%
Commercial _____	%	RR/Utility _____	%

Major Taxpayers:

Taxpayers	Assessed Value	No. of Employees
_____	_____	_____
_____	_____	_____
_____	_____	_____
_____	_____	_____
_____	_____	_____

an adequate provision for the issuing of additional bonds, all other promises are worthless. More on the resolution below.

The tool used to evaluate the bond resolution, and other aspects of the revenue bond financing, is the analytical worksheet, typically more complicated than that for a general obligation bond (see Table 1). The revenue bond analytical worksheet, illustrated in Table 5, has its widest application to "enterprise" financings for the construction, acquisition, or expansion of governmental enterprises such as water, sewer, or electric systems that rely heavily on user charges for revenues. Other kinds of state and local government enterprises include parking systems, airports, bridges and tunnels, liquor stores or swimming pools.

The worksheet in Table 5 can be modified to apply to many kinds of revenue bonds other than enterprises. However the major sections that deal with the bond resolution apply to all enterprise financings.

LEGAL OPINION

The first item of consequence on the worksheet is the Legal Opinion. These opinions have their origins in the many public defaults that followed the Civil War. Some of the best examples of these defaulted bonds were those issued by states to finance railroads. In most instances the bonds were issued without constitutional or statutory authority to do so, and were not binding obligations of the issuer. Investment bankers asked to bid on bonds began to hire attorneys from prestigious law firms to issue opinions as to whether or not the bonds were legally issued. After the federal income tax was introduced, the legal opinion included a judgment concerning whether or not the interest income was subject to the tax, or to any other tax the federal government might impose. As states began to institute their own income taxes, the legal opinion began to include judgments about those taxes as well.

Income taxes are not the only tax that can be levied in some fashion on bonds. Bonds are property, and the principal amount could be subject to a personal property tax. In the past, many states have levied a "monies and credits" tax on such things as bank accounts and bonds (sometimes an "intangibles tax," such as on an insurance policy); but the tax on bonds might be levied only on corporate bonds or, in the case of "municipal" bonds, perhaps only on those bonds issued in other states but owned by local taxpayers. In some cases, no bonds other than U.S. Treasury securities, are exempt from the state tax.

The essential aspect of the legal opinion for credit analysis purposes is the legality of issuance. The largest law firms have lawyers who specialize in the laws of state and local government. Some smaller firms, no less prestigious, deal only with such laws. The important question is, whose legal opinion is it? Opinions of lawyers associated with nationally recognized law firms enjoy the most credibility. If the purpose of a bond issue seems somewhat unclear, if the legal opinion is from an out of state law firm, and if a recognized law firm would ordinarily be the one rendering the legal opinion, caution may be called for in the examination of the legality of the bonds.

As an example, a recent financing in a large mid-western state involved a deal between the state and a "blind real estate trust," with its office located near the state capital. There are those who believe it to be the custom in this state that whenever any real estate is considered for acquisition by a governmental unit, the politicians involved in the consideration act quickly to buy the real estate and be in a position to sell it to the government, or to have it acquired under eminent domain proceedings with the price to be determined by a "friendly" court.

In this particular financing, the legal opinion of a prominent local firm was not sought. Instead, the opinion of a New York firm was solicited. Credit analysts wondered if local firms, familiar with the ways in which state politicians often conducted business, might have detected a conflict of interest indicated by the blind trust—of which beneficiaries were not disclosed.

PURPOSE

Aside from the considerations of purpose discussed above, it is important to know if a new system is being built, additions are being added to an existing system, or "retrofitting" or modernization is the purpose of the financing. Fully understanding purpose in this way should lead the analyst to expect other, particular characteristics of the financing to appear on the worksheet.

CAPITALIZED FUNDS (AND RESERVES)

These are monies that are provided from the sale of bonds (or, infrequently, from cash), and constitute what is often referred to as "up front" money. As noted before, the nature of the financing's purpose should lead the analyst to expectations about capitalized funds. Among the most important expectations is concern as to whether or not any money should be borrowed except for construction costs and the costs of issuance of the bonds. The nature of the purpose may signal whether or not money will be available from any other source. For example, in financing for enterprises, borrowing money for interest, and for a Bond Reserve (debt service reserve), may be necessary and/or desirable.

To fully consider questions such as these, the analyst must also understand the concept of reserves. In the public enterprise domain reserves are ordinarily thought of as being "funded," i.e., cash reserves, whereas in the corporate sector reserves are usually a valuation offset, such as a Reserve for Depreciation, or a segregation of equity for liabilities in the future. If the cash position of the entity is less than the required amount on some reserves, and if the reserves must be drawn on, then assets must be liquidated to provide cash for the draw. In some cases in the public sector, the corporate type reserves may appear, depending on the accounting system and auditors. The credit analyst is generally, however, most interested in cash reserves.

The most desirable and most frequently found reserve is the Bond Reserve, which serves as safety valve if pledged cash flow is inadequate. A second cash reserve that is desirable but less frequently seen is a Reserve for Renewal and Replacement, the "R & R Reserve." This fund is used for extraordinary expenses not encountered in the normal operation of the facility. A third cash reserve is a Depreciation Reserve (not to be confused with the accountant's Reserve for Depreciation). Ideally an amount would be deposited annually into this fund equal to the cost of the plant and equipment divided by the number of years of the estimated useful life, so that the end of the useful life an amount is on hand with which to replace the facility (without inflation).

In the real world this rarely occurs, though occasionally one does see a bond resolution requirement for such a fund that may require periodic deposits until a balance equal to, say, 10 percent of the cost of the facility is accumulated. Frequently a Reserve for Depreciation actually functions more like an R & R Reserve. If both reserves appear, the Reserve for Depreciation is likely to be programmed for major renovations or replacement of major components of a facility. The desirability of a Bond Reserve speaks for itself. What may not be so self evident is the utilitarian value of the other two reserves, particularly if they are substantial in amount. Their value lies in minimizing the need to borrow money in the future— a need that analysts prefer not seeing.

When is capitalizing of interest and a bond reserve necessary or desirable? When a new facility is being financed. Without "outside money coming in" there is no source of income from which to make required interest payments to bondholders. Interest must be capitalized during the estimated period of construction, and normally for six months beyond in case construction is delayed. In some types of construction, six months may not provide an adequate margin of safety. In such cases, the Bond Reserve is useful, and its capitalization is desirable, usually in an amount equal to maximum annual debt service.

If an existing, money-making facility is being expanded in order to serve more users, but full interest may not be earned until the expanded facility can serve the additional users (after construction is complete), capitalizing a portion of the interest is necessary. How much? Only the amount that cannot be earned during construction.

If an existing facility being expanded has debt outstanding, it usually also has a Bond Reserve. It may be desirable in such a case to bring the reserve up to a new requirement immediately by capitalizing the deficiency. Some bond resolutions may require providing a prospective deficiency from bond sale proceeds.

A healthy facility may already be earning its future annual interest and principal requirements. If so, there is no need to borrow at all during construction, and the Bond Reserve can be increased over a period of time (which should not exceed five years) from current surplus earnings. But needless borrowing does often occur, especially unless there are some other restrictions built into a past financing, which limit debt by reasons other than the ability to service it. This happens for three main reasons:

1. Many investors without analytical skills with which to judge credit feel that the more money up front the better, and may be willing to pay a higher price for the bonds (lower interest rate).

2. Investment bankers and bond attorneys make more money when there are more bonds to sell.

3. Prior to the Tax Reform Act of 1986, arbitrage was a significant factor. If the entity could borrow at tax exempt rates and invest at higher taxable rates, there was money to be earned by borrowing more than was needed for actual project costs.

SECURITY

It is easy to be misled by the paragraph describing Security in an official statement, if the paragraph is not carefully examined. The lien status of the bonds is seldom described in the title of the bond issue, and may only be vaguely explained in the Security paragraph(s). Here is how a junior lien might show:

> The bonds are secured by the revenues of the project after first deducting the expenses incurred in the operation and maintenance of the project, and after payment of principal and interest on Series A Bonds dated January 1, 1978.

The same thing could have been stated as follows:

> The bonds are secured by a pledge of the net operating revenues of the project, which is subordinate to that securing Series A Bonds...

> Net operating revenues is defined as gross operating revenues of the project less necessary expenses of operation and maintenance before payment of interest on debt and before charges for depreciation.

Sometimes Security is described in a paragraph stating that "the bonds are secured by the funds created under the resolution authorizing their issuance." From here one has to travel to another part of the official statement that covers the matter in a section on the bond resolution, under the heading "Flow of Funds." In that section the analyst hopes to find find a statement that revenues from the operation of the project will be deposited into the Revenue Fund, from which there shall be paid, in order of priority, (1) expenses incurred in operation and maintenance of the project, (2) interest and principal on the bonds, etc.

In the case of a junior lien, (2) would read "interest and principal on Series A Bonds," and (3) would read, "payment to Series A Bond Reserve to maintain its required level," and (4) would read, "interest and principal on these series B Bonds," or "interest and principal on the Bonds" (meaning the subject issue).

GROSS REVENUE VS. NET REVENUE PLEDGE

There is a myth of sorts that holds that a pledge of gross revenue of a project is stronger than a pledge of net revenue. That argument is valid only if "outside money coming in" is available to pay expenses. Otherwise the gross revenue pledge may pay only the first coupon if there is not enough left over to run the facility on a revenue producing basis.

DEBT

The worksheet entries under Debt are typically uncomplicated. An exception is the rare situation in which the analyst encounters a bond issue outstanding that is junior to the issue being analyzed, unless a prior lien issue has an open lien, and additional prior lien bonds are the issue under study. This is seldom the case in "municipal" finance. It is important to know if there are junior lien bonds outstanding because the default remedies in the junior lien could have a possible effect on bonds ranking ahead of them, such as making all debt immediately due and payable.

JUNIOR LIEN BONDS

These constitute the most maligned kind of debt in the field of public finance. Many underwriters and investors avoid dealing with junior lien bonds. In most cases the aversion is not warranted. Many original bond resolutions were written with exceptionally restrictive additional bond clauses. With the high rates of inflation that existed in the nation from the late 1960s to the early 1980s, expansion of public facilities involved inordinately high capital expenditures, and borrowing requirements exceeded those allowed under tight "ABCs" (additional bond clauses). If the ABC required historical coverage of future maximum debt service of, say, 1.5 times, an enterprise could be hard pressed to meet the test without having raised rates substantially two years before the anticipated additional borrowing.

Two possible solutions arise in such a situation. Junior lien bonds could be issued, or the outstanding bonds could be refunded (perhaps at a higher interest rate), and a refunding issue that would include the new capital requirements could be sold under a new, weaker bond resolution. The complications of this type of refunding are too numerous to mention here, but, needless to say those whose compensation from a borrowing program is based on the amount of the borrowing would benefit substantially. In the long run, the cost to the issuer of higher coupon refunding may have exceeded the costs of issuing junior lien bonds. A junior lien bond that is adequately protected by its bond resolution can be marketed on favorable terms. The prior lien(s) must be closed out, of course, and coverage of debt service adequate for the nature of the enterprise should be demonstrated on a pro forma basis, which usually entails a rate increase.

The Anchorage, Alaska, Telephone System, once sold 14 issues of bonds with the last issue involving a 14th lien on the net revenues of the system. Each lien was closed out with the issuance of a new series of bonds, and all of the issues were rated the same by the credit rating agency due to the fact that the earnings of the system supported all the debt on the same basis as when the first lien bonds were sold.

In a similar case, Seattle Power and Light sold out to 5 or 6 issues. When a research report on Anchorage was sent to the Board suggesting the capping off of the lien ladder, all of the bonds were refunded under a new resolution. The refunding may or may not have cost more money. Seattle topped its lien ladder with the issuance of a series with provision for parity bonds.

An important consideration about junior lien bonds is that with the closing out of a prior lien, the junior lien moves up in status as the prior lien bonds are retired. Of course, this would not have comforted analysts in the case of Anchorage's 14th lien, but would have done so in the case of the second lien bond.

In 1965, the New Jersey Turnpike Authority contemplated a refunding of outstanding bonds in order to accommodate a new, large financing for turnpike expansion. At the time, a first lien bond was anticipated to bring a coupon of 5 percent. A junior lien bond would have sold at no higher than 5 1/2 percent. This sounds sensible, but a large amount of prior lien bonds were outstanding, and bearing coupons between 2 3/4 percent and 3 1/4 percent. In addition, the prior lien bonds would have to have been called at a price of at least $102. The investment bankers with whom the authority was negotiating were enthusiastic about the underwriting. One of the managers was so exuberant that the firm had been quietly buying the low coupons that were selling at a large discount in the 5 percent market with the idea that it would have them called at a premium. The financing eventually raised questions that led the governor to withhold his approval of it. Meanwhile the market was falling away, and junior lien bonds were subsequently sold with a coupon higher than would have been attached at the originally contemplated sale. The exuberant dealer who owned all the small coupon bonds went bankrupt.

CONNECTIONS

The right-hand column on the worksheet under Connections is an analytical tool analogous to Per Capita Debt for tax supported bonds. Its usefulness is limited to such enterprises as water, sewer or electric systems, for which there is a head count of connections. Where a master meter might serve an apartment complex, the connections can be measured in the number of units in the complex or, as a competent engineer does in a feasibility study, by reducing the consumption of the complex to "residential equivalents," or "domestic equivalents," by dividing the single meter consumption of water or electricity by the average consumption of a metered single family dwelling. The same can be done for any large user such as a hospital, school or a large industry.

The only significant problem associated with a connection count is when a utility system provides more than one kind of service; if separate charges are imposed for each service the problem is addressable. Although a house may be both a water and an electric user, it is a connection to separate systems and should then be counted twice if the utility system provides both water and electricity. A city or village system may serve water only within its limits but may provide electricity to adjacent areas. Similarly water and sewer service may not be to the same customers across the board. A single charge for two services is sometimes used for water and sewer if the service areas are identical.

Any user of any service should be counted as a connection, regardless of any billing procedures. That way the counting method is consistent. High debt per connection usually shows up in the rates charged for the service.

COVERAGE (OF DEBT SERVICE)

The corporate accountant will measure coverage of fixed charges, particularly for an investor owned utility, but payment of principal on debt by a public facility is seldom recognized by accountants in the fashion that makes most sense to a municipal analyst. The carrying cost of debt (interest) is an expense, but not the retirement of it. The main reason for this is that most corporate debt has single maturity in the future, while most municipal debt is paid in installments, or in mandatory annual payments to a sinking (debt retirement) fund, effecting the serialization of principal payments. Debt service, to an investor in tax exempt bonds, is the required annual installments of principal and interest on the bonds.

The analytical worksheet illustrated in Table 5 lists a number of important items under Coverage. Operating Revenue means just that for an enterprise. It includes no gains from sale of assets, no investment income, no receipt of charges for connection to the system. It includes the revenue derived from the imposition of rates, fees and charges to the users of the service.

Operating Expense of a public facility is another category that creates problems for the corporate accountant. As indicated, expenses are before payment of interest and charges for depreciation. They should not include any items of capital outlay (depreciable assets), nor should they include any expense other than those incurred in the year to year operation of the system. For purposes of this particular worksheet format, non-operating revenues and expenses are netted out under Other Revenue. Of course, if the amount, or its components, are significantly large, special note should be taken and special analysis undertaken.

The reason for excluding non-operating income and expense in order to arrive at net operating revenue is that frequently, large items of a non-recurring nature can enter in, and if not shown separately they can distort an earnings picture. Connection charges are too often included as operating income and used for computing debt service coverage, when the best way to account for them is to do so separately and use them for system expansion to minimize borrowing. Investment income may be misleading in that it can be unduly large if it is derived from unexpended bond sale proceeds, etc.

Annual Debt Service means that occurring in the year designated in the column heading. Maximum annual debt service refers to the largest annual payment in any future year.

PRO FORMA OR PROJECTED COVERAGE

Projected Coverage is an area in which information provided investors can be very misleading. An example of pro forma projections is the case in which

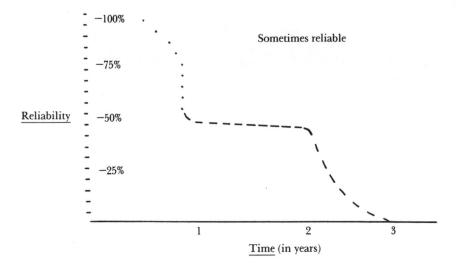

Figure 2. Hausker Curve of Reliability of Projections

a rate increase has been put into effect and additional gross revenues will result. Another example is the case in which a number of connections will be added to the system as a result of the financing. In this latter case both gross revenues and operating expense will increase, and, hopefully, net revenue.

Pro forma in this instance is performed by taking the per connection income and per connection expense for the past year and multiplying by the number of new connections to get the adjusted figures. This assumes, of course, that the new connections will be essentially the same in character as the existing ones, and that no new variables come into play.

Projections can be accomplished using a number of forecasting techniques, ranging from simple extrapolations to highly sophisticated prediction methods. The "Hausker Curve" (illustrated in Figure 2) is a simple tool for use by credit analysts that might be described as "The Curve of Reliability of Engineers or Consultants Projections." It works in the following way. In the case of, for example, projections of next year's residential connections to a utility system, if the projected number is based on the number of building permits issued for which construction is not complete, the figure is reasonable. If however the number is based only on last year's additions, cut the number in half. If that number of additions will produce the revenue needed to service debt for the project in question, the proposed financing is generally credit worthy (assuming no other problems). If that number of connections is not adequate to produce the needed revenues, how much of an increase in charges against the new number of connections is necessary, and is the increase reasonable or one that will discourage consumption?

Coverage of debt service is probably the first thing to come to the mind of most analysts in reviewing a bond issue. This raises the question of how much coverage is necessary for a bond issue to be considered minimally investment grade. The answer is that the purpose of the bond issue (as well as the strength of the source of funds) is the best guide to the adequacy of coverage (see the discussion of Purpose).

In general, where a source of funds is judged to be relatively stable, the pledged revenues should be 110 percent of maximum debt service—analysts refer to this as a 1.10 ("one-ten") cover. For a public system meeting its pledge requirements, the coverage factor tracks with what is referred to in the bond resolution as Rate Covenant (see Covenants below). Saying that a 1.10 cover is adequate is not to say that such a cover cannot indicate a high grade bond. There are factors other than coverage that can indicate high grade credit quality (see the Appendix on Chicago Water Revenue Bonds). A coverage factor of 1.25 is quite respectable for most revenue bonds where the issuer has control over the generation of pledged revenues, particularly when that coverage requirement applies only to the debt service, and the bond resolution requires additional revenues for reserve requirements.

A somewhat narrow based source of funds such as a fixed rate sales tax should provide a 1.50 cover. The only protection for this cover factor is provided by the coverage test for additional parity lien bonds. Unless an additional amount of tax is provided, where a pro forma test could be used the test should be based on historical coverage of future maximum debt service.

BOND RESERVE(S)

The Bond Reserve information requested by the worksheet illustrated in Table 5 is often vague or incomplete in official statements, and analysts should take special care in assessing this aspect of a financing. If prior lien bonds are outstanding they undoubtedly have a reserve requirement. The analyst should be able to ascertain what the requirement is, if it is met from a balance on hand, or if periodic deposits are required, and if those payments are current. Occasionally, several series of bonds issued on parity with each other each have a separate reserve. This happens frequently in Florida. An issuance of bonds on parity (or, in legal terminology, issued pari passu) with outstanding bonds, will show an existing reserve that must be increased to a new requirement level, either from bond sale proceeds or periodic payments.

DEPRECIATION RESERVE AND REPAIR AND REPLACEMENT RESERVE

This section of the worksheet was discussed above, in connection with an explanation of Capitalized Funds. Normally these reserves are available for debt service if the bond reserve is depleted, but this should be ascertained. Of considerable importance for any reserve is the replenishment of any drawn down reserve and the method for doing so. This can be ascertained by referring to Flow of Funds in the bond resolution.

ADDITIONAL BONDS CLAUSE

As noted above, the Additional Bonds Clause, or "ABC," is an extremely important section of the bond resolution, because it can prevent a dilution of the initial security of a financing. Without an adequate provision for the issuing of additional bonds, all other features of the resolution are worthless. A bond with 5.0 cover (pledged revenues are 500 percent of maximum debt service), and other credit strengthening features, can be diluted in quality if the additional bonds test permits parity bonds subject to a 1.10 cover. As important as the test itself is the method by which the test is applied. Ideally, future maximum debt service, reflecting the new bonds, would be covered historically in at least the most recent fiscal period.

Normally the numerical factor of the coverage test is the same as that in the Rate Covenant (see below). The test is more likely to state that historical revenues, adjusted for something like a rate increase, additional connections, or (back to the Hausker Curve) projections of future pledged revenues (e.g., with airports), will cover annual or maximum debt service the required number of times.

COVENANTS

In the bond resolution the section called Particular Covenants may extend over several pages. The information called for in the worksheet involves aspects of the Covenants that are of most interest to the credit analyst. The Rate Covenant, along with Coverage, the Additional Bonds Clause, and Reserves constitute the essence of the contract with bondholders. The rate covenant is a factor only in those situations where the issuer has the legal authority to impose rates, charges and fees for service to the user.

Minimally, the covenant should provide that charges will be imposed that will produce net operating revenues (when net revenues are pledged) that will meet all the requirements of the bond resolution, but at least a stated coverage of interest and principal payments as they come due. No free service should be provided to any user except where a service of comparable monetary value is received in exchange. Any existing prior liens should be closed out.

FLOW OF FUNDS

This section of the worksheet describes the order in which revenues coming into the organization fill each of the funds to required levels and then flow on to other funds. Ideally all funds left after providing for the listed requirements (surplus funds) should be retained within the system and used for system expansion, or to call bonds or purchase bonds in the market. All too often the resolution will state that surplus funds may be used for "any lawful purpose" without defining what such a purpose might be. The analyst should seek an answer to that question.

In some southern states, Alabama and Texas in particular, it is customary for surplus utility revenues to be transferred to a city's general fund. The reason for this is that local tax rate limits are quite stringent and the utility systems must be depended on by cities to provide operating funds. A rate covenant may provide only a 1.50 cover, while actual coverage may be 2.25 or 2.50 times debt service. This practice is often used by utilities serving areas outside city limits, and it is often controversial because outside users are charged higher rates than users inside the city. The State Supreme Court has ruled, however, that the practice is not unconstitutional in Texas.

Part II

CREDIT RATING PERSPECTIVES

Chapter I

*The Context of Credit Analysis**

Credit analysis is a highly subjective evaluative art, in which an attempt is made to judge the likelihood that an issuer of debt will be able (and willing) to make timely payments on interest and principal.

In order to understand the techniques of credit analysis, it is useful to know something about the financial and political context in which this activity takes place. That context has been changing recently in ways that make credit analysis more important than ever to all of the participants in the underwriting-investment process. Unfortunately, those changes have also made the process of credit analysis much more complicated and generally difficult.

The dramatic growth in the issuance of municipal securities by state and local governments, and by governmental authorities and agencies serving those governments, confronts the analyst and investor with a large array of tax-exempt investment instruments, with different credit and security provisions.

In 1975, according to statistics compiled by *Credit Markets,* less than $30 billion in municipal bonds was issued by states, cities, counties, public authorities and related kinds of government entities that issue debt obligations with the interest income not subject to federal income taxes. By 1984 that figure had grown to over $119 billion; by 1985, the annual total had peaked at $218 billion in anticipation of tax reform. In the wake of tax reform market volume has returned to pre-1985 levels, but new tax rules have further complicated the number and types of municipal securities that may be issued in tax-exempt form.

This essay describes the nature of this changing context of credit analysis, and provides an overview of some of the many different types of analytical models and techniques used.

INCREASED INTEREST IN CREDIT ANALYSIS

Most of the same factors that have contributed to broad structural changes in the tax-exempt municipal bond market have also contributed to an increased appreciation of the value of fundamental credit analysis among Wall Street investment firms, as well as investors. The growth in size and complexity of the market, rampant inflation, deep recession, severe cuts in federal grants, the taxpayer revolt, and rapidly deteriorating state and local government infrastructure have all helped to create an air of increased risk in investing in municipal securities.

New York City

Undoubtedly the most important factor contributing to a revitalization of credit research was the financial crisis of New York City in 1975. Actually, that crisis was a series of credit shocks that followed in rapid succession throughout the state, and which stunned the investment community. In February of 1975 New York State's Urban Development Corporation defaulted on $135 million of its short-term notes (which were not secured by the so-called "moral obligation" pledge of the state).

Although the New York State quickly appropriated funds to redeem all UDC notes within 90 days of the default, repercussions were felt throughout the state. Almost immediately lending institutions refused to continue financing New York City's short-term borrowing needs. The City had financial troubles of its own, complicated by what have now become classic examples of accounting and budgetary "gimmickery." The City had been issuing tax anticipation notes (TANs) for capital projects, routinely placing hundreds of millions in operating budget items in the capital budget, and continually rolling over billions in short-term debt to finance over ten year's worth of operating deficits in its operating budget. In 1975 the City's short-term debt needs amounted to roughly 30 percent of the nation's total short-term debt.

With the cutoff of further borrowing in the spring of 1975, the City could not service its outstanding debt and faced the prospect of curtailment of services and the inability to pay employee salaries or money owed to vendors and suppliers. Yonkers, New York State's fourth largest city, experienced a similar crisis, and investors generally became reluctant to purchase New York State or local securities of any kind. The impact of New York City's crisis on municipal credit research was dramatic because before 1975 most investors were not much concerned about the likelihood of a major default—there had been very few since the Depression years. The investment community as a whole tended to rely on the opinions of credit rating firms—Fitch, Moody's and Standard & Poor's.

WPPSS

In 1981 a second series of difficulties faced by a major municipal securities issuer challenged the credibility of the rating agencies and demonstrated to many other members of the investment community that their credit analysis capabilities still had not received the kind of financial and personnel support that was required. This time the problems were faced by the Washington Public Power Supply System (WPPSS), which by 1981 had become the nation's largest issuer of tax-exempt securities.

The WPPSS case has been a highly complicated example of difficulties faced by an issuer of tax-exempt debt, and has highlighted for analysts and investors alike a variety of types of risks faced by the holders of such debt. The difficulties faced by WPPSS and their full meaning for credit analysis are likely to remain unresolved for some time (the WPPSS case is discussed in considerable detail in another chapter).

WPPSS has become a notorious example of nearly all that can go wrong with such a project, including inaccurate estimates of future power demand, failure to react in timely fashion to revised estimates, construction cost overruns, schedule delays, general management failures, and more than anything else, the disenchantment of ratepayers who elected their state supreme court justices. Credit agency ratings on the projects remained high during the 1970s, even though it began to become clear to some observers that a number of the nuclear plants would (or should) never be completed, and that the Supply System would likely have difficulties paying enormous construction shut-down costs, not to mention debt service on bonds for plants not generating revenues.

By the end of 1981 a small number of Wall Street analysts were becoming concerned about the risks involved in the complicated WPPSS financing arrangements and generally concluded that the ratings issued by Standard & Poor's and Moody's were overly optimistic, particularly about WPPSS Projects 4 and 5. (Fitch did not rate the bonds.) The Supply System had already issued an incredible $6.5 billion in long-term debt, and institutional investors were beginning to reduce or eliminate their holdings of WPPSS securities.

And aside from highlighting a lack of speed and accuracy, WPPSS also illuminated other problems with Wall Street analysis. Chief among these was probably the fact that analysts employed by dealer firms were often viewed primarily as marketing tools, to be used to help sell their firms' municipal calendars. A glaring example of this came with the appearance on July 24, 1981, of a WPPSS credit analysis prepared by Merrill Lynch's fixed income research department. The report was entitled "Washington Public Power Supply System: At the Crossroads," and was probably the most careful, in-depth, and critical investigation of WPPSS financing done to that time. Unfortunately for the authors of the report, it did not support the efforts of Merrill Lynch's "sell side," which at that time was preparing for an upcoming $750 million bond sale, for which it was named lead underwriter. While Merrill Lynch promoted the bond sale with blue campaign buttons saying, "I'm bullish on the Supply System," the authors of the credit report were told not to talk to the press—a fact which in itself later became a noteworthy item in Seattle newspapers. For whatever reasons, the authors of the report soon left Merrill Lynch and took enhanced analytical reputations with them to positions of responsibility at other firms.

PURPOSES OF MUNICIPAL CREDIT ANALYSIS

The approach taken to credit analysis depends on who is doing the research and why. The analysis of governmental finance generally falls into either of two broad purposes—to evaluate performance, or for credit appraisal. Many analysts agree about the very general outlines of credit analysis—that debt factors should be examined, that certain broad economic "environmental" factors must be taken into account, etc. But investment firms and analysts do not always agree about the importance of one factor relative to another.

It is important to note that credit analysis is just one variety of a much larger family of municipal research studies that focus on the analysis of financial condition. Besides investment reasons, this kind of study is undertaken for basically one of two other possible reasons. In the first place, state and local politicians and managers are becoming increasingly interested in a sophisticated assessment of the financial condition of their governmental units. This is not technically credit analysis as such. Government managers are increasingly interested in improving the managerial efficiency of the governmental unit, and in projecting future costs of issuing debt, the interest rates for which will be based in part on an independent appraisal of their credit worthiness. In some cases, municipalities use their own analyses of financial condition as a basis on which they attempt to appeal unfavorable credit ratings issued by credit rating agencies. A host of studies and guidebooks have been published recently that are designed to enable municipal managers to better gauge their financial condition.

In the second place, analyses of financial condition are commonly used to assess the eligibility of a given municipality for intergovernmental aid of various sorts. Many different formulas exist for the dispersal of such aid, and a large number of studies have been published that test the adequacy of these formulas, and suggest areas of improvement.

For many years, roughly up to the time of the mid-1970s national economic problems, as well as some near financial disasters at the state and local levels, the analysis of financial condition was largely the province of Wall Street credit analysts and professional investors. But because of the small number of municipal defaults since the time of the Depression, their work was highly subjective, with a large number of "rules of thumb" that had really never been adequately tested, and a narrow focus on ratio analysis of debt burden measures. The general inadequacy of this approach was highlighted, as we noted in our introduction, by the fact that two of the three major credit rating agencies, as well as many investment firms, failed to predict the New York City financial problems of 1975.

Since that time, Wall Street investment firms have increased their municipal credit analysis staffs, and broadened their analytical approaches. The number of the other kinds of financial condition analysis mentioned above also increased as factors other than those in routine credit reports came under observation, including politics, demographics, etc. Many of their analytical techniques have their origins in credit analysis, but they have been supplemented and tested by other statistical and data-gathering methods of the social sciences, as required by the different purposes of these studies. These studies tend to be widely published and well known, whereas with the exception of the general analytical frameworks used by the credit rating agencies, credit analysis frameworks are considered proprietary information by investment firms. It is, however, possible to suggest ways of distinguishing different approaches to credit analysis, and to list some of the specific analytical techniques commonly used.

ANALYTICAL TECHNIQUES AND PROCEDURES

Having described the purposes of credit analysis, and who does it, it still remains to begin classifying the specific kinds of techniques, objectives and procedures used.

Solvency

Credit analysis typically focuses on a municipality's ability and willingness to make good on its debt service obligations. The ability to do this depends on the financial solvency or health of the municipality. But this raises the question of how to define financial health or solvency. The International City Management Association (ICMA) has suggested the following list of the types of solvency that may be the focus of any investigation into the nature of financial health:

1. *Cash solvency.* This is financial health in a narrow accounting sense. It refers to the "liquidity" of a state or local government—its ability, over 30 or 60 days, to generate enough cash to pay its bills.

2. *Budgetary solvency.* This refers to the ability of a state or local government to generate, over its normal budgetary period, revenues sufficient to pay its expenditure obligations, without creating deficits.

3. *Long-range solvency.* This refers to the ability to pay all the costs of doing business, whether those costs involve regular expenditure obligations, or irregular, extraordinary expenditure obligations such as pension costs or capital replacement or maintenance costs. In other words, is the governmental unit financially healthy enough to withstand all.of its expenditure demands over the long term?

4. *Service level solvency.* The ICMA study defines this as the ability, over the long term, to provide all services required for the "general health and welfare of a community." Obviously, this kind of solvency is difficult to measure with precision, but it is nevertheless a very real phenomenon— especially in the minds of citizens, whose willingness to help pay for the costs of debt service obligations must be a consideration of the analyst or investor.

It should be noted that the kind of solvency that is to be the focus of research depends on the kind of risk that is acceptable. Bond dealers, interested primarily in liquidity risk, might be interested in long-range solvency only to the extent that it (or a wide-spread perception of the lack of it) might affect their chances of "turning over" their portfolio. On the other hand, an investor interested in a secure, long-term investment, would be more interested in long-range solvency and even service-level solvency.

Analytical Format

Any analysis of municipal financial condition, whether focusing on credit analysis or any of the other purposes mentioned above, can make use of any one of a number of analytical formats. A number of such formats have been distinguished by public finance expert Roy Bahl, and are listed below. It should be noted however, that different authors use different terms to identify these formats.

1. *Comparative quantitative studies.* This name is sometimes given to basic research studies that attempt to determine cause and effect relationships between external environmental factors confronting a municipality, such as broad economic, demographic, or social factors, and the actual fiscal performance of municipalities. These kinds of studies may be the most influential in areas other than credit analysis.

Cross sectional studies constitute a variety of the comparative quantitative studies. They are usually characterized by (1) assumptions about cause-effect relationships between external environmental factors and fiscal performance; (2) the assemblage of environmental data for a large of number of states and/or localities; (3) the analysis of this data to develop rankings among the governmental units in terms of their levels of financial stress; and (4) the identification of "outliers" that are in imminent financial danger.

2. *Case studies.* These tend to be detailed studies focusing primarily on the specifics of a single city, state or region. The advantage to such a study is that it does not have to restrict itself to external environmental factors, but can also examine budgetary and accounting data that may be available. But by the same token, these kind of detailed analyses are very hard to compare for different municipalities, because of differences in the nature of the data available.

Comparative case studies would seem to be natural solutions to the problems of comparability encountered with the detailed case study approach. The difficulty comes in deciding how to limit and standardize the detail in such a way that comparability results, without loss of explanatory and predictive power.

Credit analysis is not typically limited to any particular analytical format. It may involve any or all of these formats depending on the nature of acceptable risk, and the kind (or kinds) of solvency the analyst is interested in, as well as the level of confidence a particular firm has in its case study techniques, its cross-sectional data base, etc. Credit rating agencies seem to be interested primarily in comparative credit risk. Although they are ostensibly concerned with long-range solvency and even service-level solvency, they have a limited time in which to analyze a great number of credits. They also change their ratings whenever they feel such changes are called for. Their analytical formats tend to be less like case studies and more cross sectional in nature. They do examine detailed accounting and budgetary data but depend on certain "rules of thumb" to enhance the comparability of such analysis.

In a municipal bond insurance firm, on the other hand, the relative emphasis on the two basic kinds of formats is reversed. These firms are not interested in comparative ratings of credit worthiness. And because the insurance coverage typically extends for the life of the bond issue, and cannot be altered or terminated any time prior to full retirement of the debt, a long-range perspective is a necessity in their analysis. As a result, they focus on careful, detailed case studies of the financial health of their clients, and supplement these with cross-sectional data that seems relevant.

Standards of Assessment

Each general type of analytical format implies by its design an emphasis on certain kinds of standards for use in measuring whether or not a municipality is experiencing robust fiscal health.

1. *Absolute standards.* Almost everyone agrees that there exist no "absolute" standards of municipal financial performance. State and local governmental units are simply too different, one from another, in many ways, and the on-going activities of government are too complex and dynamic to allow for the establishment of standards that unfailingly gauge financial health or distress. Efforts to develop standards of municipal financial performance are also hindered by the lack of agreed upon definitions of financial health or distress. The credit analyst focuses on whether or not a municipality will make timely debt service payments. The worst possibility is of course default. This involves not having the cash to pay one's bills on time. But which standards of performance can predict this state of affairs ahead of time?

2. *Comparisons.* Because such standards are lacking, a comparative approach is often used. This was the method described above in connection with cross-sectional studies. It involves comparing a number of municipalities on the basis of criteria that can be applied to all, identifying those municipalities that are in some way out of the ordinary, and ranking all of the entities studied in terms of someone's judgment about how extraordinary performance relates to fiscal health. This approach depends on accumulating comparable data on as large a sample as possible. It should be noted, however, that comparisons are just that and nothing more. Whether or not fiscal health is actually being measured really depends on the health of the larger sample. The approach is also limited by the fact that the large size of the sample, and the consequent need for a relatively small number of highly comparable indicators, easily leads to neglect of unique specific and hard to compare characteristics of units involved.

3. *Bench marks, rules of thumb, intuitive or a priori indicators, etc.* As we saw above, case studies and comparative case studies offer a way of taking into account the unique specific characteristics of governmental units, but the ability to compare with precision large numbers of units is sacrificed. The pragmatic way out of this dilemma used by credit analysts is to employ "rules of thumb" as standards against which performance can be judged in the hard to compare areas. Some of these rules presumably have been established on the basis of many comparisons over a long period of time. One piece of conventional wisdom has been the classic caution that local indebtedness should not exceed 10 percent of assessed valuation. Other rules

of this kind involve non-specific danger signals that are based more on an intuitive understanding of fiscal distress than on specific numbers or percentages drawn from past experience. Examples of these kinds of rule might involve whether or not the governmental unit in question has a capital improvement plan, what kind of accounting and reporting systems are used, and whether or not it engages in financial "gimmickery."

4. *Trend analysis.* Finally, any or all of the above kinds of standards can be examined over time, to establish whether or not trends exist that may affect the future financial health of the municipality. The existence of an operating deficit, for example, may have little meaning if the governmental unit has a record of occasional deficits followed by careful managerial countermeasures. A low ranking for a given municipality, relative to many others in a research sample, may carry little weight if it shows a record of steady improvement. And time series data can give weight to characteristics of a municipality that otherwise would be impossible to assess. For example, the population of a given city may be meaningless, except to determine in a general sense if the city is large or small. But a steady decline in population could be one indicator of approaching problems and would have to be examined carefully by the analyst.

Analytical Indicators

No matter what the analytical format, most credit analysis frameworks make use of four different kinds of specific indicators. John Petersen, Director of the Government Finance Officers Association's Government Finance Research Center, has described three kinds of indicators, all of which are now commonly used by social scientists and government analysts, as well as credit analysts.

1. *Financial statement indicators.* These indicators offer measures of operating fund performance (e.g., deficit or surplus), and balance sheet liquidity. As the name implies, these indicators use the summary data from the operating statements, or comparisons of these figures. Petersen points out that this kind of indicator possesses a kind of rigor and symmetrical structure that seem to produce unambiguous assessments of the financial performance of governmental entities (e.g., either there is an operating deficit or there is not). But he goes on to argue that unless they are subjected to trend analysis and examined in the light of supplementary data, their meaning is anything but clear. And as we have already noted, these kinds of figures are sometimes difficult to obtain and highly dependent on the particular accounting basis and accounting practices used to produce them. Finally, it is worth noting that financial statement indicators tend to show

the immediate financial position of the governmental enterprise and provide little from which future financial behavior can be projected. In this sense they tend at best to show the effects, rather than the causes of financial distress.

2. *General financial indicators.* These measures usually consist of ratios that either relate fiscal behavior to various measures of magnitude (e.g., debt outstanding as a percentage of personal income), or simply combine financial variables for the purposes of comparison among municipalities (e.g., annual debt service as a percentage of annual own-source revenues). As Petersen notes, these measures lack the rigor and symmetry of the financial statement indicators, but they rely on information that is more easily obtainable and comparable. But by the same token, these ratios must be compared among municipalities before they make much sense, or compared against benchmarks which themselves should have been established by cross-sectional analysis. And in the process of exploiting the relative easy availability of ratio data, the analyst must be cautious of using information collected and summarized by supplementary sources. Petersen and others have pointed out that commonly used sources such as the Government Division of the United States Bureau of the Census provide data that is often unreliable for financial analysis (and the Census Bureau admits this). This is because of omissions and distortions resulting from summarization.

3. *Socio-economic indicators.* These indicators attempt to measure the overall impact of external environmental factors on municipal financial health. Such factors include population size, median age, personal income, property values, etc. These factors are usually subjected to trend-analysis and often combined to form ratios for comparative purposes (e.g., number of public assistance recipients as a percentage of total population). These kinds of indicators have often been used in large cross-sectional studies of municipal financial condition because of the need to use a limited number of quantitative indicators in such research. Because the basic information is easily attainable, and because external economic changes appear to be having an increasingly important impact on municipal financial performance, these kinds of indicators are now an important part of most credit analysis frameworks. It should be noted, however, that except for extreme cases (the loss of a principal tax paying industry, sudden widespread unemployment, etc.) there is as yet no widely accepted theory that demonstrates specific causal links between external economic factors and municipal financial performance.

4. *Administrative factors.* These are playing an increasingly important role in credit analysis, coming to the fore in political and managerial problems prevalent in the financial difficulties of New York City in the mid-

1970s, and WPPSS in the late 1970s. The significance of these variables depends very much on the experience or point of view of the individual analyst. These tend to be qualitative factors that are somewhat difficult to identify, obtain information about, and assess, especially within frameworks that tend to be primarily quantitative in nature. In most cases they involve general political or managerial characteristics or practices that must be assessed somewhat subjectively (the degree of centralization or managerial professionalism, the nature and extent of long-range planning, etc.). In most cases they also include "red flags." These are characteristics or practices— usually directly associated with financial management, but not necessarily so—that require careful and immediate consideration by the analyst. Typical "red flags" would be the use of short-term borrowing to cover an operating deficit, deferring capital maintenance, as well as various kinds of accounting "gimmickry," and their pattern of use.

Few empirical studies have been conducted to determine what specific analytical indicators are actually used by credit analysts. Obviously most investment firms consider the details of their analytical procedures to be proprietary. The credit rating firms give somewhat general pictures of the kinds of procedures used, and occasionally they give an opinion on the use of a specific indicator—as have Fitch, Moody's and Standard & Poor's with regard to their decreasing reliance on per capita debt ratios.

Studies, like one completed by Boyett and Giroux in 1978, have asked financial analysts, underwriters and institutional investors to respond to survey questionnaires that required them to rank a large number of information items, or indicators, in order of their importance for credit analysis.

Most of the indicators ranked in these surveys, can all be developed from information suggested for disclosure by the Government Finance Officers Association's, *Disclosure Guidelines,* but typically they do not include the kinds of managerial variables discussed above. Indicators ranked in these studies are listed below in a rough order of preference, according to analysts surveyed in the various studies.

1. Total debt outstanding
2. Debt to actual value ratio
3. Overlapping debt outstanding
4. Debt per capita
5. Tax collection history
6. Changes in financial position
7. Population trends, income, etc.
8. Actual value of property in tax jurisdiction

9. Operating revenues
10. Assessed valuation
11. Tax rate limits
12. Operating expenditures
13. Debt to assessed value ratio
14. Accounting policies used
15. Principal taxpayers
16. Portion of tax rates applicable to debt
17. Tax rate history
18. Sinking funds applicable to outstanding debt
19. Bond rating
20. Current assets and liabilities
21. Fixed assets

CONCLUSION: LIMITATIONS ON THE "SCIENCE" OF CREDIT ANALYSIS

In spite of the efforts of Wall Street firms and institutional investors to improve their credit analysis capabilities, errors in judgment will continue to be made. Unlike techniques used in the credit analysis of taxable securities, tax-exempt credit analysis is still as much an art as a science, due to the lack of a large number of standards with broad applicability to government entities.

Almost everyone agrees that there exist no "absolute" standards of municipal financial performance. State and local governmental units are simply too different from each other in too many ways, and the on-going activities of government too complex and dynamic to allow for the establishment of standards that unfailingly gauge financial health or distress. Efforts to develop standards of municipal financial performance are also hindered somewhat by the lack of agreed upon definitions of financial health or distress. Governmental units, within the limits of their resources (and applicable statutes) respond to needs articulated by their electorates. Differences exist in the quantity and quality of resources, and the managerial skills available to deliver services. The credit analyst focuses on whether or not a municipality will make timely debt service payments. The worst possibility is of course default. This involves not having the cash to pay one's bills when due. But which standards of performance can predict this state of affairs ahead of time?

As has been noted, part of the problem in predicting default is the fact that so few municipal defaults have occurred in the United States since World War II. Little information about the defaults that have occurred has been systematically gathered and analyzed for the purpose of refining the nature and use of existing indicators of financial condition. In other words, there are few existing standards with which municipal performance can be measured, and default predicted. Many of the reasons that led to default in the 1930s simply do not exist today. In large part, this is due to a variety of safeguards that have been adopted to reduce the chances, and limit the damage, of the kinds of defaults that occurred during the 1930s.

The fact that there have been but few recent municipal defaults does not necessarily mean that there will be few defaults in the future. Many analysts feel that the problems of issuers like New York City, Cleveland, WPPSS, and others, are the problems that could face other issuers in the 1990s or later.

* *Source:*   James Leigland

BIBLIOGRAPHY

Roy W. Bahl. "Revenue and Expenditure Forecasting by State and Local Governments," in *State and Local Government Finance and Financial Management: A Compendium of Current Research*, Petersen, Spain, and Laffey (Eds.) (Washington, D.C.: Government Finance Research Center, 1978).

Arthur S. Boyett and Gary A. Giroux. "The Relevance of Municipal Finance Statements for Investor Decisions: An Empirical Study," *Governmental Finance* (April 1978).

Sanford M. Groves, W. Maureen Godsey, and Martha A. Shulman. "Financial Indicators for Local Government," *Public Budgeting & Finance*, Vol. 1 (Summer 1981).

James Leigland and Robert Lamb. *WPP$$: Who is to Blame for the WPPSS Disaster* (Cambridge, MA: Ballinger Publishing, 1986).

John Petersen. "Simplification and Standardization of State and Local Government Fiscal Indicators," *National Tax Journal*, Vol. 30 (September 1977).

Chapter II

Special Assessment Bond Topics*

What are special assessment bonds?

Simply stated, special assessment bonds are debt instruments secured by a pledge of an additional or special charge to property owners within a defined area.

How are assessments levied?

Usually the assessments are levied as a result of local action, either by property owners or by a municipal council. Charges are allocated by a common formula, typically using acreage, front footage, or similar physical measures.

How do these bonds differ from bonds secured by an ad valorem tax?

First, in most cases, the assessment is not a tax, although it is often collected with ad valorem taxes. However, it is not usually based on the value of the property but on the benefit derived from an improvement. Second, with a strict special assessment bond, there is no general obligation pledge. The revenue stream provided by the assessments usually must cover debt service payments.

Are there any other ways special assessments differ from property taxes?

In most states, since special assessments are not regarded as taxes, they are not tax deductible for the property owner. The reason behind this seems to be that improvement adds value to the property rather than incurs costs for the owner. But, in most cases, the assessment has more in common with ad valorem taxes than not, including the same collection agent and schedule, equal lien on property, and the same delinquency and foreclosure practices.

What are benefits relative to general obligation financing?

Special assessment bonds are not usually subject to municipal debt issuance caps because they charge beneficiary property owners directly rather than act as a charge against the municipality's general fund. Additionally, the political burden of deciding which neighborhood will be improved is reduced because property owners decide and pay for the improvements they want.

What improvements are most commonly financed?

Municipalities generally choose special assessment financing for water and sewer lines, sidewalks, streets, lighting, and similar small-scale infrastructure improvements. There have also been cases where these bonds are used to provide landscaping, neighborhood parks, commercial parking structures, and even police and fire stations.

When is a special assessment bond most likely chosen as a financing tool?

The real test of the appropriateness of special assessment bonds is the potential public benefit weighed against property owners' ability to pay for these benefits.

Do many states authorize special assessment bonds?

At least 19 states have legislation on the books. Although procedures differ slightly from one state to another, they all have much in common in their method of establishing districts assessing properties, collecting assessments, and issuing bonds—Alaska, California, Colorado, Florida, Hawaii, Idaho, Illinois, Kentucky, Louisiana, Maryland, Michigan, Montana, Nevada, New Mexico, North Dakota, Ohio, South Dakota, Wisconsin, and Wyoming. Other states may issue special assessment bonds by offering either a general fund or ad valorem tax pledge which, in effect, makes them general obligation bonds. Also, some states allow for a millage levy to augment the debt service reserve fund.

Where is an increased use of this type of debt financing likely?

It is most likely in high growth areas. Since the bonds are used for infrastructure purposes, we would expect that as increased pressures on general revenue mount with growth, more municipalities will turn to special revenue financing. California has a long history of issuance and we would not be surprised to see more issues there as well as in Florida and Colorado.

What makes a strong special assessment district?

The best conditions are a strong economic base, a stable labor market with diversification among employers, good wealth and income indicators, and increasing property values. It is important, from a financial standpoint, that projected cash flows cover debt service even in adverse conditions, such as nonpayment by a large property owner or an industry susceptible to cyclical downturns. Strong municipal management is needed to administrate the improvement project as well as to monitor assessment collections.

What are other potential weaknesses?

The greatest weakness, perhaps, lies in the relatively small size of most special assessment districts. A small number of property owners, a few property owners who make up the bulk of assessment revenues, or a concentration of property owners within one industry can detract from the financing. Thin coverage margins, small debt service reserves, and weak delinquency or foreclosure procedures can have a negative impact on the bonds. And, of course, low value-to-lien ratios indicate a greater incentive for property owners to walk away from their assessment obligations.

What documentation is necessary to evaluate a special assessment bond issue?

The documentation is similar to our requirements for most general obligation and revenue bonds. We require an official statement and bond indenture. It would be helpful, in addition, to have copies of state enabling and implementation legislation as well as any pertinent case law. Feasibility studies on the project to be financed as well as the consulting engineer's recommendations and findings are also necessary. Copies of outside contracts, agreements, or grant commitments are also requested, if the case warrants it.

What other information is required?

Essential requirements are economic and demographic descriptions of the project area, and information on the largest employers and assessment payers in the district is essential. We also ask for a five-year history of properties within the assessment district to examine tax levies, collections, delinquencies, foreclosures, land uses, and property values. A market study to demonstrate the value and demand for district property is also beneficial. Finally, projected cash flows for best estimate worse case scenarios for special assessment revenues, expenses, debt service, and coverage ratios are required.

* *Source: Standard & Poor's CreditWeek.*
  Reprinted by courtesy of Standard & Poor's Corporation.

Chapter III

*Airport Revenue Bond Criteria**

Deregulation of the airline industry and the cyclicality of airline profits have affected the creditworthiness of the nation's airports in several respects.

Operationally, deregulation resulted in more variable enplanement and airline service patterns at individual airports. In general, major air carriers cut back service at smaller airports with commuter airlines stepping in to offer a greater frequency of flights with fewer seats per flight. At many larger airports, passenger activity and airline service grew at record high rates, significantly influenced by airfare discounts and other airline marketing strategies.

At many of the airports experiencing the greatest recent growth in passenger traffic, cash flow improved markedly due to increases in parking and other concession revenues. However, capital requirements also increased and future financing estimates rose. Consequently, the long-range financial picture at many of the airports experiencing the greatest operational growth since deregulation in 1978 has not significantly improved.

In the legal area, as airlines become more competitive, they are increasingly unwilling to commit to use agreements equalizing rates across all air carriers or to approve major airport capital improvement programs. Moreover, as some airport directors seek to more aggressively manage their facilities and capture, in terms of earnings, the benefits of operational increases, a growing number of airports approach the markets with airline use agreements shorter than the term of their bonds, or with no use agreements at all.

Administratively, the greatest impact of deregulation occurred at airports where management moved away from the procedural setting afforded by use agreements to a more flexible management approach. The ability of airport administrators to function effectively in this new environment is still largely untested. Most airports that use this approach for any length of time have historically strong operations. A lengthy record of experience, through good and bad times, has not yet been accumulated by airport management teams recently opting to forego the protections of traditional use agreements.

In light of these developments, S&P refined its approach toward rating airport revenue bonds. The key to this evolution in rating policy is the recognition that passengers, not airlines, are the true users of an airport, and that the viability of an airport is mostly a function of demand for the entire facility. This approach now places more emphasis on underlying air traffic and less emphasis on airline use agreements.

AIR TRAFFIC DEMAND

The first step in evaluating air traffic demand is defining the local service area. An airport's reach frequently exceeds the boundaries of its city's limits, or even an entire metropolitan area. Competitive facilities within or near a service area are a source of concern, especially if the competition offers a better level of service, as passengers may be willing to travel farther on the ground to get cheaper fares or more frequent air service.

The local economy's direction and strength are related to past demand patterns and help identify future trends. Factors analyzed include historical and projected population growth. A growing population is likely to require more air service, and will thus add to airport revenues. Employment growth and mix are also critical in evaluating the local economy. Reliance on one industry or a history of cyclical economic activity are basic weaknesses that can exaggerate the effects of any national recession. Another key variable is the wealth of the service area, as affluent populations typically can support greater air service levels.

The breakdown between business and recreational travel is also important. Airports that rely on business travel will be most affected by the strength of local employment, while those serving tourist economies will rely upon vacationers whose numbers may fluctuate with swings in disposable income. For this reason, S&P considers those facilities not reliant upon tourism for traffic generation to be stronger. However, the existence of tourist attractions is considered positively as one component of a diverse economy.

TRAFFIC DIFFERENCES

The local economy's importance to the rating relates to the nature of the airport's traffic. If most of the airport's traffic is of the origination and destination (O&D) variety, the local economy will dictate the level of service demanded of the facility. On the other hand, an airport used heavily for connecting traffic is dependent on service area economics. Connecting traffic is a vulnerability since the connecting hub is dictated by the airline, not the passenger, and is therefore related to that carrier's viability and route decisions. In cases where the largest carrier represents more than half, or the top two account for more than two-thirds of enplaned passengers, and half of these are comprised of connecting passengers, S&P perceives a significant additional susceptibility. In these situations, a noninvestment grade S&P rating on the hubbing airlines traffic raises considerably more concerns that in an O&D facility.

A direct means of evaluating air traffic demand is an examination of historic airport utilization trends versus those of the nation. The key variable is enplanements. A facility that underperforms other airports during expansionary periods and outperforms them during recessionary periods is viewed more positively than one that grows spectacularly in good times but experiences above-average declines during retrenchment.

An independent feasibility study by a consultant experienced in the field is useful in estimating future airport utilization. The consultant typically makes a projection of future enplanements and aircraft operations and then derives a financial forecast. S&P closely examines and evaluates the consultant's assumptions and methodologies to arrive at an estimation of future utilization. While not always agreeing with the consultant's assumptions or conclusions, the reports usually play an important role in arriving at a rating determination.

USE AGREEMENTS

Use agreements between an airport and its carrier serve two major purposes under the broad goal of providing a reliable stream of revenues for debt repayment. The first purpose is to guarantee certain revenues; and the second is to establish procedures for administering revenue collection. Evaluating the strength of a particular airport's use agreements involves determining how much revenue is actually protected, how effective the procedures outlined in the agreement are in producing a reliable revenue flow, and how long the protection and procedures are in place.

In the past, S&P emphasized the existence of use agreements that would be in effect and provide revenue protection for the entire life of a bond issue. The main argument supporting this position was that the bondholders had a right to know that the various covenants and obligations between the signatory air carriers and the airport would not change—just as the bond resolution would not change—and revenue protection would not be reduced while the bonds were still outstanding. However, in the past, airlines were stronger financially and more stable in delivering service. Routing was regulated, and airlines could not quickly pull out of an airport. Moreover, major airlines were not filing for bankruptcy. Increased vulnerability in the airline industry causes S&P to reevaluate the revenue protection afforded by the typical use agreement.

AGREEMENT TERMS

In typical agreements, the signatory air carriers bear most of the risk of revenues falling below expectations or expenses increase above projected levels. The agreement specifies the manner in which landing fees, terminal rentals, and other charges are set, as well as the airport's flexibility in changing rates to recover costs. Terminal rentals are typically set on a per square foot basis. Landing fees are charged on the basis of airline landing weights and their revenues vary with the level of airline activity, while terminal rentals are more fixed.

No matter whether a compensatory method of computing airport fees is used, the level and quality of revenues locked in by use agreements must be examined to determine their value to bondholders. It is critical to note that the existence of use agreements does not ensure that an airport will experience any prescribed level of airline usage. An air carrier's financial obligations under a use agreement are very small in comparison to potential operating losses incurred by serving an airport with poor demand. An airline's decision on which airports to use is based more on fare levels and factors other than airport costs. Those costs typically constitute less than 7 percent of overall airline costs.

In the extreme, if one assumes that all airlines serving an airport land no planes and, therefore, pay no landing fees but continue to make terminal rent payments according to the use agreements, debt service payments in many cases could not be made or, at best, would be significantly jeopardized. Thus, while use agreements may provide an additional level of comfort in case a particular airline ceases to operate or alters its routing structure, the inherent demand in the air traffic market is the ultimate security for the bondholder. A strong market will continue to attract carriers to serve that demand, while even the strictest use agreement will not, in and of itself, insure timely payment of debt service.

The primary value of use agreements lies in establishing procedures for operating the airport and methods of charging rates and fees. Once this framework is established, even if the use agreements expire, the same procedures of revenue collection and management will likely be used to run the facility. Because procedural elements are not inherently tied to the use agreement's term, it follows that the actual term of these agreements assumes less importance in determining a credit rating.

It still remains preferable, however, for the bondholder to have use agreements, and for these agreements to extend for the life of the bonds. But barring, that in strong demand situations, an airport having no use agreements or short use agreements is not precluded from receiving investment grade ratings. Even so, such an airport may not be rated as highly as it might otherwise have been, especially if the use agreements were extremely strong.

AIRPORT-AIRLINE INTERRELATIONSHIP

S&P believes that passengers are an airport's customers, not airlines, and if there is sufficient demand, financial incentives will exist for a carrier to provide service. For this reason, S&P separates airport ratings from airline ratings, which are typically, but not exclusively, non-investment grade. This effectively treats airports as a special type of utility, rather than as lease obligations of various airlines. This general approach is not new; for years, S&P has rated airports higher than the airlines serving the facility. Nonetheless, the strength of the particular air carriers involved cannot be totally overlooked. Some tradeoffs between demand and legal factors are involved.

The mix of carriers serving an airport becomes increasingly important as any airline's share becomes greater. Dependence on one or two airlines creates a short-term vulnerability, as a strike could cripple an airport temporarily and have a significant short-term impact on financial operations. This problem can be mitigated, however, through careful construction of the legal documents by providing for ample reserve funds and coverage levels, mid-year flexibility to raise rates, and the ability to recover deficiencies occurring in the prior year.

For this reason, while one or two dominant air carriers may expose an airport to temporary problems, it is S&P's position that the critical rating factor is still the quality of air traffic demand, as this determines the exposure to a prolonged loss of airport activity. Uncertainties introduced by the volatile airline industry are reflected in the fact that no "straight" airport revenue bond is rated higher than 'A'. S&P currently rates approximately 75 airports based on airport revenues alone. From a rating perspective, it is best to have both strong air traffic demand and strong legal provisions; neither can be totally ignored. The rating will likely reflect cases where either underlying demand or legal provisions in the indenture and use agreements are weak.

OTHER CONSIDERATIONS

The concentration on the relative importance of demand and legal factors should not be construed as meaning these are the only two elements examined in rating an airport revenue bond. The size and purpose of the financing program undertaken and need for additional financing are also extremely important. The diversity of revenue sources, rate flexibility, and historical record of debt service coverage are also critical. Management considerations, such as the influence of local politics, the experience of senior management, and the presence of budget controls, to name some examples, are important. In addition, the role played by general obligation financing must be noted. G.O. debt paid from airport revenues but subordinate to revenue bonds provides a debt service cushion for those revenue bonds. G.O. debt paid from general tax sources is viewed as a type of equity contribution to an airport and strengthens the overall financial position.

While airport revenue bonds are different from other revenue bonds due to the existence of a private intermediary between the users of the service and the entity that pays debt service, the problems of airline intermediaries and the volatile industry within which they operate can be largely alleviated by strong airport demand factors, solid legal documents, and prudent financial operations.

* *Source: Standard & Poor's CreditWeek,* June 23, 1986.
Reprinted by courtesy of Standard & Poor's Corporation.

Chapter IV

General Obligation Debt Ratings*

G.O. RATINGS

After several years of decline, general obligation (G.O.) bonds made a strong comeback in 1985. Bonds backed by the full faith and credit of the issuing states and municipalities totaled $48.4 billion in 1985, a 75 percent increase over 1984. This volume represented 30 percent of the $161.5 billion tax-exempt debt total in 1985. The G.O. market share is the highest since 1980 when these issues captured 35 percent of the total.

Through the mid-1970s, G.O.s had dominated municipal capital financing. Various factors at that time forced a shift away from G.O. debt. These new measures included California'a Proposition 13, Michigan's Headley Amendment, and Massachusetts' Proposition 2 1/2. Nontraditional debt such as housing revenue bonds, industrial development financing and health care issues grew rapidly as a result. These new capital-raising techniques quickly overshadowed the traditional capital-market instruments. It was not until 1985 that significant indications of a sustained G.O. comeback appeared.

An issuer selling a G.O. bond secured by its full faith and credit attaches to that issue its broadest pledge. This security encompasses such things as its ability to levy an unlimited ad valorem property tax or to draw from other unrestricted revenue streams, such as sales or income taxes. However, the issuer's ability to actually generate any such revenue depends upon numerous factors. For S&P's analytical purposes, these factors have four classifications:

- Economic
- Financial
- Debt
- Administrative

ECONOMIC BASE

The economic base is the most critical element in determining an issuer's rating. A community's fiscal health derives from its economy, affecting such major revenue sources as sales, income and property taxes. Economic conditions also dictate the quantity and quality of services delivered in such categories of expenditures as welfare, community development, health care and the like.

Two kinds of criteria are brought into play in evaluating the economic base: general factors and specific comparisons.

General factors include issuer characteristics, demographics, tax base, employment base, income levels and diversity, and sales activity. Each contributes importantly to the evaluation process.

Issuer characteristics.   This first step in effect is a full camera sweep, taking in the issuer's location, transportation network, infrastructure, natural assets and liabilities.

Demographics.   Population analysis extends over a four-decade span. It embraces the impact of annexations and the effect of migration, inward and outward. The population is profiled in terms of age, education, wealth and income levels.

Tax base.   The initial focus is on diversity and growth. The tax base's composition is studied to establish proportionate contributions from residential, commercial and industrial sources. To determine the degree of concentration, the top 10 taxpayers are identified. Focus also is on the housing stock—i.e., its age and the extent of owner-occupancy. Significant changes in the tax base are reviewed in terms of both its composition and growth. Measurements of growth include assessed and market value trends as well as building permit activity.

Employment base.   Diversity and growth of the employment base also are prime considerations. This scrutiny includes:

- Composition by sector (manufacturing, durable and nondurable; trade; construction; fire and police; community services; government administration).
- Shifts within these sectors.
- Concentration, to determine relative reliance on single employer or industry.

- Employer commitment to the community, trends in work forces (expanding or contracting), business development plans, age of plants, vigor of industry.
- Employment trends, to measure local-economy performance during recession with special focus on local employment vis-à-vis general labor force trends.

(The quality of the local labor force—i.e., the match between the skills and education levels of the labor force and the employment base—has become an increasingly important consideration owing to the shift to a service economy and the loss of traditional entry-level jobs).

Retail sales. Analyzed for growth and market share, this activity can indicate a community is locally or regionally important as a shopping center. This factor increases in importance if a point-of-sale formula determines the sales tax receipts.

Comparative Criteria

Specific comparisons of the general factors outlined above then are made with overall data at the state and national level. These criteria, where appropriate (wealth and income levels are examples), also are compared with SMSA data.

Sources

Data for economic analysis must come, in part, from the issuer itself. Other sources include the Bureau of Census, Departments of Commerce, Labor and Agriculture, the State Labor Departments, and from such publications as *Sales Management and Marketing Magazine*. Additionally, S&P uses as an in-house data bank Interactive Rating Support System (IRSS).

Summary

Generally, those communities with higher income levels and diverse economic bases have superior debt repayment capabilities. They are better protected against sudden economic fluctuations than communities less fortunately situated. But even when economic change is slower its impact can be persistent. Thus an issuer's ability to meet long-term debt service must be a long-term consideration. A high current capacity to pay may not translate into a long-term strength.

FINANCIAL INDICATORS

Financial analysis involves several areas within this broad category: (a) accounting and reporting methods; (b) sources of revenues and uses and expenditures; (c) annual operating histories; (d) balance sheet history; (e) budget and financial planning; and (f) such miscellaneous variables as pension fund position and other long-term obligations. The combination of these factors will present a clear indication of the financial strengths and weaknesses of an issuer.

Accounting and Reporting

The first and possibly most important variable is the accounting and financial reporting methods. Predicated on the basic guidelines of Generally Accepted Accounting Principles (GAAP), S&P assesses the treatment of revenues and expenditures as well as assets and liabilities.

The accounting methods utilized are examined with the modified-accrual basis most often employed for governmental funds, i.e., general funds, debt-service fund and special-revenue fund. Governmental Accounting Standards Board (GASB) interpretations of accounting rulings are considered in evaluating the organization of funds, accruals and other financial methods. GAAP reporting is considered a credit strength, and the ability to meet Government Finance Officers of America's (GFOA) Certificate of Conformance requirements is also viewed favorably. A Comprehensive Annual Financial Report (CAFR) should include significant financial data, information on debt and other long-term liabilities and various statistical charts.

Although S&P does not perform an audit, it expects issuers to supply adequate and timely financial reports, preferably prepared by an independent certified public accountant. Lack of an audited financial report prepared according to GAAP could have a negative impact on an issuer's rating. Offsetting factors such as an extremely strong reported financial position or consistently strong cash-flow history may be given positive consideration in view of nonGAAP reporting. If audits are prepared by state agencies or other internal government units, S&P is interested in the independence and timeliness of such reports. A copy of the management letter which accompanies an independent audit is also requested along with the issuer's plans to meet any cited problem areas.

Current Account Analysis

Account analysis includes an examination of operating trends focusing on the composition of revenue sources and expenditure items, primarily within the general fund and debt-service funds. If other funds are tax-supported or include revenues relative to general government purposes (i.e., highway or park and recreation funds), they, too, will be carefully considered. Revenue-source diversity lends strength to financial conditions; if the income stream is dependent on one or two revenue sources, economic downturns could severely affect revenue flow. A balanced composition of revenues gives an issuer the maximum flexibility to meet all its obligations, not just those due the long-term bondholder. Recent history indicates that in order for an issuer to remain a viable entity, it must be able to operate day-to-day, meet operating expenses, and pay debt service. Major revenue sources such as property, sales and income taxes, intergovernmental aid, investment income and user-charges are analyzed over a three-to-five-year period. S&P looks for shifting proportions or decreases in revenue sources that could lead to future financial difficulties.

Similarly, expenditures are analyzed in relationship to revenue patterns. The growth of operating budget expenditures is viewed in the light of the pattern of population changes, and tax base increases or decreases. Large expenditure items are identified and examined to determine their possible burdensome effect. Changes in expenditure classifications are examined carefully. Debt-service costs as a part of total expenditures are evaluated to assess the burden of debt retirement. Revenue and expenditure balance or imbalance over a period of years is analyzed. The balance sheet is reviewed to determine the cumulative effect of each year's revenue and expenditure position.

The financial-position examination focuses on liquidity, the fund balance position and the composition of assets and liabilities. In S&P's consideration of fund balance size, several variables are important: the cash-flow of an issuer (i.e., tax collection patterns versus spending patterns); other reserves or contingency funds available to meet unforeseen expenses, and the philosophy of government officials and the overall community toward large government revenue surpluses. Since the fund-balance position is a measure of the flexibility of an issuer to meet essential services during transitionary periods, S&P does consider an adequate fund balance a credit strength. Finally, in reviewing the operating fund and financial position, the effect of any transfers of revenue is considered. Where the general fund (and/or debt-service fund) is supported by transfers from other funds, S&P looks to determine the policy guidelines and transfer practices historically.

The analysis of the financial performance takes into account the role of short-term financing and its implications. As outside fiscal (state and federal) aids decrease, and since taxing calendars do not always meet expenditure patterns, cash-flow difficulties can become more prominent. S&P's staff has been rating short-term debt since 1982 (see page 103). This understanding of cash-flow patterns is carefully integrated into the flow-of-funds analysis.

Creative management and financial strategies can enable an issuer to minimize cash-flow problems. But S&P is ever mindful of issuers' ventures into risky strategies—i.e., those which may prove reliable in the short-run but problematic in the long-run. In reviewing an issuers cash-management and investment practice, the types of investments, security precautions and uses of investment income are considered.

The budget documents are reviewed and compared with actual operations. This is a significant indicator of financial and managerial strengths. In budget development and planning, assumptions and forecasts are extremely important. S&P is interested in the strategies built into future budgets and the monitoring systems utilized to determine budget execution.

Pensions and Other Long-Term Liabilities

Other factors have become increasingly important in considering the financial condition of a municipal debt issuer. Pension fund position, other long-term liabilities and risk management have significant impact on financial performance. While all areas of expenditure growth are important indicators, pension fund requirements are particularly noteworthy. S&P expects issuers to provide recent and ongoing actuarial valuation reports. The emphasis of the pension fund analysis is toward the trends and ratios of asset accumulation versus accruing benefits.

While "unfunded accrued liabilities" generally is considered a major indicator, it is often clouded by the assumptions and funding methodologies involved. Furthermore, the rate or return on investments may be predicated on various assumptions whose accuracy could affect significantly the level of unfunded liabilities. Recent GASB rulings regarding computation methods are designed to standardize pension fund reporting for the public sector. However, in view of current limitations and lack of standardization in valuation studies, no system-by-system comparison analysis can be undertaken. S&P's effort involves trend-data analysis on individual systems, with the direction of such trends closely monitored.

Long-term contingent liabilities are examined to determine the issuers exposure to financial pressures. Accrued sick and vacation pay costs should be accounted for at least as a footnote within the financial statements. It is considered a strength for a reserve fund to be established to cover some or all of such costs.

Risk management for governmental issuers has become increasingly more complex. In light of the difficulties of assuring that sufficient coverage can be provided by traditional insurance programs, this area has become of greater significance. S&P is interested in the types of coverage, and where self-insured programs exist, the amount of insurance reserves set aside to meet claims. Sound management and financial planning can effectively meet concerns where long-term liabilities face an issuer—if resources are available and allocated to meet such liabilities.

DEBT FACTORS

The analysis of debt focuses on the nature of the pledged security, the debt structure, the current debt burden and on the future financing needs of an issuer. Because debt level and structure are important credit factors, an issuance pace that overburdens a municipality may lead to rating downgrades. Conversely, a low debt burden may not be positive. Low debt could evidence underinvestment in infrastructure, which could impede economic growth. Indeed, fiscal crises in the 1970s left some large cities with a backlog of capital needs that is placing downward pressure on their credit ratings. Long-term debt issued to finance operating expenditures or to fund deficits has a negative credit impact. While deficit financing may ease a crisis, it is not a cure for financial problems.

To analyze debt, S&P focuses on four factors:

- Type and strength of security pledged.
- Maturity schedule and whether it matches the life of the projects being financed.
- The degree of reliance on short-term debt or variable-rate put bonds.
- Current debt burden and future financing needs.

Type of Security

A G.O. pledge takes various forms which provide different degrees of strength.

Unlimited ad valorem tax debt, secured by a full faith and credit pledge with no limit on tax rate or levy, carries the strongest security. However, during a period of fiscal stress, debt service must compete with essential services such as police and fire protection.

Limited ad valorem tax debt, or a limited tax pledge, carries legal limits on tax rates that can be levied for debt service. S&P views this type of security more as a means to limit debt than as a strict cap on revenues available to retire debt. In a limited tax situation, the tax base's growth and the economy's health are more significant credit factors than the limited source of payment. In fact, a limited tax bond can be rated on par with unlimited bonds if there is enough margin within the tax limit to raise the levy or if other tax revenues are available for debt service.

Double-barreled bonds are secured by an enterprise system's revenues, such as by water or sewer user charges. They also carry a full faith and credit pledge, but taxing power is used only if the enterprise's revenues are insufficient. S&P's approach is to rate both pledges—the government and the enterprise—and to assign the higher of the two ratings. A well-run enterprise system can enhance the general government's credit by making substantial financial contributions to the general fund, or because the enterprise has greater flexibility in setting its rates than the government has in setting its tax levy. However, a troubled utility can severely drain the general fund.

Credit implications may be positive when the enterprise has:

1. A solid track record of self-support.
2. Covenants to maintain rates.
3. Other provisions which would work to prevent a potential fiscal drain upon the general fund.

Special assessment bonds are now rated based on their own creditworthiness. Such bonds may have some speculative characteristics. But a lien on parity with or ahead of ad valorem taxes, legal protections, economic incentives for timely payment, in addition to low risk associated with the particular project, can mitigate concerns. If the assessment can be reallocated in the event of bankruptcy of one or more of the participants, credit protection is improved. The project's importance to those paying the assessments is critical in determining if timely payment will be made. Water, sewer, or street improvements generally meet this test, while landscaping might not. A high ratio of property value to debt is another indication of the likelihood of timely payment. A debt service reserve fund or other security feature that will cure problems associated with delayed collections is essential.

A moral obligation pledge occurs when an issuing entity relies on another to make up any deficiency in the debt service reserve fund. That pledge is most often given by a state to the debt of its agencies or authorities. The promise of the state to appropriate money to the debt service reserve fund usually enhances the creditworthiness of the issuing authority. Close attention is paid to the public purpose being served by the project (the more essential it is, the more likely it is that successive legislatures will appropriate funds for debt service). In most cases, S&P rates moral obligation debt one category below the G.O. debt of the guarantor.

Maturity Schedule

The maturity schedule can become important in some circumstances. Prudent use of debt dictates that the bond's term matches the useful life of the facilities being financed, even though the legal obligation to repay exists. For example, 15-year bonds issued to finance police cars would be viewed negatively.

An average maturity schedule for capital projects is one in which 25 percent of the debt rolls off in five years, and 50 percent is retired in 10 years. A faster maturity schedule is viewed positively only if it does not place undue strain on the operating budget, or if the expected life of resources paying off the debt is shorter than the facility's useful life.

Debt Structure

Short-term debt is now a permanent part of many municipalities' cash flow management and capital structure. To accommodate the different types of short-term debt being issued, S&P has three sets of symbols: municipal notes rated 'SP-1' to 'SP-3'; tax-exempt commercial paper rated 'A-1' to 'D'; and variable rate put bonds with dual ratings, for example 'AAA/A-1'.

In the 1970s, municipalities under the greatest stress had the heaviest short-term debt burdens. If properly used, however, short-term debt is a valuable management tool that evens out the flow of receipts and disbursements. The short-term market also provides lower interest costs when the long-term rates are temporarily high. It does carry risks: Limits on the period during which notes can be outstanding may force an issuer into the long-term market when rates are higher.

Excessive reliance on short-term debt can result in a lowered credit rating. Such is the case of Camden County, New Jersey. The county guaranteed the project notes of its Municipal Utilities Authority being used to finance construction of a large regional sewage treatment facility. Contingent liability that accompanies the guarantee is projected to exceed the county's bonded indebtedness by project completion in the next two to three years. This market-access risk was the primary reason why the county's rating was reduced to 'BBB' from 'A' last year.

Balloon or bullet maturities expose the bondholder to market access risks which are not present in serial maturities. Because balloons must be refinanced to assure timely repayment, a large amount of debt comes due at one time. However, several circumstances provide a degree of comfort. S&P prefers small balloons to large ones, and prefers a long maturity to a short one. Moreover, an issuer with a high long-term rating, good operating record, and satisfactory plan for dealing with the balloon is viewed more favorably.

Put or variable rate demand bonds may have a final maturity in 25 years, but holders have the right to demand the entire principal and interest within a short period of time (for example, every seven to 30 days). S&P assumes all holders simultaneously will exercise the put option. Therefore, credit quality of both the long-term serial maturity and the demand portion are analyzed, and two ratings are assigned. For example, an issuer may have variable rate demand bonds rated 'A/A-1'. The 'A' reflects the likelihood of timely repayment of the serial maturity, and the 'A-1' may be based on the rating of the bank providing liquidity support for the put. The issuer's ability to honor the put or possible onerous repayment terms from a bank providing the liquidity support can negatively impact the long-term debt rating.

Debt Limitations and Needs

S&P looks for realistic debt limitations that permit the issuer to meet its ongoing financing needs. A city near its debt limit has less flexibility to meet future capital needs—but, more importantly, may be unable to borrow money in the event of a financial emergency. Restrictive debt limitations often result in the creation of financing mechanisms that do not require G.O. bond authorization or voter approval.

S&P examines the community's future financing needs, in particular, evidence of regular needs assessment as well as planning for capital improvements is sought. History of past bond referendums indicates the community's willingness to pay. S&P also measures the debt burden against a community's ability to repay, that is, against the tax base, the disposable income of the community, and total budget resources. In general, a debt burden is viewed as high when debt service payments are 15 percent-20 percent of the combined operating and debt service fund expenditures.

ADMINISTRATIVE FACTORS

As municipal operations expand and become more complex, an understanding of the organization of government is a prime requisite. It establishes an entity's ability to execute autonomous actions, with the focus being the entity's degree of autonomy including home rule powers, legal and political relationships at state and local levels.

The range and level of services provided by the issuer also is examined in relation to the capacity to provide such services. Tested, too, is the ability of officials to make timely and sound financial decisions to meet both economic and fiscal demands. Tenure or term of office, frequency of elections and the background and experience of key members of the administration are important considerations, to the extent that they affect continuity and ability to formulate and execute plans.

There are several elements in the organization of government beyond the control of the administration, (e.g., state statute, voter initiative or political reality). But even where constraints exist, a strong and innovative administration will find ways to lessen this effect. The ability to work with what is available, and gain maximum results is a key factor in this area.

Documenting the Planning Goals

Long-range financial planning goals and objectives should be well documented, and should include projections for fund and cash balances as well as anticipated sources of revenues and expenditures. Revenue requirements must be able to respond to the needs of expenditures. Total reliance on one or two revenue sources could be of concern. Ability to make accurate short-range requirements, is a consideration. Financial planning goals and objectives should be closely aligned with the same format as that of the operating budget, to reflect proposed or projected future revenues and capital and other expenditures. Adherence to long-range financial plans is considered a reflection of good forecasting and planning.

Financial Management

Financial management is a major factor to be considered in the evaluation of state and local governments creditworthiness. Historical trends, the organization in place, experience and qualifications of personnel, all have an impact on the "bottom line."

Financial management, by definition, has two basic and broad considerations: financial and managerial. Within these areas exist several distinct disciplines. Major financial aspects include debt, tax policy, economic base analyses and forecasting, governmental accounting and financial reporting. Knowledge of interest rate movements is important in management of cash and other assets, as well as pension costs. Increasing attention is paid to risk management, which includes adequate insurance for accidents, health, and potential law suits for public officer's liability. The language and use of data processing are vital requirements. The need to develop a meaningful balance between taxes and user charges is often a volatile political issue. Politicians need the support of qualified professionals to establish and carry forward their priorities. The national mood in recent years has reduced the scope of governmental resources, and major considerations for the future will be how to cope with cuts, fewer resources, and managing the phase-out of certain services previously taken for granted. This may include recreation programs or outreach programs for the aged or handicapped.

Effective management includes training in the political process and the interpersonal relations so vital to the achievement of goals. Management of one's time, effective decision-making, and knowledge of details are necessary ingredients for successful management.

Annual Budget

A budget and budget-preparation policy statement, along with three years of audits are required documentation in the debt-rating process. S&P views the budget as an expression of administrative capability. Timeliness of budget adoption is another factor considered. A smooth budget-formulation process is reflected in a history of passing budgets on time. Late budgets are a hindrance to planning and an indication of political difficulty. Timely adoption reflects cohesiveness in both the administrative and political process.

Also weighed are budget oversight controls or guidelines e.g., tax and revenue, and expenditure limitations as they affect an administration's flexibility. Expenditures limits are less of a concern, unless they impair the ability to issue or service debt.

A sound budget plan should identify those elements which lie outside of the administration's control e.g., the condition of the economy and its effect on a major revenue source, such as sales taxes. The administration is expected to exhibit a willingness to make revenue and expenditure adjustments to ensure a realistic operating budget. S&P's experience shows that where these adjustments have been made, serious situations have been resolved. Continuous monitoring and surveillance should be carried out once the budget has been adopted, preferably monthly, with any deviations reported to S&P, and responded to in a timely and effective manner.

Capital Improvement Program

As part of the debt rating process, S&P requires a well documented capital improvement program (CIP), which should be reflected in the capital budget. Funding sources in the CIP should be identified, and the positive or negative impact on the operating budget in the capital improvement plan should be discussed.

Benefits Statement

A pension and employee benefits policy statement, explaining the degree of participation by both employer and employees and describing appropriate actuarial methods and assumptions, should be made available to S&P. There should be some discussion on funding policy and levels, and investment guidelines. Periodic actuarial reports and review of the financial position of the program by independent professionals should be submitted to S&P.

In cases where bonds are issued to fund the unfunded portion of the employee retirement pension obligations, attention will be focused on the impact of additional debt on already outstanding debt. Keeping in mind the limitations and lack of standardization in evaluation studies, no system-by-system comparison analysis is undertaken. The effort involves trend data on individual systems, with the direction on such trends closely monitored.

Property Tax Administration

Administrative factors analyzed by S&P include the issuer's property valuations and assessment trends, changes in assessment ratios, and assessment procedures. S&P looks at the valuations by categories—industrial, commercial, utility and residential—and at how the assessment ratio is applied to these different classes of properties. Tax rates, levies, collections (on both a current basis and a total basis, including delinquencies) and procedures are examined over a ten-year period. Tax-due dates and delinquency rates are noted for their possible effect on cash flow. An administration's taxing flexibility, or the ability to raise taxes without any political or other obstacles, is an important rating factor. Inability to collect taxes is viewed negatively.

Labor Settlements and Litigation

Full disclosure of labor disputes and settlements should be made. There should also be full disclosure on budgetary implications in terms of funding and on the impact on future budgets. Relationship between employer and employees, timely resolution of negotiations, settlement at levels the municipality can support, and a lack of work stoppages or strikes, also are important rating factors. Possible litigation against local municipalities has become a reality, and this area is analyzed for any fiscal vulnerability. The focus here is on whether insurance coverage is adequate, and on the implications from a budgetary standpoint in terms of near and long-term liabilities.

STATE RATINGS

The approach to rating the general obligation bonds of states is similar to that for local government units. However, state governments have sovereign powers and therefore possess certain unique options and flexibility. These options and how they are exercised will affect the creditworthiness of a state's general obligation bonds. Conversely, the states' functional responsibilities are more widespread than those of local units, increasing the likelihood of expenditure pressures.

Changing Relationships

In recent years, states' relationships with their localities have changed. In California, for example, the local units' dependence on state aid has grown since 1978, when voters approved Proposition 13, a constitutional amendment that limited property tax revenue. Similarly, in Massachusetts, local governments came to rely more on state aid in 1980 when voters passed Proposition 2 1/2, also a property tax limitation measure.

S&P's general obligation worksheets includes the factors considered in any general obligation rating under the four broad categories discussed on page 29. The discussion below highlights areas of difference between state and local ratings.

Economic Base

As with local units, the economic condition of a state defines its ability to generate tax revenue, perform its functions, and retire debt. Thus economic base analysis is the most critical element of the rating process.

A state's economy is generally more diverse than that of a local unit. It encompasses central cities with major tax and employment bases and generally lower-income levels as well as wealthier bedroom communities and cities incorporating both elements.

The creditworthiness implication of this difference between states and local units can be both positive and negative. The larger nature of the state's economic base may avoid the problems of concentration, low income, and economic dependency on a neighboring community that can exist for local units. But the state's greater diversity can leave it more vulnerable to downturns in a larger variety of industries. Also, a state must find a method to handle effectively the diverse needs of the various areas within its boundaries.

Financial Factors

Since states can unilaterally establish funding levels for certain local programs (such as education), they have an increased degree of control over expenditure levels. Funding levels are usually statutorily, not constitutionally, determined. However, the political reality is such that once a certain level has been established, it may be difficult to change. Nevertheless, states enjoy considerable discretion in establishing or changing major disbursement dates and funding levels for state assistance. States also enjoy a similar flexibility in setting and modifying tax rates and their collection timing. These discretionary powers can immediately and favorably influence a state's cash flow calendar, as well as its fiscal condition.

Debt Considerations

States generally issue a wide variety of tax-supported debt in addition to general obligation debt. Such issues include authority debt that is secured by state lease rental payments, subject to annual or biennial appropriation, moral obligation debt, and debt secured by general taxes such as the sales tax.

When S&P examines the debt burden of a state it looks not only at the direct general obligation debt but also at these other types of debt and at all the obligations incurred as local government debt. A calculation is then made of the S&P index, which is per capita total debt divided by per capita personal income. The index yields a measure of the debt burden relative to the income level. The S&P index also can be used as a balancing indicator, since states differ in their relationships with local governments. Some states issue a great deal of general debt for local purposes (roads, schools, etc.), and others very little, leaving these functions to the local units. The S&P index evens out these jurisdictional variations.

To deal with timing differences between receipts and disbursements, some states enter the public short-term debt market because of prohibitions against-or limitations on-interfund borrowing. Others borrow to the maximum interfund and then issue short-term debt as necessary. S&P looks at both internal and external liquidity supports to fully assess the effect of the alternative used on creditworthiness.

Administrative Factors

Administrative factors are as important to state creditworthiness as they are to local governments. Tax structure, or the ability of a state to benefit from the economic activity within its boundaries, is an important rating factor, as is the degree of flexibility existing in this structure, both legally and politically. Expenditure pressures and disbursement schedules are also important, as state officials deal with the needs of a wide variety of local communities.

Many challenges exist for state governments today as they strive to create a workable balance between their tax structures and service demands. Federal revenue reductions have intensified this struggle since needs at both the state and local levels continue to expand. Tax reform of any sort also creates additional burdens as state and local governments face uncertainty and possible revenue losses. For states, these challenges have become particularly acute as local units turn to them for assistance.

* *Source: Standard & Poor's Debt Ratings Criteria,* 1986.
Reprinted by courtesy of Standard & Poor's Corporation.

STANDARD & POOR'S GENERAL OBLIGATION BOND EARLY WARNING GUIDELINES*

Check and date any that apply:

_____	_____ Current year operating deficit
_____	_____ 2 consecutive years of operating fund deficit
_____	_____ Current general fund deficit (2 or more years in last 5)
_____	_____ Short-term debt (other than ban) at end of fiscal year greater than 5 percent of main operating fund revenues
_____	_____ Short-term interest and current year debt service greater than 20 percent of total revenues
_____	_____ Total property tax collections less than 92 percent of total levy
_____	_____ Declining market valuations—2 consecutive years on a 3-year trend
_____	_____ Overall net debt ratio 50 percent higher than 4 years ago
_____	_____ Current year operating deficit larger than previous year's deficit
_____	_____ General fund deficit in the current year—balance sheet—current position
_____	_____ 2-year trend of increasing short-term debt outstanding at fiscal year end

____	_____	Property taxes greater than 90 percent of tax limit
____	_____	Net debt outstanding greater than 90 percent of debt limit
____	_____	A trend of decreasing tax collections—2 consecutive years on a 3-year trend
____	_____	Overall net debt ratio 20 percent higher than previous year
____	_____	Other (specify) _____

* *Source: Standard & Poor's Debt Ratings Critera,* 1986.
Reprinted by courtesy of Standard & Poor's Corporation.

Chapter V

Rating Tax Allocation Bonds*

Tax allocation bonds have become an increasingly popular financing technique to encourage development in blighted and distressed neighborhoods. To accomplish this purpose, tax allocation (or tax increment) bond proceeds are used to finance projects ranging from land acquisition to infrastructure improvements which encourage private development in the distressed area. For the community the investment hopefully results in assessed value growth and new employment opportunities. The additional property taxes generated by this growth-the tax increment-are then pledged to pay for debt service on the tax allocation bonds. Moody's analysis of the credit quality of a tax allocation bond focuses on the legal structure of the debt instrument and the ability of the project area to generate a sufficient flow of revenue to provide for debt service.

THE "PURE" TAX ALLOCATION BOND

Tax allocation or tax increment financing is authorized in many states. However, in many situations, tax allocation bonds are issued with back-up security provided by the issuing municipality's general obligation tax pledge. In those instances, Moody's evaluates credit quality based primarily on the ultimate security-the general obligation pledge with the analysis also considering any tax collection timing delays which might potentially affect the ability of a municipality to pay bondholders on a timely basis. In this article, we will focus our comments on how Moody's evaluates pure tax allocation bonds, those secured only by the incremental revenues generated in the project area.

Moody's rates such tax allocation bonds in numerous states including California, Iowa, Minnesota, and Oregon. California has the longest history of tax allocation bond issuance and the broadest market with over $2.0

billion in tax allocation bonds outstanding. Because of the broader base of experience in California, our comments will further focus on the tax allocation bond process in California with reference to other states' experience where relevant.

CAPTURING THE INCREMENT

The mechanics of capturing incremental property tax revenues are fairly simple. In California, a municipality forms a redevelopment agency which typically includes the members of city council serving ex officio as the board of directors of the agency. Staffing is provided by existing city employees. The agency can then designate redevelopment project areas within the city based on a finding of blight or economic distress within that area. A redevelopment plan for the project area is developed and, when approved by city ordinance, the project area tax base is frozen. Property taxes generated by the increases in assessed value over the frozen tax base flow to the agency and can then be used to pay for debt incurred by the agency.

A redevelopment agency can designate numerous redevelopment projects within a city. Each individual project area will have its own redevelopment plan, frozen tax base and stream of incremental property tax revenues generated by the increases in assessed value. Tax allocation bonds issued by a redevelopment agency are issued for a specific project area and are separately secured by the incremental property tax revenue generated by that specific area.

LEGAL CONSIDERATIONS

Tax allocation bonds are instruments whose security benefits solely from the product of a growing tax base and established tax rates. Redevelopment agencies typically have no ability to set tax rates or to control tax reform legislation that may be approved at the state or local level. As a result, the revenue stream securing the bonds can be viewed as "passive." Because of this feature, Moody's views tax allocation bonds as an inherently weaker debt instrument than a general obligation or revenue bond. Although there is no fixed rating ceiling, currently Moody's rates no tax allocation bond higher than A, although many carry that rating.

California's experience with Proposition 13 shows how vulnerable tax allocation bonds can be to legislative change. With Proposition 13's rollback of tax rates to 1 percent of full market value and assessed values to 1976 levels, many redevelopment agencies found their stream of incremental property tax revenues substantially cut. Similarly, changes in California property tax law exempting business inventory from taxation caused a reduction in assessed values, particularly in project areas with significant manufacturing or retail land use.

Beyond these structural legal issues, Moody's evaluates the specific legal provisions of the resolution authorizing bond issuance. Again, basic security is provided by the pledge of incremental tax revenues. Typically this is a sum sufficient pledge, although historically up to 125 percent of debt service was pledged with the surplus accruing in a reserve to be used for the early retirement of debt. Additionally, the property tax cycle in California frequently requires that capitalized interest be provided to cover the period from the issuance of the bonds until sufficient revenue is received by the agency to provide for debt service payments.

Tax allocation bond debt service should have a first claim on incremental revenues, senior to the lien of any non-bonded obligations of the agency. However, Moody's has rated junior lien tax allocation bonds secured only by the incremental revenues remaining after payment of the senior lien bonds. Credit quality is obviously affected by the more narrow margins of coverage provided to these junior lien securities.

Legal provisions which further strengthen credit quality include a reserve fund and additional bonds test. We evaluate reserve fund requirements to determine the level and method of funding with a reserve fully funded at closing at a level equal to maximum annual debt service providing the strongest security. Additional bonds tests are evaluated to determine the protection they afford bondholders from future dilution of security.

In recent years, redevelopment agencies have issued an increasing number of tax allocation bonds which anticipate depositing a portion of bond proceeds into an escrow account. These proceeds are released from escrow only when incremental revenues grow to provide a specified level of aggregate debt service coverage. Typically, if required coverage is not provided within a set period of time, escrowed proceeds are then used to redeem bonds. Such structures should not diminish credit quality assuming the terms of the escrow account are stringent enough so that proceeds are released only when debt service coverage is sufficient or to redeem bonds and escrowed funds are safely and prudently invested.

PROJECT AREA CONSIDERATIONS

Equally important as a review of the legal provisions is the analysis of the project area itself. The analyst's most basic concern is to determine whether incremental property tax revenues can cover annual debt service. Existing revenues should provide at least one times coverage of maximum annual debt service when the bonds are issued. Obviously, higher coverage ratios provide greater bondholder security and can contribute to higher bond ratings. Recent changes in California state law requires that 20 percent of incremental tax revenue be set aside for low and moderate income housing. The stream of incremental revenues can also be reduced by reimbursement agreements which the agency has with underlying units. Such agreements are not uncommon, as underlying units of government are frequently reluctant to give up any growth in property tax receipts. Moody's calculates debt service coverage net of these required expenditures.

Moody's also evaluates the redevelopment project area on a micro-level to determine the strength and significance of the neighborhood. We examine the size of the project area, existing land use and the unique features that will encourage or discourage future development. We also examine city-wide and regional demographic and labor statistics to assess the vitality of the overall economy supporting continued development. Historic growth of assessed value and incremental revenue from the project area are evaluated as is the trend of tax rates.

Overall property tax delinquency rates are examined as are major taxpayers and their proportion of assessed value. Because redevelopment project areas typically include relatively small tax bases, they can be fundamentally affected by the strength of major taxpayers. Assurance must be provided that major taxpayers are stable operating entities that will enhance the incremental tax base.

If debt service is not fully covered by existing incremental tax revenues, assurance must be provided that assessed value growth will occur to provide coverage by the time the initial debt service payment is due.

As a basic measure, the amount of undeveloped land in the project area is evaluated to determine the physical limitations to future development. Projections for project area growth over the next five years must be based on reasonable and conservative assumptions about assessed value growth and changes in the tax rate. If major new development projects are expected to contribute to significant increases in assessed value, Moody's requires that construction be substantially underway before this growth in valuation is included in the various debt service coverage tests used by the analyst. Development and disposition agreements, between city and developer outlining their respective roles and responsibilities in a project, are required as proof of a developer's commitment.

CONCLUSION

Tax allocation bond financing provides a method for cities to address the problems of blighted and distressed neighborhoods and acts as a means to spur economic development. From the issuer's point of view tax allocation bonds can be considered a "self-supporting" financing mechanism because ultimate security is provided by the tax base growth they encourage rather than drawing on the existing tax base. An analyst views such debt as an additional tax-supported obligation drawing on the issuer's tax base.

Moody's evaluates many factors in its determination of the credit quality of a tax allocation bond. Although the basic structure of the debt instrument places a limit on the ultimate security afforded bondholders, the existing strength of the project area, the prospects for future growth and the specific legal provisions of the bond issue all contribute to a final evaluation of credit quality.

* *Source:* Nancy Barbe. *Moody's Municipal Issues,* 1986.
Reprinted by courtesy of Moody's Investors Service.

Chapter VI

Rating Airport Revenue Bonds*

The federal government's October 1978 deregulation of airline routes and fares pushed the nation's air carriers into a new and unfamiliar era of competition. Deregulation has greatly changed the way the industry does business and in a less dramatic way has also affected Moody's analysis of airport revenue bonds.

Since 1978, air carrier competition has generally been a beneficial force, bringing over 50 new air carriers into the market, lowering air fares, and encouraging operating efficiency to the degree that the successful airlines are now enjoying some of their most profitable years ever. Carriers quickly learned and institutionalized a variety of new competitive mechanisms, including the use of innovative marketing techniques such as the "frequent flyer" customer bonus programs, and efforts to boost labor productivity. The latter has ranged from union representation on airline boards and the use of a Chapter 11 filing to escape constrictive labor agreements, to the development of two-tier wage structures.

Another major innovation has been the hubbing of traffic through a given airport to achieve convenient and numerous flights that are also full, and hence more cost effective. Deregulation has been so successful in these terms that pressure is now building in the European economic community for similar action. But the positive effects of deregulation were won at a price, of course—change was necessary for survival, and many carriers including several large airlines, succumbed to financial pressure and went bankrupt.

It is worth noting, as a measure of deregulation changes, that half of the nation's present 12 largest air carriers were much smaller operations in 1978. Moreover, the industry-wide changes wrought by deregulation are far from complete. In discussing a fare war that is expected to begin in 1986 among carriers with western routes, reports from industry officials indicate that they had learned only the rudiments of operating in a competitive environment.

117

ROLE OF THE AIR CARRIER

Despite the impact of deregulation, it affects the analysis of municipal airport revenue debt mainly in a shift in focus. For the analyst, deregulation has highlighted what has long been the dominant issue in rating an airport revenue bond—the relative risk and unpredictability inherent in the air transport industry. While the rating of a particular airport revenue bond still depends on individual credit factors—notably the level of debt and its projected coverage by pledged revenues, the strength of specific legal and security provisions, and the record of financial and operational management—the analyst must focus increasingly on the role of the air carrier as the primary generator of pledged revenues and, ultimately, the source of bondholder security.

Because the unpredictable performance of an air carrier is largely beyond the control of the municipal airport or the issuing authority, it introduces a range of structural credit factors that are endemic to airport revenue financings, and which tend to define the upper limits of security for this type of bond.

KEY QUESTIONS

Why is there risk and unpredictability inherent to an air carrier, and how is this transferred to municipal airport debt? To begin with, an airport revenue bond constitutes a somewhat unique type of municipal debt only because it is secured by the revenues of a single and limited economic activity. Unlike a water or electric revenue system the revenues of which derive from a diverse mix of residential, commercial, and industrial users, the pledged revenues of an airport bond—typically landing fees, concessions, and space rentals—all depend on the carriers' success or failure.

An airport revenue bond by definition lacks a diverse revenue base, and has inherent credit vulnerability analagous to a general obligation bond whose supporting tax base is dominated by a single manufacturer. This would be less of a credit issue if the air transport industry were not historically volatile and unpredictable, but it is, unfortunately, a classic example of an inherently risky industry where performance is likely to change radically due to economic conditions. The reasons for this are not difficult to discern. Air carriers are heavily leveraged, and have high fixed costs, with expensive and sophisticated equipment that must be operated and maintained by skilled personnel, and replaced or modernized as technological change dictates. Equally important is the sensitivity to energy prices and economic cycles that affect both personal and business travel. In this light, the dramatic price wars and the births and deaths of airlines that followed deregulation simply reflected the addition of competition to an already risky business. Moody's corporate ratings reflect these long-term credit issues; only a handful of air carriers carry debt ratings in the A category, with most falling in more speculative ranges.

That Moody's ratings on municipal airport revenue bonds are somewhat higher reflects a number of moderating factors that reduce to some degree the riskiness associated with air carriers. These include the simple public necessity for an airport, as well as the credit factors, as well as the credit factors, mentioned earlier, that are specific to and are controllable by the issuing airport—level of debt, financial and managerial quality, and the security provided by a reserve fund, additional bonds test, and other legal provisions.

The most important moderating factor, however, discussed in some detail below, tends to be the strength of the passenger market served by the airport, since this provides some assurance that an air carrier will continue to provide service even if another has failed. Even with these moderating factors, Moody's at present does not carry airport revenue bond ratings higher than A1 except where the debt is secured by supplementary, non- airport derived revenues or where there has been credit substitution. The latter include letters of credit and bond insurance, and the former include deficiency tax pledges, or mixed revenue pledges such as from a comprehensive transportation or port authority whose different facilities sufficiently diversify the revenue stream. All in all, the industry has too short a horizon of predictability to support the highest quality ratings on long-term debt. Not the least of these concerns is the probability that technological change will continue to increase the capital needs of an airport, which will most likely alter its future debt position.

ANALYTICAL FOCUS

Within the credit limitations imposed by the characteristics of the air transport industry, there are a number of issues that the analyst must address as part of the rating process that have become increasingly important with deregulation. While these issues vary from airport to airport, they are structural in nature, shaped less by the managerial actions of the airport than by the circumstances of the industry and the economic necessity that an air carrier act in its own self-interest.

The single most important of these is the nature of the airport's passenger market, and more specifically whether the airport primarily serves as an origin-destination (O&D) or national gateway facility, or acts as a hub, wherein most passenger traffic makes through connections for flights to other locations. An airport's O&D market is generated by its own economic hinterland, and if it is sufficiently strong, it reduces the problem of air carrier vulnerability to one of timing; if the passenger market is strong, another airline will take the place of the one that just failed, although the intervening interruption may affect revenues to an uncertain degree. An airport with a small or relatively weak O&D market poses more serious risks, in that at some point it may not be able to sustain competitive, efficient airline service, resulting in fewer flights or higher fares that would alter the revenue stream more permanently.

A hubbing airport presents a more complex problem because the hub activity brings to the airport passenger traffic that has little to do with the airport's immediate economic base. While hubs are selected partially on the basis of regional location, the point is that another location may serve just as well; as carriers can and have shifted their hubs. For this reason, the issuance of debt by an airport to address expanding hub traffic, as opposed to O&D activity, can be seen as having a more inherent risk. A hub airport requiring significant capital expenditures for physical expansion faces the dilemma of either losing revenue if it cannot meet air carriers' need for more space, or of incurring a large amount of debt that may be inadequately secured if hub traffic moves to another airport that offers air carriers more favorable terms such as lower fees, rentals, and labor costs.

A further, but lesser issue concerns the number and condition of air carriers serving the airports. The presence of a larger number of air carriers obviously reduces vulnerability of the revenue stream to the fortunes of a single carrier. Deregulation has benefited a number of airports in this way by increasing the number of carriers, although this is indirectly a result of passenger market strength. While current financial performance of air carriers is of limited predictive value, poor operating results may be a significant indicator of problems associated with serving a particular airport.

Finally, with deregulation, lease or facility use agreements between the airport and air carriers becomes less significant a rating factor. They are only as strong as the air carrier's financial health and economic self-interest in continuing operations of the airport.

Nevertheless, agreements are still an important tool for capital planning, and provide the basis for the legal pledge of revenues. However, such agreements cannot by themselves make up for or erase the inherent risks of the air transport industry. Economic limitations to the practical worth of agreements similarly extend to other users of airport facilities, such as car rental agencies, that contribute to the revenue stream and which are directly affected by fluctuation in passenger traffic. In the case of smaller airports that are adjacent to a commercial area, however, these users may also be affected by discount competitors located in cheaper, off-airport facilities.

OTHER FUNDAMENTAL CONSIDERATIONS

Beyond these series of externally imposed structural issues are more fundamental but nonetheless important credit concerns. Financial performance, debt, and legal structure are often the final determinants of credit quality for airport revenue financings, because these factors are particular to and largely controllable by the airport. More specifically, they are the key indicators of how well an airport will mange its debt obligations in the future, within the overall uncertainties of the air carrier industry. While the analysis of these issues is not mechanically different from that for other types of revenue debt, it still bears some review.

Provisions concerning the revenue pledge, funds flow, reserves, and additional bonds test establish the legal parameters for the debt. Unless the pledge limits revenue in an unusual way, perhaps the most important of these provisions is a reserve fund typically comprising a year's debt service. This is a favorable, if standard credit feature, and is essential given the structural uncertainties discussed earlier. While a strong additional bonds test also enhances bondholders' protection by preventing the dilution of debt service coverage, a very conservative test—based on historical net revenues alone, for example—may be impractical because it too severely limits the airport's ability to respond to growth. A related analytic concern is the degree to which legal provisions allow the issuance of variable rate, tender, or other new forms of debt, and the way in which these may affect reserve and revenue coverage. Finally, as with other forms of revenue debt, there is no significant difference in credit quality between net and gross revenue pledges. Long-term bondholder security is not well served by the payment of debt service at the expense of routine maintenance of proper operations.

The issues of debt and financial performance are clearly intertwined, since a given amount of debt and the structure of required payments over time must be balanced by the airport's ability to generate sufficient revenues. The assessment of this balance—the determination of whether debt is excessive or forecast revenue growth too optimistic—has much to do with the dominant issues of passenger market type and growth discussed earlier. In general, large increases in debt must be matched by reasonable expectations of growth to sustain credit quality, and further, must be structured so as not to constrain future operations; increasing or ballooned debt service, therefore, is problematic, particularly given the short horizon of predictability for air carrier operations.

In assessing the projected revenue debt balance, the airport's previous financial record provides an important analytic tool. While historical financial performance alone does not guarantee future operations, particularly when indebtedness is increasing, it is nevertheless a valuable indicator of the level of an airport's ability to manage its financial and material resources. Given the future unpredictability of air carrier operations, historical performance in a year of declining passenger traffic and revenues can provide a much deeper insight into strengths and weaknesses of the airport, and provide a better measure of its ability to deal with the uncertainties inherent to the industry.

* *Source:* Al Medioli. *Moody's Municipal Issues,* 1986.
Reprinted by courtesy of Moody's Investors Service.

Chapter VII

Schools:
*Analyzing Bond Credit**

The nation's recent reemphasis on basic education provides an appropriate backdrop for a reexamination of the fundamental elements of school district credit analysis. Since the postwar baby boom surge in school construction, much about school district finance has changed. Mandated state redistribution of resources has moved toward substantially equalizing school spending, while uneven economic shifts and the anti-tax militancy displayed by many taxpayers have heightened credit distinctions among school districts.

The analysis of debt issued by school districts continues to follow the standard approach used by the Municipal Department of Moody's Investors Service. The ability and willingness to repay debt obligations are evaluated both in terms of economic capacity and administrative capabilities and on the basis of the actual track record of debt management and financial operations.

RECENT TRENDS

This reexamination of new concerns in school district analysis is particularly timely given recent capital market trends. Borrowing for school purposes has remained at a near constant $5.0 billion level for nearly a decade, with school bonds comprising nearly 21 percent of all municipal bonds issued in 1974, but dropping to only 9 percent in 1981. Recently, there has been an upsurge in new financings, $4.3 billion in 1981 to $8.7 billion in 1983, although school issues' share of the market in 1983 was only half the level of 1974. While part of this trend is fueled by certain regions of the country that are still undergoing rapid growth (contributing to the need for new facilities), today we are also typically seeing more financing for renovations to meet fire, health and safety requirements.

Financings for school districts have also mirrored recent trends in the market of revenue bond issues; witness the growth of lease sales by school districts. The expectation is that bond issues for school purposes will continue to comprise a moderate amount of total long-term bond issues brought to market and that the structure and security of these issues will increasingly resemble the innovative financing techniques now seen in the municipal market.

NEW FACTORS AND FOCUS

Probably the most significant change seen over the past decade, which has had an effect on Moody's analytical approach to rating the debt of school districts, has been the change in revenue sources and expenditure items brought about by the landmark judicial decisions of the 1970s. The change toward greater equalization of resources and more comparability in programs offered is clearly seen in those state-aid programs and distribution formulae which were adjusted to recognize local taxing abilities.

Nationally, education spending is now less dependent on local wealth, as states funded 45 percent of 1982 local school expenditures, compared to 38 percent just five years earlier. Between 1977 and 1982, state aid increased over 70 percent, while local tax support grew by just 35 percent. Credit analysts, however, continue to find significant distinctions between school districts within each state, in addition to credit differences from state-to-state.

CREDIT FUNDAMENTALS

Local management is one important determinant in differentiating credit quality as each district must exert tight control over limited resources. However, local economic capacity and individual district spending requirements remain equally important determinants of credit quality. Tax base strength, a determining factor in most aid formulae, cannot alone explain local economic capacity or current and future needs. Personal income measures indicate a community's ability to afford local school spending while population characteristics, particularly age distribution, provide insight into a community's willingness to support local schools. Each of these factors will be discussed in terms of the rating process.

In school debt analysis what is measured is 'control'—the ability to manage resources so that obligations are met in full and on time.

The highest levels of control are demonstrated by a school district with a prospering economy, unlimited revenue-raising capability, a great deal of discretion in terms of programming and staffing, and a proven track record of careful management that has provided for the build-up of an adequate financial reserve to address certain contingencies. Conversely, when a district has insufficient funds to meet an obligation that is due and payable, the situation is clearly out of control. The vast majority of school districts whose bonds we rate falls somewhere in between.

DEBT FACTORS

School financings have been accomplished in a number of different ways across the nation. A significant portion is done directly through issuance by an independent school district; dependent school systems have had to rely on the creditworthiness of a municipality. In still other cases, special authorities or school building corporations have been created, often to circumvent borrowing restrictions on the district although the ultimate responsibility for repayment remains with the district.

Regardless of the vehicle used to finance capital projects, the analyst must evaluate the same basic credit fundamentals. The nature of the security being pledged for debt repayment is carefully studied as is the relationship of the revenue being pledged to the total budget and to the debt servicing obligation created. Certain accepted standards of debt measurement are used including indicators of per capita debt, debt relative to taxable valuation and rate of debt retirement. However, it is important to note that these selected indicators should be considered as broad guidelines only. Performance relative to the guidelines is not an absolute indicator of credit quality, and a bond rating cannot be inferred within this narrow context. Debt and capital planning is a good way of demonstrating control of future debt position. Multi-year capital improvement plans showing project priorities, expected costs and benefits, and probable means of financing have become a critical tool for debt analysis. More and more school districts are preparing multi-year capital improvement programs, but often the out-year projections are unrealistic or not well prioritized. As to capital plant conditions, much needs to be done to develop coherent means of documenting remaining useful life, replacement costs and required maintenance programs. These are particularly important to consider for districts that have had to defer borrowing for several years at the same time that budget constraints also lead to a substantial reduction of all current capital outlays.

ADMINISTRATIVE FACTORS

The powers and abilities which a school district possess can be key determinants in assessing how well its debt is secured. The school's organization, diffusion of responsibilities, degree of professionalism and ability to perform required functions must all be taken into account. Management controls and the timeliness and quality of financial documents, annual reports and planning documents add to impressions of administrative performance.

Most school districts that we study have two things in common: they must contend with some form of limitation on local powers, and operations are generally subject to numerous fixed costs and program mandates.

REVENUE STRUCTURE

The revenue structure of most school systems involves some mix of property tax and state aid. In a credit evaluation, the analyst knows that the ability to levy property taxes may be limited in any number of ways, i.e., with levy ceilings, growth limits on levies, or limits on the tax rate itself. Voter approval may be necessary in each fiscal period for setting the tax rate and adopting the proposed budget. From a state aid perspective, schools commonly operate under per pupil formulae and categorical grants. The former can be a problem where enrollments are dropping and cost cutting measures have not been adopted nor save-harmless provisions instituted by the state. The latter may be subject to the whims of annual legislative appropriation.

EXPENDITURES

On the expenditure side, it is not unusual to see a broad array of fixed or mandated costs, many of which apply only to schools. Aside from debt service, pension program contributions or other contractual obligations to teachers and their union, school administrators must comply with mandated pupil/teacher ratios, teacher accreditation, curriculum requirements, and minimum standards for the length of the school day and term. It is not surprising, given this type of environment, that tightly balanced budgets and low operating margins are quite common. For schools where these administrative restraints are predominant, quality of management becomes the key variable in determining actual financial condition.

Budgetary planning and projecting; together with day-to-day spending control is crucial to maintaining balance. The absolute level of current financial resources is not nearly as important as the established trend of financial performance. Long-term financial trends demonstrate how school administrators use their powers and adjust to changing conditions. The ability to consistently achieve budget targets and successfully implement programs of cost control, increased productivity and revenue enhancement demonstrate the degree of control that a school district can exert over its financial condition. Large financial surpluses are not very impressive if they result from the inability to execute spending expansions or new program start ups. Conversely, a planned drawdown of a surplus is often acceptable and may not necessarily signify problems. Policies on spending for growth, use of surplus, and shortfall contingency plans are all important to the analyst.

The goal of Moody's financial analysis is to determine whether annually recurring resources are, in fact, available to meet ongoing spending. Our analysts often find that under conditions of rising costs, high interest rates and limited revenue growth, deficit projections are inevitable. However, in discussions with school officials, alternative strategies can be shown to demonstrate commitment to maintaining balance and to fiscal integrity.

The role that state government plays in capital financing cannot be underestimated. A large number of construction aid and debt reimbursement programs are now in operation.

These programs take many forms and add an additional dimension to credit analysis. In some of the programs, the state's involvement may extend to assumption of responsibility for debt service payments. Others provide for some level of reimbursement of debt payments and may or may not be subject to annual legislative approval. Still other programs are geared to assistance in marketing of the debt and include some form of reserve, guarantee or pledge to withhold state aid in support of a school district debt payment.

ECONOMIC FACTORS

Economy is probably the most uncontrollable and often the most unpredictable factor in our analysis. The recent recession has emphasized how little a community can do to counter national economic trends. Recent economic volatility has taught us that even the most sophisticated econometric models are not very accurate in projecting the length and depth of a cycle within any local community. Measures of relative economic control are, nevertheless, very important to our analysis. Basic credit strengths are attributed to diverse and growing economies, while especially in small communities, overdependence on a single industry, the dominance of a single employer or an older and less mobile population are viewed more negatively.

Population trends and shifts in age distribution tell the analyst something about expectations for future enrollment and can help gauge a likely pattern of school programs and service provisions, and offer signals on potential needs for education budgets and programs.

Control is also measured in how sensitive financial condition is to the performance of the economy. Those communities that are property tax dependent can see higher tax delinquency rates during economic downturns.

Many school districts are particularly sensitive to interest rates. Some rely heavily on interest earnings and are hurt by falling rates, while others rely on projected growth from commercial and residential construction and are hurt by rising rates.

IN CONCLUSION

Although Moody's analytical approach to the rating of school district bonds is consistent with our overall approach, the focus here begins with an assessment of governmental structure and its particular effect on finances. Almost more than any other type of local government, school districts are creatures of a superior level of government, whether that be the state, county or city, due to the nature of the service provided-education. Because of the existence of federal and state requirements for educational services, school districts, as a class of governmental units, can be more dependent on factors out of their direct control. Nevertheless, management's ability to exert control over budgets and other variables is the key to determining credit quality.

* *Source:* Daniel Heimowitz and Howard Mischel. *Moody's Municipal Issues,* 1984.
Reprinted by courtesy of Moody's Investors Service.

Chapter VIII

*Credit Analysis**

LONG-TERM OBLIGATIONS

Credit analysis is the assessment of the relative strengths and weaknesses of those factors which have a bearing on the likely repayment of debt obligations. Ultimately, the repayment of a debt depends on both the borrower's ability and willingness to make repayment. To judge ability to pay, what is really measured is the degree of control that the obligor can exert to call forth and manage its resources so that its obligations can be met in full and on time. Determination of relative degrees of control or measurement of ability to pay is a major focus of the rating process.

The other component of credit analysis, the one that is less easily measured, is willingness to pay. Tax expenditure limitation initiatives, voter rejection of millage budgets and bond issues, or the unwillingness of officials to make the often difficult decisions to assure budget balance are looked upon as symptoms of a possible unwillingness to pay. A consistent trend of positive performance, particularly when achieved in an environment of economic stress or under restrictive bond covenants, can provide the analyst with strong evidence of willingness to pay. An analyst's determination of credit quality, expressed in a credit rating, is based on an assessment of those factors affecting ability and willingness to pay.

These fundamental concepts of bond analysis, ability and willingness to pay, apply equally to general obligation, special tax bond analysis, and to the analysis of enterprise revenue bonds. The analysis of more limited liability revenue bonds also encompasses additional considerations relating to the future sound operation of the enterprise over the life of the bond issue. Both sets of analytical approaches are summarized in this chapter. It is important to note, however, that no one single factor in the process can be considered as most important. It is also important to note that tax-status has no bearing upon credit analysis. Moody's Municipal Department applies the same analytical approach to the rating of municipal obligations, whether they are issued as tax-exempt or taxable debt.

ECONOMIC FACTORS

The economy is probably the least controllable and often the most difficult factor to predict in municipal credit analysis. Local performance during recent recessionary and inflationary periods has emphasized how little any one community can do to offset the effects of national economic trends. Even with these limitations, measures of local economic control are nevertheless very important to credit analysis.

Decennial U.S. census statistics of population and housing characteristics and various measures of employment, unemployment, and economic production provide a profile of the community's economy and the well being of its residents. These basic statistics are necessarily augmented by locally-derived information. Especially in smaller communities, this information is needed to determine a community's dependence on a single industry or the dominance of a single employer.

Analysts are also interested in what the management of a municipality can do to encourage economic activity. In the case of a revenue bond, information on competitive factors relating to the service being provided by the enterprise is vital to the analyst. The size of the primary and secondary service areas and what duplication of services by other competitive units existing within those service areas are key issues which are reviewed.

Economic control can also be measured in terms of how sensitive a municipality's or enterprise's financial condition is to the performance of the local economy. Cyclical sensitivity of revenues, such as personal and business income taxes and sales taxes or fees and charges to industrial or commercial users, can be an indicator of financial vulnerability. Economic downturns are also reflected in higher property tax delinquencies and increasing accounts receivable.

Many municipalities have also shown particular sensitivity to interest rate movements either because of reduced investment earnings when rates fall or because of reduced private investment when rates rise.

ADMINISTRATION OF SERVICES

To be able to evaluate the ability of a community or enterprise to control financial conditions, it is particularly important to understand the scope and powers of the municipality's administration. How is the government organized? Are powers, particularly financial and budgetary responsibilities, clearly delineated? Are powers vested in a chief executive or are they spread among several offices? Is there a professional manager who can supply continuity between elected administrations? Are municipal enterprise operations supervised directly by the general government or are they managed by a professional administrator? What services are the government responsible for? U.S. municipal governmental arrangements vary widely and this is a key reason why it is difficult to quantify standards of municipal performance.

Intergovernmental relationships become important considerations when provision for services to a common group of taxpayers is shared. At one extreme are relatively independent units that provide all local government services that in other places are traditionally provided by multiple layers of government. At the other extreme are governmental arrangements where even such basic services, as police and fire, are the responsibility of independent special service districts, or where regional financing authorities, such as those for transit and sewer purposes, legally separate the financing of a service from the responsibility of service provision. Intergovernmental relationships are particularly important to understand in joint action agency financings where the benefits of using the financing approach can be outweighed by the risks; that can be true primarily when there is lack of centralized responsibility or when a large variety of units participate, many of which have different objectives to be achieved by the financing. Experience indicates that membership in a joint action agency should be undertaken cautiously by the governmental participant, and such membership is carefully examined by the municipal analyst.

In addition to understanding the scope of municipal services, it is also important to understand the degree of flexibility in providing these services. Some proportion of any budget's expenditures is likely to be fixed, including the servicing of debt and other contractual obligations and contributions to employee pensions. Certain costs, particularly pension expenses or maintenance of municipal facilities, can be deferred without immediate consequences; however, the prudent funding of these accrued expenses is critical to building a solid base for future operations.

THE REVENUE COMPONENT

Just as it is important for the analyst to examine the degree of spending flexibility, revenue-raising powers must also be considered in the assessment of financial performance. Some governments have broad powers to raise tax rates and other fees independently, providing a strong means of controlling future financial condition. The analyst is particularly interested in the way revenue-raising authority is utilized. Some communities undertake a revenue review as part of the annual budget process and implement marginal tax rate adjustments as needed, while in other communities tax rate increases tend to be traumatic events, usually implemented only when crisis conditions are at hand.

Different types of enterprises, i.e., hospitals versus water systems, operate under widely different regulatory climates. Some must comply with separate rate review agencies while others are able to set rates at their own discretion, with covenants made to bondholders and competitive forces the main constraints.

When constrictions on revenue-raising authority exist, they take on greater significance in credit analysis because of the already inherent limitations to revenue structure of all governmental units.

DEBT MANAGEMENT

Control of debt position is particularly critical to any kind of credit analysis. Honoring the promise to repay and the fulfillment of all legal convenants with bondholders are the ultimate tests of a borrower's ability and willingness to pay. The starting point for debt analysis is the pledged legal security and other bondholder protections, and it is the task of the bond analyst to determine whether the borrower will meet these commitments. Although legal security for the debt provides the foundation and remains a central component of debt analysis, other analytical considerations are equally important. The economic feasibility and necessity of the magnitude of debt to be repaid and the perceived benefit to be derived from the uses of that debt has become very critical.

Empirical evidence strongly suggests that when public indebtedness becomes too burdensome, an inability or unwillingness to pay may follow.

Analysts employ certain measures of relative indebtedness to measure the burden of debt. Key measures of debt factors are further described in Moody's Debt Median Booklet, which we publish annually (and is available on request).

The analyst is concerned with the impact of all debt obligations and the ability of taxpayers to meet them. Capital planning for future debt can be a very meaningful way of demonstrating control. For tax-supported debt analysis, total debt includes not only the debt obligations issued by the borrowing government, which is called the direct debt, but also the proportionate share of the debt obligations of overlapping governmental units. The analysis here must cover all debt supported by the same group of taxpayers, regardless of who issues the debt. This overall debt is then related to population and to the broadest and most generally available measure of the wealth of the community—the assessed valuation of all taxable property adjusted to reflect market value as nearly as possible.

For revenue debt analysis, coverage of annual debt service by net revenues[1] affords the analyst the ability to trace the trend of coverage over time, an indicator of both debt protection and sound management practices. Coverage calculations can also act as a supplemental indicator of the margins of protection available to bondholders, with the primary indicator of protection being the debt service safety margin ratio.[2] The ability of a municipal enterprise to repay its debt is always evaluated on a net revenue basis. We take this "harshest" test view in order to assure ourselves that sufficient revenues are available to operate and maintain the enterprise over the life of the debt. We also need affirmation that all covenants to bondholders have been met as a basic indicator of willingness to pay.

Another indicator is the rate of debt retirement relative both to tax base growth projections and the purposes for which the mix between the debt was issued. A key indicator is the mix between long-term and short-term debt. Reduced control of financial position is usually associated with an overreliance on short-term debt. The need for future market access always introduces some degree of vulnerability. Heavy reliance on bond anticipation notes that require subsequent refinancing and on annual operating loans or heavy use of variable rate debt with demand options reduce the level of financial control by increasing vulnerability to market uncertainties.

FINANCIAL PERFORMANCE

Annual operating performance and resultant year-end position are the ultimate measures of management's control. Regardless of economic, spending and taxing realities, a municipal government is expected to balance its budget. Financial results are deemed satisfactory when annual revenues meet or exceed annual expenditures and sufficient financial resources have been accumulated to meet unforeseen contingencies and normal liquidity requirements.

Important to the analysis of any enterprise is clear evidence of the sound maintenance of plant investment. Operations are judged by the quality of annual balance as measured by a multi-year trend of results and through detailed analysis to determine that ongoing expenditures are financed by recurring revenues. Normal costs should be covered from basic charges for service, without reliance on one-time connection or other such fees; analysts expect any increased costs to be quickly addressed through timely rate adjustments. Regular rate review prevents the occurrence of periodic large rate increases and potential customer resistance.

The level of fund balance is related to the likelihood of drawing upon these accumulations. Generally, a fund balance of 5 percent of the budget is deemed prudent. A smaller balance may be justified by a long-term trend of annual budget surplus, while a larger balance may be warranted, particularly if budget revenues and expenses are economically sensitive or otherwise not easily forecasted. While positive operating results and a large fund balance provide financial strength, a planned drawdown of balances and actual performance consistently close to original budget estimates are evidence of strong management control. Prudent management will also insure that the investment of cash balances is done carefully and conservatively.

Accumulated balances should provide for the maintenance of debt service and other reserves at covenanted levels and also for the availability of monies for unforeseen contingencies, extraordinary maintenance needs and certain capital improvements. The outflow of surplus from the enterprise's funds flow, to finance other governmental purposes, is viewed cautiously to assure that all of the needs of the enterprise are fully met prior to any transfer.

LEGAL FACTORS

Critical to any analysis, particularly for revenue bonds, are the legal provisions contained within the resolution, indenture, state statute or local law authorizing the debt issuance. The analyst evaluates the specific revenue that has been pledged for debt repayment. Also reviewed are provisions concerning the flow of funds, additional bonds' test governing further debt issuance, the required level of any reserve, and the "rate covenant." The latter three are essential components of any analyst's review of a revenue bond as they can have a direct bearing on overall security.

A liberal additional bonds' test offers weak protection in the future against significant further borrowing. A weak rate covenant, i.e., a low coverage requirement, offers little security in terms of added financial operating cushions. Finally, a weak reserve requirement also provides little comfort, particularly in the event an issuer enters an unexpected period of financial stress.

At the same time, analysts clearly recognize that legal provisions should not be structured to overly restrict an issuer's ability to operate efficiently. Rather, legal provisions should represent a fair balance between the legitimate security concerns of a bondholder and the issuer.

SUMMARY

Ideally, the analyst looks for a municipality or an enterprise to be in a position to exert maximum control over its ability to repay its debts and to demonstrate a clear willingness to honor its commitments. The local economy should be strong and prospering. There should be no constraints on revenue raising abilities; in fact there should be a great deal of discretion in determining service levels. A proven track record of careful management should exist which has provided for the build-up of financial reserves to address unforeseen contingencies. What the analyst looks for is a clear trend of sound performance, both financially and operationally, that is reinforced by a record of management's responsiveness to bondholder needs.

* *Source:*   Reprinted by courtesy of Moody's Investors Service.

NOTES

1.   Revenue bond debt service coverage is one of the most commonly used statistics within the municipal market. It is the ratio of net revenues to debt service requirements. For example, 1.50 times coverage refers to net revenue equaling 1 1/2 times debt service. In most resolutions authorizing the issuance of revenue bonds, it is standard for the issuer to offer bondholders added protection by a covenant to maintain rates and charges to yield net revenues sufficient to achieve at least a minimum coverage level. The requirement that certain coverage levels be met before additional debt may be issued is also standard.

2.   Defined as net revenues less debt service for the year divided by gross revenue and income.

Chapter IX

Municipal Defaults and Bankruptcy:

Myth and Reality*

There is a saying that "while doctors bury their mistakes, in municipal financing, they are refunded." There comes a time, however, when certain mistakes cannot be refunded. Given present conditions, the probability has increased that a municipality will be faced with a bond default and will consider instituting a proceeding for municipal debt adjustment under Chapter 9 of the Bankruptcy Code. It is important that certain myths that exist concerning municipal bond defaults and municipal bankruptcy are dispelled and that the municipal bond market is aware from an historical and legal basis of the true reality.

Reasons for Default

Before discussing myths and realities, it is important to note briefly that defaults occur for at least one of the following reasons:

1. *General Economic Conditions* are such that the municipality pay from its current revenues its current obligations as they become due and provide the type of service necessary for operation of the municipal body. The "Proposition 13" mentality is one of the manifestations of the difficulties of continually increasing tax levies in order to pay for increasing costs of municipal services.
2. *Incompetency of Management* of the municipal body in failing to increase revenues to meet costs.
3. *Fraud and Dishonesty* by municipal officials by either abusing their powers and misusing municipal financing for their own political profit and gain or by actually converting municipal funds to their own personal benefit.

The problem of municipal default and bankruptcy is today more of a concern than it was in the past 40 years. There currently exist a number of factors which tend to make it more difficult for certain municipalities to be able to meet their municipal obligations as they become due. These factors include the following:

1. Movement in both population and manufacturing capabilities from the snowbelt to the sunbelt. (This is due not only to climate but also to the perception of individuals and corporations that there are higher tax levies in certain snowbelt states.)
2. The decline of urban areas and the present need in the 1980s for major capital improvements and repairs in many metropolitan areas.
3. The increasing percentage of municipal budgets devoted to the cost of personnel and personnel-related expenses which for the most part have been tied to cost of living increases and at times somewhat unrealistic union contracts.
4. The growing unrest among taxpayers in the face of increasing taxation without commensurate increase of benefits. "Proposition 13" mentality is just the beginning of that manifestation which should continue during the 1980s.
5. Adverse effects of inflation which have significantly increased the cost of maintenance, repair and operation of a municipality beyond what was projected at the time many municipal obligations were assumed.

It was the defaults in the latter part of the 1800s and the beginning part of the 1900s that brought about changes in procedures, documents, and structuring in municipal finance in order to reduce the rate of municipal defaults. Any future increase in municipal bond defaults most likely will be met with appropriate corrective action mandated by the municipal bond market as was done in the past.

MYTH 1: THE DEFAULT RATE FOR MUNICIPAL BONDS IS APPROXIMATELY THE SAME AS THAT FOR CORPORATE BONDS

Reality

The first recorded default of a municipal obligation was the city of Mobile, in 1839 which was a default of an issue in the principal amount of $513,000. After 1839, numerous municipalities and states failed to pay their debt obligations. During the 1850s and 1860s, such cities as San Francisco,

Philadelphia, Detroit and Chicago defaulted on their municipal bonds. One of the causes was the excessive cost of municipal financing. Another reason for municipal default was speculation by municipalities in real estate and other ventures unrelated to necessary municipal services that such bodies were established to perform.

Approximately 77 percent of all municipal defaults occurred during the 1930s when 4,770 municipal units defaulted in the payment of interest or principal on some 10 percent of the then outstanding total of $15 billion of municipal bonds. The default rate for corporate bonds was greater. By the way of comparison, for example, in 1932 there were defaults in 1.8 percent of all municipal bonds, 3.5 percent of railroad bonds, 5.4 percent of public utility bonds, 7.2 percent of industrial bonds and 19.4 percent of all foreign bonds. Thereafter, in the 1930s, the respective percentages increased, but, for the most part, the lowest percentage of principal amount of outstanding bonds in default was in municipal bonds.

Approximately 75 percent of all municipal bond defaults have occurred in bonds issued by a municipality to finance revenue producing enterprises (i.e., highways, bridges, utilities, swimming pools, harbors, etc.). During the 1940s, there were only 79 defaults by municipal bodies on indebtedness; during the 1950s, 112; and during the 1960s, 294. As we progress into the present economic times, the defaults increase.

Between 1945 and 1970, there were $450,000,000 of principal amount of municipal bonds which went into default constituting .4 percent of the principal amount outstanding of all municipal bonds in 1970. In one year, 1970, .9 percent of the outstanding of all corporate bonds or $1,005,000,000 of corporate bonds went into default.

While the default rate per principal amount of outstanding corporate bonds went down from 3.2 percent in the 1930s to 4 percent in the 1940s, .04 percent in the 1950s, .03 percent in the 1960s, it has risen to approximately .2 percent in the 1970s and appears to equal or exceed the 1940s rate in the first part of the 1980s. Between 1966 and 1977, there were over $2.5 billion in principal amount of corporate bonds which went into default as compared with 1986 when the Petition filed in the LTV Bankruptcy resulted in the default of $2.2 billion in long-term debt, mostly debentures held by many mutual funds. The Texaco filing in 1987 has triggered $1.2 billion in corporate debt defaults already this year.

The Pacific States (Alaska, California, Hawaii, Oregon and Washington) had 654 municipal units default in the payment of principal or interest from 1839-1969; of these 520 (79 percent) occurred during 1930-1939; 5 during the 1940s; 1 during the 1950s; 13 during the 1960s. The Mountain States (Colorado, Idaho, Montana, Nevada, Utah and Wyoming) had 329 municipal units default in the payment of principal or interest from 1839-

1969; of these, 270 (82 percent) occurred during 1930-1939; 6 during the 1940s; 4 during the 1950s; 3 during the 1960s.

It has been true in the past that the percentage of principal amount of municipal bonds that are in default is less than the percentage of principal amount of corporate bonds that are in default. This fact is due in part to the constructive response which the municipal bond market has made to the problems of the past.

The total principal amount of the WPPSS Bonds of approximately $8.3 billion is equal to approximately 2.4 percent of the U.S. municipal debt currently outstanding. In 1975, New York City had approximately $14 billion of principal amount of Bonds and Notes outstanding of which approximately $6 billion was Short Term Debt (Notes). In 1976, with the help of the federal government, New York City proceeded to avoid bankruptcy and to workout of the troubled situation. The LTV Bankruptcy triggered defaults in more than $550 million of outstanding tax-exempt pollution control bonds. Technically, Texaco's municipal debt has not been included in the bankruptcy filings of Texaco, Inc., the holding company, and its two finance subsidiaries, Texaco Capital and Texaco Capital N.V. The subsidiaries responsible for paying the municipal debt, Texaco Refining and Marketing (R&M) and Texaco Convent Refining, Inc. have not been the subject of Chapter 11 filings. As a result, Texaco has indicated it will continue to make payments on its Parish of St. James 9.00 percent Pollution Control Revenue Bonds, and on its Port of Port Arthur Navigation District Pollution Control Revenue Bonds, both of which are secured by agreement with Texaco Convent Refining, Inc.

MYTH II: MUNICIPAL BANKRUPTCY IS JUST AS COMMON AS CORPORATE BANKRUPTCY

Reality

From 1937 when the Municipal Bankruptcy Act was passed to 1972, there were over 362 cases filed involving municipal bodies. These 362 cases involved admitted debts of approximately $217 million. The amount paid on such debts exceeded $140 million and the amount of the loss was approximately $77 million. For the most part, municipal bondholders in such Chapter 9 proceedings received principal and interest on their bonds, the only modification being either an extension of the maturity date or a reduction in the interest rate. It was the trade creditors and employees of municipalities who for the most part suffered the losses in such proceedings. Between 1972 and October 1, 1982, nine cases were filed under Chapter 9 by municipal bodies. Since the enacting of the Bankruptcy Code which became effective on October 1, 1979, there have been only 23 Chapter 9 bankruptcy proceedings instituted involving special tax districts and small municipalities or counties. In contrast, there were over 24,442 business bankruptcies filed in the United States in 1986. Bankruptcy has been viewed by some financially troubled corporations as a safe harbor; however, there are serious adverse effects to financially troubled municipalities instituting a Chapter 9 proceeding.

MYTH III: MUNICIPAL DEFAULTS HAVE LITTLE EFFECT ON THE MUNICIPAL BOND MARKET AND THE DEFAULTING MUNICIPALITY'S ABILITY TO OBTAIN FUTURE FINANCING

Reality

At the time of the first municipal default in the city of Mobile in 1839, commentators were quite apologetic for the city citing two major fires in 1839, the panic of 1837, and a resulting yellow fever epidemic as some of the factors that caused this then unprecedented municipal default. There after, there were defaults by various cities in the 1850s and the 1860s. A somewhat graver situation was the fact that in the 1840s, 1850s and 1860s, a number of states repudiated their indebtedness to bondholders. The first such repudiation was by Mississippi in the 1840s. Florida, Alabama, North Carolina, South Carolina, Georgia, Louisiana, Arkansas, Tennessee, Minnesota, Michigan, and Virginia also repudiated their indebtedness in the late 1800s. Such repudiation along with the defaults that occurred in the 1800s brought into question the security of investment in municipal obligations. It was the municipal bond market which reacted to these defaults and demanded that there be appropriate changes and assurances given in order to insure the security of investment in municipal obligations. As a result of the problems referred to above, legislation was enacted to give bondholders greater rights and protection in order to prevent unnecessary defaults on municipal obligations. The municipal bond market in effect mandated changes in documentation, legal authorization, and structure of municipal financing which now are considered basic. Such changes included:

a. debt limitations on municipal issues to prevent excessive borrowing caused by speculative growth in real estate valuation;
b. clearly defined bondholder rights in the event of default supported by statutory and case law;

c. use of bond counsel to determine the legality of a bond issue before the sale to avoid technical legal defects that could allow an Issuer to repudiate the debt;

d. development of credit rating agencies as well as thorough credit review by investment firms and many institutional investors;

e. statutory restrictions against municipal issuers borrowing for chronic deficiencies; and

f. the use of indenture trustees, paying agents, and others who have certain fiduciary duties in order to protect the rights and interests of bondholders.

It is clear that whenever municipal bond defaults have become a significant percentage of the outstanding municipal bonds, the municipal bond market has reacted and demanded that there be corrective action in order to insure payment of principal and interest when such becomes due. Whenever any municipality believed it could avoid a payment to bondholders based on technical legal arguments or present economic conditions, the past has demonstrated the price for avoiding such payment is quite high and the ability to obtain financing from the municipal bond market in the future quite questionable.

MYTH IV: REMEDIES AVAILABLE TO MUNICIPAL BONDHOLDERS ARE IDENTICAL TO THOSE AVAILABLE TO CORPORATE BONDHOLDERS IN A DEFAULT SITUATION

Reality

There are significant differences between the types of remedies available to municipal bondholders in a default situation and those available to the holders of corporate bonds. In a municipal default, unlike a default on corporate bonds, the bondholder cannot seize collateral or pledge or attach property of the municipality, initiate a bankruptcy proceeding for the municipality, or liquidate the assets of the municipality. The usual remedies available to a municipal bondholder include the following:

Acceleration

The documentation for both corporate and municipal bonds normally provides that upon the occurrence of an event of default as defined in those documents, the bondholders by a certain percentage (normally 25 percent or more), or the indenture trustee may declare the principal and all accrued and unpaid interest immediately due and payable. It is important for the municipal bondholders to understand the effects of acceleration and the relative benefits and detriment to holders. It is not necessary to accelerate for the institution of equitable remedies or to file a proof of claim in a bankruptcy proceeding or to seek appropriate non-accelerated remedies. For example, in a default by a municipality in failing to comply with a covenant in the indenture such as maintaining a certain ratio between tax revenues and existing obligations, that breach can be enforced through the institution of an appropriate legal action seeking to require a municipality to comply with the terms and there is no need for acceleration. Also, if there is an impairment in the security of the issue on account of certain persons connected with a municipality maintaining that the pledge of revenues is Invalid, bondholders or the indenture trustee may institute an action seeking an appropriate declaratory judgment resolving the matter without acceleration.

Generally, acceleration is necessary if one desires to obtain: (a) an increased interest rate as may be provided for in the documents upon the occurrence of acceleration or (b) a judgment of deficiency judgment for principal and accrued and unpaid interest against the obligor. As a practical matter, acceleration decreases the ease and ability of the municipality to cure a default. The waiver of acceleration of a widely held public issue is difficult to achieve. Normally, it requires a higher percentage (50 percent or more) to rescind than to accelerate (25 percent or less). It is important for the municipal bondholder (including underwriters and dealers) to remember there are few benefits to acceleration and there are difficulties that are created by acceleration since the municipality is faced with the demand for immediate payment of the full amount of principal and accrued and unpaid interest which may paralyze the ability of the municipality to ever cure the default.

Institution of Lawsuits

Request for monetary judgment. Bondholders may institute a lawsuit requesting the municipality to take action to immediately pay all amounts due and owing to the bondholders or otherwise cure the default by a suit for money judgment, mandamus, specific performance or other equitable relief.

Bondholders have a right to sue on their bonds for past due interest or principal without requesting the indenture trustee or other party to take action. As we have seen in the case of New York City, the municipal body can take no action to seek a moratorium against suits by bondholders for past due principal and interest except to rely upon the automatic stay that occurs upon filing a petition under Chapter 9 of the Bankruptcy Code as will be discussed later. Generally, the indenture should have a prohibition of the payment upon default of coupons detached from the bonds prior to the payment of the bonds. The purpose of such a provision is to prevent the trading of coupons, the purchasing of coupons and the directing of the trustee or others to take actions based upon a discounted purchase of such coupons which had been detached from the bonds.

The collection of a money judgment. A money judgment against a municipality is complicated by the fact that, generally, the courts, on public policy grounds, do not allow the seizing of municipal property to pay the municipality's debts and obligations since the seizure would disrupt local government. Some courts have held that if there are funds which are surplus and not dedicated for any public purpose, a bondholder may be able to attach and obtain those funds which are purely surplus and not necessary for the normal operating of the municipality. Likewise, in the absence of specific statutory authority for seizure of private property in order to satisfy a judgment on a defaulted bond, there can be no remedy directed to the property held by the resident or the inhabitant of a municipal body.

Mandamus action. Given the difficulties of collecting on money judgments against a municipal body, an available and most appropriate remedy to bondholders of defaulted municipal bonds that are without recourse to specific collateral is to proceed with an action in mandamus ordering the municipal body to increase taxes sufficiently to pay the obligation owed to the bondholders. However, bondholders in a mandamus action cannot require the municipal body to levy a tax which would exceed the applicable constitutional or statutory debt limitations. There are, too, practical problems in a mandamus action such as vacancies in offices, resignation by municipal officers thereby mooting the effect of any mandamus (command to a ministerial officer to levy taxes to pay the amount due) without the bondholders or the court having a right to cause such vacancies to be filled. The only alternative the court has if a municipality refuses to act as ordered by the court in the mandamus action is to hold the officers in contempt and render civil or criminal penalties. If there have been any improper expenditures by the municipal body or if other action is taken which impairs the security for the obligation, injunctive relief may be sought. It should be apparent given the problems inherent in other forms of relief that such equitable and declaratory action should be sought first before resorting to other remedies.

Municipal Insolvency: Debt Adjustment

If a municipal body cannot pay its municipal obligations as they become due, it may consider proceeding to seek remedies under Chapter 9 of the Bankruptcy Code. Even if a court were to determine that a municipality was in fact insolvent and its revenues were not sufficient to meet its current debt obligations, as a practical matter, such determination would be of little help to the bondholders since there would be certain necessary expenses in order to generate any municipal revenue that a municipal body would have to incur and there would be a significant question of whether liquidating municipal assets in an insolvency situation is in the best interests of the bondholders. There is no authority for the proposition that poverty may be successfully interposed as a defense to the payment of lawful obligations. There is some thought that if bondholders obtain a judgment against a municipality, they have a benefit if that municipality is later declared insolvent. However, given the new Chapter 9 provisions, it appears to make little difference whether one is a bondholder or a judgment creditor of a municipality. Obviously, a municipality on its own or at the urging of the bondholders may seek relief under the federal bankruptcy law. A Chapter 9 proceeding can only be instituted by the municipal taxing body and, unlike the corporate situation, such a proceeding cannot be instituted by creditors involuntarily against the municipality.

Appointment or Use of Consultants, Financial Advisors or Financing Authorities

In troubled financial situations, where the municipality lacks the confidence of the investing public that the municipality will continue to make the right decisions with regard to its operations, there exists a possible solution whereby such confidence can be increased by the use of financial advisers or financing authorities. In such use, the municipality should be able to proceed with operations without the threat of continued default and exercise of remedies. Some defaults may have as their most appropriate cure appointment or use of a consultant or financial advisor to guide the municipality to the degree permitted by law in the operation and management of the enterprise involved. Legislatures and other governmental bodies have desired to aid in a default situation by the establishment of a finance authority with the powers to issue debt obligations and set or approve an appropriate budget for municipal bodies in question. It should be remembered that consultants, financial advisors or financing authorities cannot alter the bondholders' rights and remedies without consent. Such consultants, advisors or authorities cannot improperly exercise the power of a municipal body which they supervise or have an improper delegation by the municipal body of the powers that are vested in the troubled municipality.

Tax-exempt Conduit Financing

When the municipal bonds are based upon tax-exempt conduit financing either for industrial development or social benefits of the municipal body and its inhabitants, there is normally provided an alternative source of recovery for the bondholders other than the governmental body's ability to levy taxes to pay off the indebtedness. The collateral takes the form of a guaranty by a corporation of the indebtedness to the bondholders and a mortgage or a security interest in the collateral which is financed by the tax-exempt bonds. In these situations, the municipality should be aware that these financings are structured as revenue bond issues and that the municipal body is not liable for the indebtedness incurred but is merely used as the conduit for the public purpose financing which has been approved by that municipal body. The remedies of the bondholders should not be directed against the municipality as such remedies are outlined above but rather against the collateral and the corporation which has received the benefits of such conduit financing. Some of the specific remedies regarding conduit municipal financing are as follows: (a) request for judicial foreclosure and sale of collateral, (b) non-judicial sale of collateral, (c) suit against guarantor, and (d) right of entry.

Filing Proof of Claim in Bankruptcy

The bondholders may file a proof of claim in bankruptcy for the amount of the bonds they hold. The indenture trustee has the authority under most indentures to file a proof of claim on behalf of all bondholders whether bankruptcy be of the municipality or of the conduit tax exempt financing of the corporation which was liable on the bonds. The indenture trustee is not authorized to vote on a plan of reorganization or debt adjustment; however, the indenture trustee may object to plans of reorganization and should object to plans of reorganization that such trustee knows are woefully inadequate or not appropriate. Likewise, a municipality in a tax-exempt conduit financing is not liable on the bonds but has a fiduciary duty to the bondholders to file a proof of claim, if appropriate, or to object to any plan of reorganization which in the opinion of the municipality is not in the best interests of the municipality and the bondholders.

Security Fraud Action

One court has held that the Tenth Amendment to the U.S. Constitution does not protect a municipality's issuance of industrial revenue bonds from the application of the federal securities laws since the issuance of such bonds does not rise to the level of traditional governmental functions. There is a recent trend in case law towards increasing the use of federal security fraud actions against issuers, underwriters and others, including municipalities. The best defense to such actions is the careful consideration of tax-exempt conduit financing in order to insure that the bondholders and the municipality do not become victims of a prearranged scheme to defraud both of them. Security fraud action should be one of the last remedies to be taken.

Supplemental Indenture

Almost every indenture provides and should provide a mechanism of allowing the indenture to be supplemented or modified with or without appropriate approval of the bondholders. Modification of the indenture without consent of the bondholders is only proper when it does not affect the rights of the holders or if the modification gives additional security to the holders. Supplemental indentures have been successfully used when the approval of the holders is necessary in order to resolve the defaulted issue and the proposal is deemed to be meritorious by the holders.

Recision Of Acceleration And Waiver Of Default

Sometimes the obligor after being informed of the acceleration of an issue might be able to cure the defaults that caused acceleration but may not be able to get the required approval of the bondholders to rescind the acceleration. The indenture should provide that acceleration, notice to sell collateral or entry of final judgment or decree against a municipality can be rescinded and annulled if the obligor pays all amounts due and owing, plus fees and expenses of the indenture trustee and bondholders provided all defaults have been cured, and a majority of holders approve the recision of acceleration, sale or judgment.

Acceptance Of Default

Sometimes, in widely held public issues, it may be impossible to get an appropriate percentage of holders to direct certain action to be taken to resolve the defaulted issue. Circumstances may be that the above cited remedies are inappropriate, and it is in the best interest of the holders to accept the default. Court approval of the acceptance of the default may be in the best interests of the municipality, the indenture trustee and the bondholders. Accordingly, the bondholders should consider whether they should accept the default and proceed with discussing the resolution without taking legal action except, if necessary, court approval for the acceptance of the default.

Application of Proceeds

The indenture should have appropriate provisions with regard to how to disburse funds that are collected pursuant to the exercised remedy. Normally, such indenture provisions provide funds to be disbursed as follows: to pay costs and expenses of the indenture trustee, then to the holders, and if there is any surplus after payment of principal and interest to the holders, to the municipality or obligor. Funds collected for holders who cannot be located and who are not known cannot be paid as a windfall to known holders. Usually, any surplus money collected that cannot be distributed because the holders are not known or cannot be located goes either to the state or to the municipality.

MYTH V: A CHAPTER 9 BANKRUPTCY PROCEEDING IS THE ONLY MEANS BY WHICH A MUNICIPALITY WHICH CANNOT MEET ITS CURRENT DEBT PAYMENT OBLIGATIONS CAN RESOLVE THE PROBLEM

Reality

The municipality Bankruptcy Act was enacted in the late 1930s in an attempt to protect municipalities from a long series of acrimonious lawsuits injurious to municipalities and unproductive in furnishing funds to pay off creditors. Chapter 9 of the Bankruptcy Code was not intended as an exclusive remedy for municipal bodies who are unable to meet their current debt obligations. Since 1930, numerous states have provided for a state receiver or a state agency to act as receiver when a local governmental unit defaults on its financial obligations. A receivership is an available remedy which, given the enactment of appropriate legislation establishing a mechanism to control acrimonious lawsuits, allows bondholders and other creditors of the municipality to obtain the relief in a default situation. As recently as May 14, 1986, a Federal Judge in Chicago appointed a receiver for the beleaguered Chicago Housing Authority, but delayed the implementation of the appointment for 60 days. It is the state created agencies, such as a State Agency for Emergency Municipal Finance, which have prevented a number of municipalities from having to seek relief under Chapter 9, and have allowed a troubled municipality to work out of its problems under state supervision while providing to bondholders the assurance that the amounts due and owing to them will be paid. Another mechanism, if a municipal body finds that its function and purpose have been eliminated, is to petition the legislature for the revocation of its charter seeking an appropriate state court to supervise the liquidation of municipal assets. This remedy is probably more appropriate to special tax districts and local governmental agencies which experience financial difficulties and no current public purpose for their continued operation and existence (municipal hospital, waste treatment facilities, etc.). Given the stigma many believe to exist with regard to a municipal bankruptcy, consideration should first be given to the use of state agencies, state receiverships, supervised liquidation of municipal assets, or the enactment of legislation establishing finance authorities (to issue debt to finance and refund existing obligations) as available and in many instances preferable to municipal bankruptcy.

For example, in Pennsylvania, if a local government revenue project is in default for 30 days on the principal or interest due for any bond or note, the holders may appoint a trustee who may petition the court for a receiver to take over the operation of the project and the collection of all monies due to it. The receiver may operate, maintain, repair, and reconstruct project facilities and collect any rents or revenues due on the project. However, he shall not perform any essential government functions. One should not forget that a receivership is an available remedy which, given the enactment of appropriate legislation establishing a mechanism to control acrimonious lawsuits, allows bondholders and other creditors of the municipality to obtain the relief in a default situation.

A composition is an agreement between an insolvent debtor and the creditors to scale down the former's obligations. The Bankruptcy Code does not preclude state compositions provided that they are not binding on nonconsenting creditors. In Ohio, for example, the Local Fiscal Emergencies Law provides for the appointment of a seven member board to supervise a local government's finances upon the declaration of a fiscal emergency. Within 120 days after the first meeting of the board, the mayor must submit to the board a feasible, bona fide plan, approved by the appropriate legislative body, setting forth the time schedule and method by which the municipality will, *inter alia,* satisfy past due obligations and restore the municipality's ability to market long-term general obligation bonds. The board must report annually to the state speaker of the house and president of the senate and is subject to the supervision of the state auditor. During the emergency, the municipality may issue notes secured by a pledge of revenue from the State Local Government Fund.

In New Jersey, any petition for municipal readjustment must be approved by the state municipal finance commission, and any public debt issued as part of a plan of reorganization must be approved by the commission. Further, a board is created which is authorized to liquidate assets pledged to a special fund and to apply the proceeds to the fund. Warrants for funding or refunding indebtedness may be issued and may be secured by the proceeds of the sale of real estate acquired by the city for taxes.

Given the stigma many believe to exist with regard to a municipal bankruptcy (as demonstrated by its use in the last 36 years only by a few smaller municipal bodies), consideration should first be given to the use of state agencies, state receiverships, supervised liquidation of municipal assets, or enactment of legislation establishing finance or refinance authorities (to issue debt to finance and refund existing obligations) as available and in many instances preferable to municipal bankruptcy.

Workouts are normally tailored to specific situations, and are an attempt to see if there is a common ground on which the municipality and creditors can agree without the necessity of having Bankruptcy Court supervision. As set forth above, a workout can take various forms including:

1. Use of consultants and advisers to set rates which will be sufficient to generate revenues to pay debt service pursuant to an agreed upon debt service program.
2. Use of a refinancing authority or state composition which provides additional state or federal guarantees to refinance debt and to pay off old debt either in full or at an agreed upon discount through tender offers or exchange offers.
3. Use of state receiverships where assets are liquidated under state court supervision and proceeds are disbursed to creditors based on a court determined schedule of payment.

The advantages of a workout include: the stigma of bankruptcy is not placed on a municipal body, the bond market is anticipated to view the municipality as capable of resolving and paying off its debt obligations, making the possibility of future financing at market more likely, and the acrimony and uncertainty of bankruptcy are replaced by the certitude of an agreed upon program.

Disadvantages of a workout include: lawsuits are not automatically stayed unless there is legislation or a court order staying such during the workout; there is not necessarily an efficient and practical method whereby all creditors would be bound by the agreement of the majority (except perhaps in a state receivership where such matters could be resolved); bankruptcy puts all creditors in one forum rather than a multitude of various forums, staying litigation and providing a mechanism of binding all creditors, so a recalcitrant creditor cannot hold up the process by unreasonably demanding more than what other similarly situated creditors are receiving; and the contract clause of the United States Constitution and various state constitutions prevent a nonjudicial mandatory involuntary settlement of claim by all creditors.

MYTH VI: ANY MUNICIPALITY CAN GO INTO A CHAPTER 9 PROCEEDING

Reality

In order to institute a Chapter 9 proceeding, the municipality must be duly authorized by state law or home rule power. There is no grant to creditors of a municipality to institute an involuntary bankruptcy proceeding as such is available for creditors of corporate debtors. A municipality is a "political subdivision or public agency or instrumentality of the state." Before a municipality is able to institute a proceeding under the Bankruptcy Code, it must be generally authorized to be a debtor under such chapter by state law or by a government officer or organization empowered by state law to authorize such an entity to be a debtor under such chapter. Sixteen states have specifically authorized a municipality to so proceed. Some states have specifically prohibited municipalities from filing under the Bankruptcy Code. However, one bankruptcy court has found no such authorization in the typical statutes authorizing an entity "to sue or be sued" without any specific statutory authorization to file a bankruptcy case. With regard to an unincorporated tax or special assessment district which does not have its own officials, an action is commenced under Chapter 9 by filing a petition under that chapter by the district's governing authority or board or body which has authority to levy taxes or assessments to meet obligations for such a district. If it can be shown to the Bankruptcy Court that a petition was filed not in good faith or not meeting the requirements of Chapter 9, the petition may be dismissed.

* Reprinted by courtesy of James E. Spiotto, Partner, Chapman and Cutler.

Chapter X

Past Bond Defaults and
Municipal Bankruptcy*

A. Analysis of Past Defaults
1. Municipal Bonds
    a. Between 1839 and 1969 there were 6,195 recorded defaults of municipal issues.
        (1) The defaults between 1839 and 1969 consisted of default by 727 counties and parishes, 1,911 incorporated municipalities, 313 unincorporated municipalities, 1,372 school districts and 1872 special purpose districts.
        (2) During the period of 1929-1937 there were 4,770 defaults by Governmental bodies as shown in the following table.
    b. During the 1930s municipal units defaulted in the payment of interest or principal on some 10 percent of the then outstanding total of $15 billion of municipal bonds. Between 1945 and 1970 municipal bonds in the principal amount of $450,000,000 went into default which constituted .4 percent of the principal amount of municipal bonds outstanding in 1970.
    c. Since 1937 when the Municipal Bankruptcy Act was passed, there have been 380 cases filed involving municipal bodies. Between 1937 and 1972 there were 362 cases filed.
        (1) These 362 cases involved admitted debts of approximately $217,000,000.
        (2) In these Chapter 9 cases, the amount paid on such debt exceeded $140,000,000 and the amount of loss was approximately $77,000,000.

Table 1

Type of Govt. Unit	Number in Default	Percent of Total Number in Default	Indebtedness of Defaulting Unit	Percent of Debt in Default
Counties	417	13.7	$ 360	15.1
Incorporated municipalities	1,434	8.3	1,760	19.9
Towns and organized townships	88	.4	10	2.9
School districts	1,241	.9	160	7.8
Reclamation, levee,irrigation and drainage districts	944	28.2		
Other special districts	646	12.4	400	25.0
Total	4,770	2.7	2,690	17.7

See: A Commission Report "City Financial Emergencies: The Intergovernmental Dimension," Advisory Commission on Intergovernmental Relations, Washington, D.C., July, 1973.

    d.   Between 1954-1972, 17 of the 362 bankruptcy cases were filed and between 1972 and 1979 there were 9 Chapter 9 petitions filed by governmental bodies. Since the effective date of the Bankruptcy Reform Act of 1978 (October 1, 1979) there have been 9 Chapter 9 petitions filed.

    e.   In contrast, during the 1940s, there were only 79 defaults by municipalities. However in the 1950s the defaults by municipalities increased to 112 and during the 1960s to 294. As we progress into present economic times, defaults increase.

    f.   Approximately 75 percent of all municipal bond defaults have occurred in bonds issued by a municipality to finance revenue producing enterprises (i.e., highways, bridges, utilities, swimming pools, harbors, etc.).

    g.   Given recent legislative restrictions on taxation combined with economic factors of increasing costs of providing minimal municipal services there is an increasing difficulty posed to municipalities in meeting their debt obligations.

  2. Comparison with Corporate Bonds

    a.   Debt obligation of U.S. corporate business, commercial banks and financial borrowers totaled $112.9 billion in 1965, $346.8 billion in 1977 and estimated to exceed $400 billion in 1981.

    b.   In years 1900-43 U.S. corporate bonds defaulted at an average annual rate of 1.7 percent of the outstanding; from 1944-65 at an annual average rate of less than 0.10 percent and after 1965 the annual default rate is gradually rising towards pre-1943 level (See Smith, Barney, Harris, Upham & Co. Corporate Bond Research: Special Report dated April 26, 1978).

   c. Present economic conditions including higher interest rates and recent financial troubles of major U.S. corporations lead some to conclude corporations will and are experiencing difficulties in meeting debt obligations which may pose difficulties for municipal "conduit" financing.

   d. The 1983 Annual Report of the Director of the Administrative Office of the U.S. Courts indicate that in fiscal 1983 there were 85,439 business bankruptcy estates as opposed to 77,503 business estates in 1982. Focusing on Chapter 11 estates alone, in 1983, there were 21,039 Chapter 11s filed, an increase of 55.5 percent over 1982. Bankruptcy has been viewed by some financially troubled corporations as a safe harbor; however, there are serious adverse effects to financially troubled municipalities instituting a Chapter 9 proceeding.

B. Probability of Defaults in Corporate and Municipal Bonds: The 1930's Experience.

   1. In 1932 there were in default 1.8 percent of all municipal bonds, 3.5 percent of railroad bonds, 5.4 percent of public utility bonds, 7.2 percent of industrial bonds and 19.4 percent of all foreign bonds; thereafter in the 1930s the respective percentages increased. The average default rate for municipal bonds in the 1930s was approximately 10 percent.

   2. Defaults are a function of not only the then economic condition but also the competence and honesty of the management of obligor and the negative trends in the related industry.

C. Analysis of Defaults Reveal Necessary Changes

   1 It was the defaults in the latter half of the 1800s and early 1900s which brought about the procedures, documents and structuring of municipal financing which are now taken for granted. An analysis of present defaults and the problems related to defaulted bond issues will lead to the necessary required changes and safeguards.

   2. The analysis of past defaults has revealed and caused necessary changes in the documentation for municipal and corporate financing, including:

      a. Debt limitations on municipal issues to prevent excessive borrowing caused by speculative growth in real estate valuations.

    b. Clearly defined bondholders' rights in the event of default supported by statutory and case laws.

    c. The use of bond counsel to determine the legality of the bond issue before the sale to avoid technical legal defects which could allow the issuer to repudiate the debt.

    d. The Trust Indenture Act of 1939 (hereinafter referred to as "TIA") specifying needed requirements of providing bondholders in certain issues with an independent indenture trustee to protect the rights and interests of the investing public. (However, the TIA is not applicable to municipal bond issues).

    e. Development of credit rating agencies as well as through credit review by investment firms and many institutional investors.

    f. Statutory restrictions against municipal issuers borrowing for chronic deficits.

(See H.R. No. 1016, 76th Congress [1939]; Section 302 of the TIA; Feldstein, The Daily Bond Buyer, May 12, 1980, pp. 3, 12.)

D. Remedies

    1. Acceleration of principal and interest.

    2. Institution of lawsuit.

       a. Request monetary judgment;

       b. Request specific performance;

       c. Mandamus action;

       d. Request foreclosure of security conduit financing;

       e. Request other legal or equitable relief.

    3. Sale of trustee estate of collateral in conduit financing (judicial and non-judicial).

    4. File proof of claim in bankruptcy.

    5. Use of supplementary indentures to cure or waive defaults (with consents of bondholders).

    6. Acceptance of defaults with court approval in unusual situations.

    7. Security fraud actions.

    8. Acknowledgment of default and consent of judgment.

    9. Right to entry.

    10. Supplemental indenture.

    11. Rescision of acceleration and waiver of default.

* Reprinted in part by courtesy of James E. Spiotto, Partner, Chapman and Cutler.

Chapter XI

*State Bond Defaults**

Debt defaults by our American States, and for that matter by our municipal or local governments, may loom large when viewed briefly down the aisles of history. Any grouping of them makes them seem important and makes them look portentous. The same thing occurs with intergovernmental debts, which makes Great Britain out as a defaulter on World War I obligations, and Russia out as completely callous to all financial promises, with almost all other world governments involved in one way or another.

Actually, the record on the debts of our American States is rather modest, when it is placed in its proper setting. And every state that has defaulted, either of necessity or by the much more ominous road of repudiation, has learned that default is far more expensive in the end than prompt payment. It would be foolish to predict that defaults never will occur again. But it can be said that they have become historically less frequent over the years, to the point almost of disappearance.

But let's look at the record, as Al Smith used to say. For convenience, the debt negligent States can be listed as repudiators and innocent defaulters. The line of demarcation sometimes is thin and involved with legal questions.

Mississippi led the procession, with repudiation in 1842 and 1852 on $7,000,000 Planters Bank and Union Bank bonds. This incident was recently reviewed by J.T. Brown, president of the Mississippi Bankers Association, whose report was reprinted in *The Daily Bond Buyer* of March 25. Mr. Brown ended his report on the note that "Mississippi may have grievously erred, but if she did, lavishly did she pay for her error."

Florida is regarded as a repudiator of $7,000,000 bonds in 1845 and 1876, issued to establish banks and for railway guarantees. Alabama, in 1876 turned thumbs down on some railway guarantee obligations, regarding which no reliable estimates are available. Georgia, in 1872, and again in

157

later years of that post Carpet Baggers decade, refused to pay about $12,700,000 railway guarantee obligations. South Carolina failed to pay an estimated $6,000,000 securities, details of which are not available.

Louisiana, in 1874 and subsequent years, shrugged off some $6,000,000 "Baby Bonds," railway guarantees and claims under a debt settlement. North Carolina, in 1879, turned down some $12,600,000 special tax bonds and railway guarantee obligations. Arkansas, in 1884, defaulted on about $8,000,000 railway guarantees.

There was skullduggery involved in the debt incurrence of all of such States. Each and every one felt justified at the time in refusing to recognize their debts. But this did not help innocent creditors, of whom there were many. The British Council of Foreign Bondholders, which recently revived its agitation on repudiated Mississippi bonds, used to proclaim that "a bond never dies." But debts often have to be compromised, as even the Government of Great Britain has learned.

Several other States must be mentioned, less as repudiators than as victims of circumstances. Michigan authorized, in 1837, a loan of $5,000,000, but the underwriters failed and the State received only $1,387,000 for the bonds. In 1842, that State offered a compromise proportionate to the sum received. Minnesota issued, in 1858, as a Territory, $2,275,000 bonds in aid of railroads, with a provision that the railroads were to service the debt. The railroads failed and the State scaled down the debt by about 50 percent.

Virginia, which is held in highest regard by every informed investor, got into a hassle on debts with West Virginia, when that territory receded from the Old Dominion and preferred to stay with the Union in the Civil War. Some scaling down of debt was occasioned, and the matter was not fully settled until 1919, when West Virginia heeded an advisory opinion of the U.S. Supreme Court.

There were other instances, on which the record is brief or obscure. Even the great Commonwealth of Pennsylvania had difficulty in meeting its obligations after the panic of 1837. By 1843 it was almost $3,000,000 in arrears on interest payments, as the Federal Reserve Bank of Philadelphia notes in its business review of March, 1958. But such episodes were fleeting and never have rated as defaults.

Arkansas requires a second mention, for that State decided early in the 1930s that it would halt debt service on more than $140,000,000 road bonds. This occasioned one of the most interesting legal battles in all our history. It was and is a commonplace that, as William L. Raymond put it in his book, *State and Municipal Bonds*, in 1923, "There is no legal method of forcing a sovereign State to pay its debts against its will."

No one would admit this more readily than David M. Wood, senior partner of Wood, King & Dawson, and dean of the municipal bond legal experts. But Mr. Wood went to the Federal bench and obtained a writ which required the Treasurer of the State of Arkansas, as an individual in his official position, to set aside gasoline and other designated taxes for payment of debt service. This led to a prompt settlement and a refunding which was aided by the Reconstruction Finance Corporation, to its own substantial financial advantage.

Thus, in almost 80 years, only the one State of Arkansas defaulted and Arkansas tried it twice. That State was shocked and chastened and has paid from ample revenues much of the debt which it defaulted in the Great Depression. Some other States found the going rather rough at times during the 1930s, but not even a hint of any other State default ever appeared.

It should be mentioned, perhaps, that there are still a half-dozen or so of States which do not have a direct bonded debt. After the banking and railway aid troubles of the last century the subsequent waves of reform led to constitutional provisions in various States against any incurrence of debt.

This chronicle should not be regarded as definitive or exhaustive. The brilliant analyst, Lawrence Chamberlain, when he wrote his "Principles of Bond Investment" in 1911, linked Maryland with Pennsylvania as having been slow for a time in the 1840s in meeting some obligations, and Indiana is mentioned by him in the same context. But Chamberlain was rigid in his judgments and the three States thus mentioned are not generally regarded as having a default record. Even Chamberlain, moreover, has scorn in the end only for Mississippi and Florida, because repudiation rather than financial difficulties seemed to be the motivations of their long-ago defaults.

There are also a few accidental circumstances known only in professional circles. Even in recent memory, funds by strange misadventure got deposited in banks which were not the paying agents. On one such occasion the funds were hastily made available thrice over before everything got straightened out. Such anxiety to meet payments is what really prevails in our State finances these days.—Editor.

* *Source:* *The Bond Buyer* (weekly), April 19, 1958.
Reprinted by courtesy of *The Bond Buyer*.

Chapter XII

1841 Bonds Still
Follow Mississippi*

When Mississippi treasurer William Cole went to London in July to discuss with foreign investment bankers the possibility of issuing bonds in Europe, he was reminded that the state has a little unfinished business to take care of.

In 1841, Mississippi repudiated about $7 million of bonds it sold to assist banks in the state following the financial panic of 1837. The bonds were sold to Nicholas Biddle, the Philadelphia banker, who then resold them in Europe.

One of those buyers was William Wordsworth, who in 1843 lamented the "heavy loss that had been inflicted upon many families, including my own, by Mississippi repudiation. I cannot ... but hope that the time is not distant when our brethren of the West will wipe off this stain from their name and nation."

Wordsworth's descendants are still waiting. Investors, represented by the London-based Council of Foreign Bondholders, say the debt has grown to more than $50 million.

Mr. Cole said the bankers he met told him that while the repudiation might not be an obstacle to the state selling bonds in Europe, it might limit the market for them.

"It's not really a prohibition, but there is some concern that the Bank of England would object" if Mississippi tried to sell new bonds without settling the earlier debt, he said. "It would eliminate British firms if the Bank of England objects."

The central bank earlier this year prevented British firms from underwriting a bond issue by the Bank of China, Mr. Cole said, because China is in default on bonds it sold early in the century. "The Bank of England considers it a precedent, and they don't like to change precedents."

It is not clear if the Bank of England would indeed object to Mississippi's issue, Mr. Cole said. Even if it did, he added, the state would be able to sell bonds elsewhere in Europe and in Japan.

Mr. Cole said he met with the subsidiaries of American and Japanese securities firms in Europe to discuss the possibility of Mississippi selling general obligation bonds outside the United States. The state Legislature recently passed a law authorizing Mississippi to sell GOs in foreign markets and in foreign currencies to assist private development in the state.

The state is looking at selling bonds abroad "as an option," Mr. Cole said. "I think when you talk about selling taxables it's incumbent upon you to look at all the options, both in the United States and outside the United States. Before too long, someone's going to cross that line."

The state treasurer said Mississippi had hoped to have sold a foreign issue by now, but it could not come up with an issue large enough to sell efficiently in the Euromarkets. But the state may sell a taxable issue before the end of the year, he said.

Mr. Cole said his office is also working on legislation that would enable the state to sell taxable industrial development bonds.

If Mississippi does become a frequent foreign borrower, "it's clear we should look into doing something" about the repudiated debt, Mr. Cole said. That, however, would involve amending the state constitution. In 1869, the Reconstruction government put a ban on payment of the bonds into the constitution, and it became part of the current version that was adopted in 1890.

* *Source:*   *Credit Markets.* Reprinted by courtesy of *Credit Markets* (Publication of *The Bond Buyer*).

Chapter XIII

History of State Debt Payment:

*Baby Bonds**

In the Biennial Report of the Auditor of Public Accounts for the State of Louisiana for the Years 1896 and 1897, the auditor makes the following statement, "It is gratifying to state that all debts created since the year 1880 have been paid or provided for..." This statement has been true since that time.

During the period immediately following the Civil War, Louisiana was governed by a federally appointed governor and legislature. Such period is known as the Reconstruction Era (North) or Carpetbagger Era (South). During the period such governor and legislature (known locally as "carpetbaggers") sold $100,000,000 in State bonds, k, the proceeds of which were misappropriated by such officials. After the Reconstruction Era ended, the bonds were repudiated, on the basis that since proceeds had been misappropriated (stolen) by officials (the Carpetbaggers) not of the state's choosing, the state had received no benefit from the bonds and hence had no obligation to pay the same. The state did authorize and sell some $2,000,000 in bonds to refund by exchange the bonds sold in the Reconstruction Era, with the exchange being only for pennies on the dollar of par value of the bonds surrendered.

The $2,000,000 of bonds issued subsequent to the Reconstruction Era, being in the denomination of five dollars, were called "Baby Bonds." The plates used for the original Baby Bond issue were held in the custody of the State Treasurer. During the 1880s while he was "vacationing" in Europe it was discovered that the plates had been used to reprint the bonds with identical numbers at least three times, one of the later printings being in green ink rather than the standard black or brown. It was also discovered that the treasurer had taken $420,000 of the Baby Bonds with him (another

$300,000 were found in his safety deposit box), as well as cash from the State Treasury, for which he had substituted additional Baby Bonds to keep all funds and accounts in proper balance. Since the treasurer extended his vacation permanently, he was not available to make full disclosure concerning the transactions. The state subsequently used surplus revenues in the general fund to buy up some of the irregularly issued Baby Bonds, the purchase price being fifty cents for each of the five dollar denomination bonds.

* *Source:* State of Louisiana—Official statement.

Chapter XIV

*A Generation of Change in Public Finance**

One of the most valuable assets in the trade of the municipal analyst is an elephantine memory. In some respects I hope my remarks today, along with the handout material, will provide some memory to you younger members of the Municipal Analysis Group of New York.

I would like to take a moment to look at where we have been and perhaps benefit from the view. I think a look back is important to those large numbers of this membership who have been involved in our profession but a few short years.

*   *   *

The history of municipal defaults is one subject about which many analysts probably could be more familiar. That history is too often glossed over with a reference to a small percentage of losses. I'm not even sure of exactly what is measured by the typical reference. More meaningful statistics on defaults have been gathered by James Spiotto, a partner in Chapman & Cutler in Chicago, and a bankruptcy specialist.

Between 1839 and 1969 there were over 6,000 recorded municipal defaults. Of these 4,770 occurred during the 1930s and represented 10 percent of the $15 billion outstanding. Historically, 75 percent of defaults were revenue bonds.

Between 1937 and 1954 cases involving bankrupt municipalities numbered 345. Between 1954 and 1972 an additional 17 bankruptcies were filed. In 1978 the Federal Bankruptcy Act was amended to provide that municipalities could file bankruptcy only on a voluntary basis.

Because the term "municipal bonds" today includes the issuance of so many bonds that have nothing to do with municipal or government credit, the default record of municipal bonds since 1960 could be loaded with false meaning. Bonds issued by state and local governments, or their special purpose agencies, for private hospitals, private colleges, mortgage financings, housing projects and private industry are numerous. In fact, the most numerous category of new issues listed by the Public Securities Association is "other." These instances are where virtually all the current defaults occur.

Permaneer Corporation, a wood products company, filed bankruptcy in 1977 and affected IDB issues in one city in Michigan, two in Missouri, one in Georgia and one in Arkansas. Alternative use of the buildings fortunately has saved some of these issues from default. But what if K-Mart defaults? On the basis of the number of bond issues sold on their behalf, the exposure, and threat to the good history of "munis" is very large.

A large number of IDB defaults have occurred, some in Arkansas and Mississippi where GO bonds were voted for the purpose, and some here in New York State. An IDB bond rated AAA also went into default. The AAA rating assigned was based on a state guaranty. The rater overlooked the fact that the guaranty did not come into effect until the resort project was completed—which it never was.

The experience of default in the 1930s was largely a temporary inability to pay, and most defaults were cured by refunding with principal stretched out, and/or with lower coupons attached. The type of security that could not be shored up was primarily that of special assessments without any back-up taxing power.

The most discussed historical defaults are those of states in the last century (needless to say, WPPSS will occupy center stage in history in the future). Most of these defaults had to do with state credit pledged behind bonds issued to finance railroads or canals. In most cases the bonds were declared to be illegally issued. If the states had been operating the rails and if they had been financial successes, there probably would not have been any questions raised as to the legality of the bond issues. Does this sound like anything we know today?

*   *   *

Now to the events that have occurred within my memory—that is, in my 30 years in the business.

When I came into "muni bonds" in late 1955, I started with a financial consultant in Minneapolis. During my first six months I would drive the boss around to suburban school boards or village council meetings at which he would make his presentation (we do not say "pitch" anymore) for a contract. He would invariably tell them that municipal finance was the most complicated in the nation and for that reason they needed a consultant. I did not realize the truth of that statement until my assignments took me into the neighboring states of Wisconsin and North Dakota. Each state had a different constitution and set of statutes governing debt issuance by the state and its political subdivisions. At that time there were 48 different sets of state laws, plus the territories of Alaska, Hawaii and Guam and commonwealths such as Puerto Rico.

We used to, and still do, rely heavily on bond counsel to keep us out of trouble as to the legality of bond issues. But even bond counsel have their blind spots. I can tell you about a bond counsel who approved a bond issue with a final maturity of 20 1/2 years in a state whose statutes limited maturity to 20 years.

I can tell you about a bond issue in Illinois that was approved, and I think sold, but not distributed, for a fictitious school district. But all the forged documents were properly signed including election proceedings and the bonds were approved as to legality. The perpetrators were caught in St. Louis.

Back in the old days we thought we had progressed past the point where states would undertake projects that the private sector turned down because the risk was too great. New York State broke that bubble with such things as Battery Park City, the Urban Development Corporation, Coop City, and the Convention Center. Now the state wants to squander more public money on an athletic stadium, while allowing the city to pump raw sewage into the Hudson River. Louisiana also has an affinity for losing stadiums.

In the old days, state and local governments were content to borrow to finance streets, schools, city halls and county courthouses—along with water and sewer systems, and in some instances electric systems or airports. Professional athletic team owners owned and operated their ball parks and stadiums. I guess the St. Louis and Chicago teams are the only ones who still do.

Somewhere around 1960, in every city of over 100,000, a disease I call "stadiumitis" began to spread. Perhaps it is a mental disorder, which can be called the "Edifice Complex." "If only we had a stadium all our problems would be over." If not a stadium, then a convention center. About the only stadiums that ever became self supporting were the ones in Anaheim and Philadelphia. I think Anaheim's was the first of the genre, and that success took better than 15 years.

A lot of happy marriages between teams and cities were broken up by the pirating of teams with free, or nearly free, stadiums furnished by cities with no teams. If cities could not or would not do the pirating, their states did. In the old days it would have been absurd to talk about the California Angels, Minnesota Vikings, or Patriots from New England.

In my earlier days we never saw state and local governments, or their agencies, issuing general or special obligations for the benefit of private commercial interests. It was felt that private borrowers have no business at the tax exempt window. Farming out the tax exempt privilege was tantamount to "selling one's birthright for a mess of pottage."

Tax freezes and abatements did nicely to encourage new development and construction and jobs. Why does industry prefer tax exempt financing? Could it be because that is the only way to get 100 percent, or more, financing? That is probably more important than the coupon.

Shortly after I entered the business the market went south—no cause and effect relationship. Put the blame on the Federal Reserve. In those days the Fed was always tinkering with interest rates, and sought to curb borrowing through higher rates, creating what it erroneously thought was "tight money" conditions.

Nominal rates went from 3 percent to 4 1/2 percent, and as high as 5 percent in 1957 for BB-Ba rated Bloomington, Minnesota. Municipalities wondered how they could possibly afford to pay such sky-high rates. Two years ago when some paid 14 percent they could not borrow enough. In fact, they added to their costs by flooding the market with IDBs, PCBs, and several generations of advance refunding bonds.

Speaking of "tight money," it has been my experience that the only time we really had tight money was in 1966. Banks were fighting to see who could issue the most C.D.s, and at the highest rate, and in late summer it seemed that they all had them coming due at the same time.

During all other so called "tight money" periods there has never been a shortage of money if the borrower was willing to pay the price. Some of the biggest acquisitions in our history took place with borrowed money when the prime rate was 20 percent.

Once it became known that state and local governments were willing to prostitute themselves in their tax exemption it did not take long for investment bankers from one end of the country to the other to help them dispense the largess. The great and the not so great wanted to avail themselves of 100 percent financing and lower interest rates—one of the most recent of the not so great reposes in harbor near 42nd street. Intrepid bankers, intrepid investors and the aircraft carrier are anchored down with default.

Most of these large scale "pie in the sky" financings that are natural losers seem to take in New York State. This is Rockefeller's legacy—think big and borrow big! Jump into water over your head instead of stepping slowly into the water's edge. Rocky's biographer says that he was obsessed with the idea that he could solve any problem if he threw enough money at it.

Not all grandiose schemes made it to market. In the early 1960s some enterprisers in Florida came up with another form of the old scam notion of "with my brains and your money we can really go places." Envisioned was a permanent year round inter-American "cultural and trade center," including certain trade, entertainment and amusement facilities. "Your money" included $60,000,000 in revenue bonds; the proposed sources of funds escape my memory. Uncle Sam, through HUD, would have bought $22,000,000 in parity bonds—but only if the $60,000,000 was sold. The State of Florida would have appropriated $6.25 million for a pavilion. The city of North Miami sold $12,000,000 in bonds to purchase 350 acres for the site, secured by a pledge of cigarette taxes, utilities service taxes and special assessments.

The only hitch was that nobody wanted to buy the $60 million revenue bonds. A last gasp effort was made in 1974 to market the bonds, followed by the demise of the project. I took exception to the federal loan and wrote to my then senator, Mr. Percy. I hope I helped doom it.

North Miami is still paying on the bonds. I do not know what happened with the acreage. Even when Mr. Rouse finally entered the picture as consultant, there were no takers for the bonds. Had the idea been proposed in New York State, it probably would have gone on the hook.

When I worked for Reynolds Securities I was charged with managing a research department, and with screening the proposals from the several regional underwriting offices for tax exempt negotiated deals. A Texas office showed in a proposal for a Galveston County special purpose agency to finance a machine to make waves in the surf in the Gulf of Mexico. The public purpose was to create immeasurable benefit and delight for surf board afficionados.

These particular kinds of goodies are held out to tax exempt investors, greedy for larger coupons, as "businessman's risk" type of investment. I do not know what these words connote to you, but they have only one meaning to me, and that is that not only the interest is at risk, but also the principal. The investor is asked to provide what is really venture capital for only a coupon reward. And that coupon, if it is paid, will seldom provide more than 250 basis point more yield than an investment grade bond which treats him as a creditor. Venture capital is equity-type risk and should have equity reward. No coupon with the remotest possibility of being paid is large enough to adequately reward the risk of principal.

Not that an equity reward has never been offered with tax exempts. An attempt was made back in about 1965 to do an industrial revenue bond financing in Arkansas for a Wisconsin paper company. The offering consisted of "units," wherein for each $1,000 par value of bonds purchase you would also receive a number of shares of common stock. Fortunately the Treasury blocked the deal and ruled that the bonds and stock had to be completely separate offerings.

Any taxable bond offering for a somewhat marginal borrower either has warrants attached for purchase of common, or the bonds are convertible into common. I have never heard of this type of offering—or any other taxable bond or stock offering—described as "businessman's risk." Only in munis. None but the most naive professional investor would touch bonds offered that way.

*   *   *

Change is endemic to life and perhaps one of its most outstanding characteristics. Change in the bond business is natural too, but in this business the changes are revolutionary, not evolutionary. In my brief experience, the rate of change has become geometric.

The first major market change came in 1960, when the Federal Reserve's Regulation Q, affecting bank savings rates, was changed after a long period of passbook rates of around 1 1/2-2 percent, and C.D. rates about the same. When banks were able to pay 3-3 1/2 percent or higher, to attract savings, naturally they wanted to offset the higher payout, so they became large buyers of tax exempts. What better way to buy bonds than to underwrite them and take them out of the account at the takedown. Banks really were not that big in underwriting before they became large scale investors.

The next big change came with the end run around voters with the so-called "moral obligation," which I choose to refer to as immoral.

The apparent first of this kind was the New York State Housing Finance Authority, with its first issue in 1961. A man, who in a later career subsequently went to jail, is the father of this illegitimate ruse. Following close upon that was the First Albany County GO bonds in 1966 for the infamous mall. The primary security was a lease with the State of New York.

New York was not the first in lease financings. Pennsylvania, Indiana and Kentucky had used them for several years to escape very tight constitutional debt limits, not categorically to avoid the need for voter approval. California later became a leader in lease financings, due to the fact that a 2/3 majority vote was needed to authorize GO bonds.

New purposes, new wrinkles in financing methods, security enhancement. Even those of you in the business only two or three years have seen marked changes.

The change that is most disturbing to me is the intrusion into the municipal markets by so many players who are middlemen, who siphon off large profits without encouraging sound finance on the part of state and local governments.

One of the most profound changes that has occurred in the last generation of tax exempt financing is the inclusion in the Official Statement of the section titled "bondholder risks." Imagine that. You are a creditor and you have to be warned about risk. All too often the risks are real, sometimes they are not all described. All too often they are ignored.

Another important change in tax exempts is the change made by the rating agencies for the compensation for their service as credit evaluators. In 1955, when I stumbled into "munis" the rating agencies were compensated by the subscription fees charged to subscribers. Anyone could ask an agency to assign a rating to a bond issue, or to the debt of an issuer. A fee would be charged only under unusual circumstances, such as a very small issue.

Having just come out of a brief career as a bank examiner, I was aware that there were three rating agencies, and that for a bond issue to be eligible for holding by a bank, most states and the comptroller of the currency, the Federal Reserve and FDIC required that the bonds be rated as investment grade by two of the three agencies. My new employer, the municipal finance consultant, and all other consultants that I knew, always sent the Official Statement to all three agencies.

In 1970, the agencies started to charge a fee for each new debt offering or for new debt review. From whence came the fee makes no difference. With a new bond offering it comes most naturally for the issuer to pay the fee. The only trouble with that is that a less than investment grade rating never gets published on a new offering. If the issuer does not like the rating assigned he may withhold the fee, in full or in part, or pay the fee but simply request that the rating not be published.

The only BB or Ba rating on a new offering that comes to mind is New York City. A non-rated offering would have had perjorative implications for the city.

Only in tax exempts do you see the market react so negatively to a sub-investment grade rating. I must say that I like Moody's definition of the meaning of their Baa rating. It states, or used to, that the credit characteristics of the bonds outweigh the risk factors—ergo investment grade. Today, even that fourth level rating is the kiss of death if bonds are offered to tax exempt unit trusts or mutual funds. In the old days the only people who thought that a BBB or Baa rated bond had one foot on the banana peel was the State of Wisconsin Banking Department. Personally, I like that type of bond when I can select them. That is where the real value lies.

A change that has created another new industry is, of course, insurance as to a timely payment of principal and interest on tax exempt bonds. This development did not come as a result of any defaults, but as a result of market conditions.

In 1967 when I was in portfolio work at Allstate Insurance we were approached with the concept by John Nuveen and Co. I met with the underwriting people and told them that in my estimation the underwriting would be a leadpipe cinch in so far as risk was concerned. I also told them that the market for the insurance at that time would be quite small because hardly anyone was very worried about payment on bonds. There were very few bonds that needed the insurance. Nuveen subsequently had some financial difficulties and a few heads rolled, including that of a fine gentleman who, after many labors, convinced Mortgage Guaranty Insurance Corporation (MGIC) that bond insurance might work as a business venture and AMBAC was created as a subsidiary of MGIC.

Nuveen was not the only one to approach Allstate about insurance. But at that time, it just did not seem as if there was enough of a market to bother with and therefore little profit to be made in the venture. AMBAC did get started, but with little fanfare and little business—likewise with MBIA.

What finally launched insurance as a viable industry was the purportedly tight money market of 1974-75. Like many states, Florida had a statutory interest rate limit, which was 7 1/2 percent. With that limit there were no bids for bonds that would have come at a higher net interest cost. One brave issuer tried an issue with MBIA insurance and cracked the limit at around 7.45 percent.

This was possible with MBIA because at that time, Standard & Poors gave a AAA rating to MBIA's guarantee. AMBAC did not yet, as a single insurer, have its re-insurance treaties in place so S&P only rated them at AA. Most Florida names came to market with MBIA insurance in that market, and thereby hangs a tale.

The most infamous event in the years of my experience has been the default of WPPSS due to blatant unwillingness to pay. Hopefully, this will not start a trend. I do not think anyone familiar with the case opines that the State of Washington Supreme Court decision has the appearance of anything but a political decision. In fact, there are some involved who are willing to bet on it.

Within an elected court one is tempted to wonder what the court could come up with if the electorate suddenly decided that state GO debt was more than they wanted to be burdened with. As if deliberate default were not enough to contend with, we poor analysts now look at voluntary bankruptcy on the part of local governments as a possible way out of debt. The San

Jose School District hopefully had very competent legal advice before it took the drastic step that it did.

Closer to home this year, the New York towns of Babylon and Huntington, out on Long Island reneged on promises to include in their budgets money to repay notes of their state-created Multi-town Solid Waste Management Authority. Their argument is that the payments contracts were only a "moral obligation" and therefore not binding. An Official Statement for Huntington indicates that reluctantly the payments were made before court action.

Also recently, Pike County Kentucky decided not to make a covenanted lease payment, throwing into jeopardy the only finance system the state knows.

After WPPSS, San Jose, Pike County, and two towns on Long Island, it is nice to know that there are some taxpayers willing to step up and be counted when a question of credit comes up. The best example of this is Cleveland, where the voters threw out their mayor, and voted additional taxes to pay bonds. I wish the same feeling prevailed with some New Jersey municipal utility authorities. Neither the authorities nor their back up municipalities wanted to be held responsible for rate increases and some near misses on defaults have occurred.

The name of the game used to be to borrow as little as possible. You might start making a capital levy in anticipation of expanding the school. If your revenue project was in sound shape you could pay the interest out of earnings during construction of additional facilities rather than capitalize it. If you were credit worthy you could get away with increasing the bond reserve from annual deposits over 2-5 years rather than capitalize it. Now the new game is to borrow as much as you can stretch the imagination for.

*   *   *

I would like to close with this thought, joining some of my colleagues on the gloomy side of the street named WPPSS.

The Washington State Supreme Court ruled that under the statutes municipalities and districts could not purchase the "capability" of Projects 4 and 5. The Court was strongly, perhaps pointedly, silent on Projects 1, 2, and 3. The net billing agreements provided not only for purchase of the capability, but the resale of it to Bonneville. Could they sell what they could not buy? If not, are the contracts invalid, and could Bonneville back out of paying for 1, 2 and 3 from its rate base if it chose to?

* An address by Arthur J. Hausker to the Municipal Analysis Group of New York

Chapter XV

Definitive and Other Considerations of General Obligation Bonds*

A few years back, when I worked for Allstate Insurance Company a salesman from Memphis called me about a bond. He gave me a name, a coupon, maturity and basis price. I asked him, "Wait a minute, what kind of bond is this?" There was about 30 seconds of silence at the other end, then he said, "This is an O.K. bond!" I thanked him sincerely and said, "We're not buying O.K. bonds this week, we're buying swell bonds." How many bonds offered in the market today, that are described as general obligation may really only be "O.K. bonds"?

GENERAL OBLIGATION—WHOSE OBLIGATION, A GENERAL'S?

How many here know what a Saxon G.O. is? About 15 years ago the contest between dealers and dealer banks over bank underwriting of revenue bonds first began to gather steam. A gentleman named Mr. Saxon, coincidentally from the First National Bank of Chicago, rose to the post of Comptroller of the Currency of the United States, the bank regulatory agency for banks with federal charter, or "National" banks.

In reply to requests from banks, he began to issue rulings as to whether or not national banks could deal in and underwrite certain kinds of bonds that were not secured by a pledge of the full faith, credit and taxing power of the issuer. For the most part these bonds fell into the lease obligation category and/or the so called "Moral Obligation," of which New York State

Housing Finance Agency Housing Bonds were the first of their kind. Appropriately enough, the credit of these bonds began to be described as "Left Handed" G.O.

Seemingly without exception the comptrollers' approval was given. Together the two categories of obligations were affectionately called by the street, "Saxon G.O.s." This tag is still used by those of us who have been in the business long enough to remember.

At the time Saxon G.O.s began appearing, I was working at the Marine Bank in Milwaukee in the Bond Department. I did a lot of appraisals for the Trust Department, and noted in some of the portfolios the inclusion of church bonds, described as "general obligations of such and such archdiocese." I went from the sublime to the ridiculous and suggested to the other fellows in the department that we get Mr. Saxon's approval on these G.O.s and underwrite them and sell them to the Trust Department as Holy G.O.s.

Subsequent to Mr. Saxon's reign a great many new kinds of bonds have come to market with a security aspect described as somebody's general obligation. In the period between the passage of the Glass-Stegall Act, Circa 1933, and Mr. Saxon's entry on the tax exempt stage, the apparent tradition developed that accepted "General Obligation" to mean as security, and ad valorem tax, or property tax (on all taxable property, real and personal) for political subdivisions; or full power (of whatever nature).

Better late than never—for so many actions in this best of all possible tax exempt worlds—perhaps now is not too bad a time to reflect on what changes have occurred in the tradition of our particular culture.

In this discussion the term "tax exempt bonds" shall be applied to bonds issued to provide facilities for states and their political subdivisions, or what I would call "municipal bonds." Some tax exempts are excluded from the term "municipal bonds" because the beneficiary of the borrowing may be a private entity, as is the case with so called industrial revenue bonds (including pollution control financing, non-state supported colleges, non-municipal hospitals, land developers, etc.).

The most important consideration of a municipal bond is that a "municipality" (i.e., state, county, city, village, school or other special district) is not likely to go out of existence as a result of financial distress. There are statutes that deal with bankruptcy on the part of municipalities, but the municipality will not, except under the worst imaginable set of circumstances, be dissolved, and its assets disposed of at a sheriff's sale to satisfy creditors. School districts have merged or have been dissolved, cities have merged, but for socio-political reasons, not for reasons having to do with debt.

DEFINITION OF "GENERAL OBLIGATION"

In its broadest usage the term "General Obligation" (or simply "G.O.") is used in the same context as the term "debenture" in corporate finance. G.O. bonds would then be unsecured, in the sense of involving no specific pledge of properties or revenues.

In tax exempt financing, a G.O. of a political subdivision with taxing power is usually secured by the "full faith, credit and taxing power." But let's also define "Taxing Power." Typically, a bond authorized by a referendum is issued by a borrower that has the power to levy unlimited taxes (usually "ad valorem" or "property taxes"), to pay bond principal and interest. The bonds are secured by a covenant, or pledge, to "levy ad valorem taxes without limit as to rate or amount against all the taxable property" within the territorial boundaries of the borrower.

Most states, cities, school districts, counties and special districts, such as water or sanitation districts, are empowered by their respective states' constitutions or statutes to levy unlimited taxes for voted G.O. bonds, even though tax rates for other purposes may be limited.

HOW ABOUT LIMITED TAX G.O.s?

Yes, Virginia, there are such things as "limited tax G.O.s." First, let's define "limited tax." The limit may be the tax rate imposed by the issuer that may not be exceeded, or the limit may be a dollar amount. The schedules of annual principal and interest payments are set within the amount made available under either limit.

The state of Ohio allows issuance of either unlimited or limited tax bonds. The unlimited tax bonds must be voted. The limited tax bond is not secured by a specific tax, but the tax rate imposed must be such that the aggregate total general tax rate imposed by all taxing subdivisions levying against property in the particular subdivision does not exceed a constitutional limit.

In Texas, cities are restricted to tax rate limits for all purposes and the Attorney General, who also issues an opinion as to legality of each bond issue, makes a determination as to how much of the tax rate limit may be utilized for debt service. Alabama cities, also subject to quite severe tax rate limits, issue "General Obligation bonds, additionally secured." In this context G.O. means any funds the city can legally "beg, borrow or steal"; but specific revenues, such as a sales tax, are usually pledged to "Additionally Secure" payment of the bonds.

Many states authorize special districts, such as a hospital district, or port district, to levy taxes limited by rate, all or some of the proceeds of which may be used for debt service.

TAXES OTHER THAN AD VALOREM FOR G.O. BONDS

About the only borrowers who can characteristically secure bonds in this fashion are states. Some states have no power, or currently do not exercise power, or have very limited power, to levy ad valorem taxes. These bonds are usually called "Full Faith and Credit" bonds. The phrase may or may not include unlimited taxing power of any sort, but again we are back to the "beg, borrow or steal" syndrome. Taxing powers of states that produce large amounts of revenue are sales taxes, income taxes and motor fuel taxes, but these are rarely pledged specifically.

WHEN IS A G.O. NOT A G.O.?

When an agency of a state, such as a public service corporation, or "authority" is empowered to borrow money, the resulting "G.O. bond" may not really be a G.O. Unfortunately the words "General Obligation of the Authority," when used to describe the security of the bonds, are a misnomer when applied to the real security behind such a bond issue. As traditionally used in the "Muni Bond" business (and indeed under the Glass-Stegall Act, which limited commercial banks to dealing in "General Obligation bonds"), the words imply that the borrower has taxing power, or has vast and varied sources of revenue.

In most cases the loans of the borrower, and the funds to repay the debt, are tied to a single project or group of projects which are built for and leased, or sold under contract, to a beneficiary entity which may be public or private. The source of funds is provided for under the terms of a lease or sale contract. In the case of a public beneficiary the lease obligation may have funds pledged from a limited source. Where the beneficiary is a private entity the bonds may be guaranteed by that entity and could rank as a debenture, but then the obligation is weaker than, for example, a mortgage secured bond.

WHEN IS A REVENUE BOND A G.O.?

When a non-profit corporation, or an authority, is formed to act as a financing vehicle to escape very restrictive constitutional limits against borrowing by a state or its subdivisions, the revenue bonds issued are in effect, General Obligation bonds. The borrower has no taxing power so it must issue revenue bonds, with the revenues derived from leases. The borrower incurs the debt, and builds a facility and leases it to a city, county, or school district, with the annual rentals at least equal to the principal and interest payments on the bonds.

Ideally the lease is valid and binding over its entire life, which should be stated as ending only when the last bond is retired. In some states the lease cannot be binding past the term of an incumbent legislative body and must be renewed (and is made automatically renewable) annually or bi-annually, as the case demands.

In some states the leases are payable from unlimited ad valorem taxes, the same as bonds would be if voted. School lease bonds are more likely to be supported in such fashion than are city or county lease bonds. It is difficult to not call the credit, General Obligation.

For cities and counties the lease payments are general fund expenses, which may be required to be budgeted annually, but the general fund combines monies from many sources, including an as valorem tax, which is usually limited. Are these G.O. credits too?

GENERAL OBLIGATION REDEFINED

From the foregoing it would seem that to define General Obligation is a formidable task indeed. But the Federal Home Loan Board (FHLB) has apparently taken at least federally chartered savings and loan institutions off the horns of the dilemma, if they want to buy tax exempts. The FHLB has ruled that, for the board's qualification, bonds are General Obligations if a governmental entity possessing general power of taxation has incurred a legally enforceable obligation for the payment of whatever amounts are necessary to discharge fully any obligations on the bonds.

This sounds like, and is, a good working definition for some purposes, but in the absence of a pledge of taxing power the availability of the source funds from which to fulfill that obligation, on a continuing basis must be ascertained and evaluated.

Florida cities and counties have a bad habit of pledging all receipts except ad valorem taxes toward payment of some bonds, but they do not give that pledge a lien status and they reserve the right to pledge away any amount of those receipts to other obligations.

In New York, the words "General Obligation" seem to preclude specific ad valorem tax receipts unless a tax is levied when other sources are inadequate. In Minnesota as a matter of general practice a tax levy is passed, as part of the resolution awarding the sales of the bonds, which sets the amount of taxes levied each year over the life of the bonds, and includes a 5 percent over-levy to allow for delinquencies.

Now that we have decided not to decide on a definition for all seasons as to the nature of G.O.s, let's look at a G.O. financial statement under the sections headed "Debt, Direct and Overlapping."

In practice, direct debt is the aggregate of the outstanding amounts of G.O. bonds issued by the subject municipality and, where applicable, is reduced to a net G.O. debt figure by subtraction of so-called self-supporting G.O. debt. Overlapping debt consists of debt of subdivisions which are coterminous with the subject municipality (i.e., lying within the exact same boundaries), or debt of a larger subdivision which includes within its bounds, all or portions of the subject municipality. A school district is likely, in a rural area, to include a city or village and surrounding area, while a suburban district may include all or parts of several suburbs. A county will include many cities, villages, townships and school or other special districts.

The overlapping portion of the other taxing subdivisions' debt is ascertained, at a given time, on the basis of proportional assessed or taxable value of property lying within the subject subdivision. Every city, village or township that does not operate its own school district will have overlapping debt of at least one school district and that of a county. (Cities that straddle two counties could be an exception to this.)

In these instances every taxpayer in the subject city or village will pay a proportionate share of that kind of overlapping debt. Similarly a school district will usually be located in a single county and every taxpayer in the school district will pay a proportionate share of that county's debt.

Far too often a gross misinterpretation of overlapping debt numbers, as reported, occurs. In the case particularly of a county, the aggregate debt of all school districts, all cities, villages and townships, all sanitary districts, all debt incurred anywhere in the county, is inferred by reports of statistics to be paid by each and every taxpayer in the county. But a rural township may have no direct debt and pay only its share of school and county debt.

I have heard of analysts who ask state officials for their state's overlapping debt figures. About the only really overlapping debt of a state might be the lease secured debt of a state building commission, but that should be under a sub heading of direct debt.

A gross example of this kind of fuzzy debt is the debt for the state building complex financed by Albany County G.O. bonds. By definition each and every taxpayer in the county is liable if the state reneges on its lease obligation. The mall debt at one time was greater than the assessed value of the county, and amounted to more than $2,500 per capita (at the time of this address). Is this direct or overlapping debt of the state or county, or either?

Another area of debt that lends itself to misinformation is that of self-supporting debt, and the exclusion or subtraction of it from a G.O. debt statement. Exactly what does self-supporting mean? This may vary from state to state depending on what may legally be excluded when computing debt that is subject to constitutional or statutory debt limits. In Minnesota debt may be excluded if it is issued for a purpose from which revenue may be derived. Water and sewer bonds may finance a utility, but charges need not be imposed for the bonds to be excluded for debt limit purposes.

Even where charges are imposed, in any other state, how much revenue must be derived in order to say that the bonds are self-supporting? In Tennessee virtually every water and sewer bond is a General Obligation revenue bond and the issuer covenants to impose charges sufficient to provide net revenue adequate for debt service. The issuer also covenants to levy unlimited taxes to pay the bonds, if necessary.

In how many Official Statements do we see documentation as to the self-supporting nature of deducted bonds? In how many states do covenants exist to ensure no tax liability?

Yet another area of easy misinterpretation of debt of cities, villages and eastern townships lies in the subtraction of revenue debt in a financial statement. G.O. debt may be 1 percent of assessed value, and the analyst "oohs and ahs" about the wonderful credit because tax supported direct debt is so low. But how many of you take a wide look at the community and examine how much debt is supported by that community, regardless of the source or kind of payment securing debt?

A city hall G.O. and a water revenue bond for the same city cannot be looked at as different credits. A municipal water or sewer system usually serves at least the entire municipality. The same taxpayers will pay water and sewer charges as pay property taxes. What difference does it really make then, in the evaluation of the credit of a city, if water and sewer systems bonds are paid from taxes or user charges? If the Detroit water system had the same numbers without serving a much wider area could you accept realistically a AA rating for water revenue bonds and BBB for tax bonds?

With a binding covenant to impose sufficient rates, charges and fees (that's all a tax pledge is), can a water utility bond really be a lesser credit than a G.O.? How much less collectible are delinquent water and sewer charges than delinquent taxes?

A similar consideration for an electric system that serves the entire city. Even if that electric system is investor owned, there are analytical techniques that can be applied to determine how much debt load of an investor system is paid by a given city in a large service area.

Any kind of debt that imposes a payment burden on all segments of a community should be included when looking at the debt facet of a community profile. This should include sales tax revenue bonds, particularly if the surrounding communities do not have a sales tax and the goods purchaser then has an option of where to shop.

In comparison shopping appraisal of debt statements, if a city has a total G.O. debt figure that seems inordinately high compared to an otherwise similar credit, the composition of that debt should be analyzed. More often than not a close look will reveal that funding for water and sewer service has been accomplished by G.O. bonds rather than revenue bonds. If water and sewer revenues are not used to abate tax levies for bonds which financed those services, the total amount of G.O. debt stands. Similarly a comparatively low G.O. debt structure should provoke inquiry as to whether there is any water, sewer or other utility type revenue debt outstanding.

Instead of simply measuring municipal debt, should we not be measuring all the costs of municipally and privately furnished services that make a community an attractive place in which to live and also make it an attractive place for commerce and industry?

The acid test of a community's ability to pay both revenue and tax supported debt is its economic viability. Statutes and courts generally provide protection against unwillingness to pay debt. What really counts is the ability to levy and collect taxes, and concurrently, to impose and collect service charges. A municipality that can successfully do one can do both. To try to be discriminating between tax supported bonds of a city and the necessary utility service revenue bonds (especially water and sewer), is like trying to square the circle in geometry.

* An address by Arthur J. Hausker to the Municipal Analysis Group
  of New York

Chapter XVI

*General Considerations About Bond Ratings**

When a bond issue is submitted to a rating agency for a credit rating it should be evaluated as if it was the first bond appraised. The rating should be assigned according to how the bond measures up to the quality standards indicated by the key to bond ratings of the rating agency.

Regardless of the nature of the pledge, or the particular kind of source of funds, the rating assigned to one bond must indicate the corresponding ability to pay as all other bonds with the same rating. To state that a bond deserves a particular rating among bonds of its class begs the meaning of all ratings and their symbols.

Bond ratings should not move up and down with the tides of funds available for debt service in a given fiscal year. Changes in ratings should be based on considerations that indicate a more or less permanent change in ability to pay.

A budget deficit does not categorically cast doubt on the ability to meet the next coupon, nor principal and interest to maturity. Causes of recurring deficits and resultant cash positions, along with corrective actions (if any) are the important factors about deficits. Mounting cash surpluses can mean inept government (or management) in that it is not the function of state and local governments to amass huge cash balances at a cost to their constituents. The five billion dollar surplus developed by the State of California "fired a shot heard round" the nation, and started a near avalanche of taxpayer revolts, evidenced by Proposition 13 and similar proposals in other states.

Tax exempt bonds are not necessarily "municipal" bonds, e.g., industrial development bonds, pollution control bonds, hospital bonds, etc. Within the "municipal" bond universe, the spectrum of quality is much narrower than with corporate bonds. Even in bankruptcy a governmental unit is highly unlikely to go out of existence. Defaults are much more amenable to correction and/or work out, and bondholders will seldom be left without an obligor, as they might be in a corporate venture in liquidation.

Dealers will often refer to a bond as being "double barreled." The words imply two sources of payment, one backing up the other. As most often used the words refer to a general obligation bond payable in the first instance from a user charge, usually for water or sewer service, and backed up by a tax pledge. If the water or sewer system serves an area generally coterminous with the bounds of the issuing municipality, the same source of payment is paying either the taxes or the user charge. A true "double barreled" bond would have two separate sources, not kinds of payment— one as a primary security backing the bonds, the other a secondary security. A good example would be the Arkansas or Mississippi general obligation industrial revenue bonds.

A "municipal" bond and a non-municipal tax exempt bond must meet the same quality definition for any rating. There is no bell curve of distribution which says statistically that certain percentages of the total universe of bond issues should fall into certain grades of quality. By nature of existence, and pledge, not all bonds can be high-grade virtually unaffected by unusual circumstances.

Unlike taxable securities issuers, a municipal bond issuer (as differentiated from non-municipal tax exempt borrower) is generally unlikely to come to market as a first time marginal ability borrower. The most notable exceptions to this are special districts associated with real estate development, where the developer, not a developed district, is the borrower, and the bond proceeds finance infrastructure normally paid for by the developer's capital (or direct borrowings).

With bonds secured by the credit of state and local governments units the factors that affect ability to pay are not great in number, nor widely different in effect, so that differentiation within rating symbols is not a particularly fruitful endeavor. For special obligation bonds there may be more opportunity to single out with a "+" or "-" rating the bond which exhibits the characteristics above or below the usual features within a rating category.

Because of the nature of the credit and pledge themselves, non-municipal tax exempt bonds will likely be affected by more factors than will bonds secured by government credit, and the spectrum of quality in "good" and "satisfactory" (A or BBB/Baa respectively) bonds may be broader, as is the case with corporate bonds.

Rating agencies should take into consideration special features of the issue, its relationship to other obligations of the issuer (if any), the record of the issuer and of any guarantor, as well as the political and economic environment that might affect the future financial strength of the issuer.

In assessing credit risk, rating agencies rely on current information furnished by the issuer and/or guarantor and other sources which they consider reliable.

Ratings may be changed, withdrawn or suspended at any time to reflect changes in the financial condition of the issuer, the status of the issue relative to other debt of the issuer, or any other circumstances that the agency considers to have a material effect on the credit of the obligor. The definitions of the bond rating symbols, and the implications to municipal issuers are discussed below. If a single symbol is shown, it is used by both Moody's and Standard & Poors. If two symbols are shown the first is Moody's, the second is Standard & Poors. If discussion refers to a single symbol it refers to the equivalent rating of the two agencies.

RATING SYMBOLS

Aaa/AAA (highest quality or "premium")—the issuer has the ability to service its debt under virtually any circumstance.

Within the confines of their constitutions states are "sovereign" and can generate revenues in ways in which they may be unhampered by legal restraints, thus on a categorical basis they might qualify for a rating of Aaa. Each state's credit must be analyzed though, by examining the provisions of its constitution that deal with debt, and with taxation or other ways of producing revenue. The methods by which a constitution can be amended are also important, (e.g., initiative and referendum as in California, or the lengthy tedious process required in New York).

Perhaps all states can, and some do, escape the constitutional restraints by creating extra-constitutional agencies to act as financing vehicles; and the obligation is not to pay service on debt but to make lease payments by which the agency can service debt incurred on behalf of the state. In such cases the ability to generate revenue is more important than debt restrictions.

In analyzing a state's credit, location, natural resources, demographics, economic considerations and governmental debt management and fiscal practices can dilute the strength inherent in sovereignty. The right of public employees to strike can have a serious effect on budgeting measures.

This is not to say that only states can have Aaa rated bonds outstanding. A well managed city or county with low debt and a flourishing economy may also qualify. Similarly a thriving enterprise system with special characteristics could enjoy a rating of Aaa on its revenue bonds (see Appendix—Chicago Water Bonds).

A large number of bond issues have been refunded in advance of maturity, or have been called for redemption on optional maturity dates and are secured by escrowed funds that provide monies adequate for timely payment of principal and interest on the refunded bonds. Certain characteristics of the escrow may result in a rating of Aaa. The AAA rating is also enjoyed by certain bonds which have a reserve fund of appropriate collateral equal to at least the principal amount of the debt.

Contractual payments from a federal agency can also provide additional security adequate for Aaa quality.

Bonds of very few other governmental units, or the utilities systems that serve them, enjoy the overwhelming strength necessary for prime quality. It is easy to define a circumstance which would put a high grade bond into default. It is not so easy to state the possibility of a circumstance happening. Only the reasonable probabilities or possibilities should be taken into account.

Bonds whose timely payment of principal and interest is insured can qualify for the Aaa rating, provided that the insuror/insurors' strength measures very high.

A closed lien on a dedicated tax with a high degree of coverage (3 times or better), where the taxing entity covenants to impose the tax over the life of the bonds could be a candidate for the AAA.

Aa/AA. Bonds thus rated and Aaa rated constitute the spectrum of "high grade" bonds. The ability of the issuer to service its debt, while very high, is not as high as that of a Aaa credit, and may be more subject to change while the debt is outstanding.

Very strong states not qualifying for the AAA fall into the AA standing in most instances.

Categorically, it is more difficult to achieve a rating of AA or higher on hospital or other user charge revenue bonds than it is for general obligation bonds. A significant portion of a hospital's gross operating revenues is reimbursed under cost-basis entitlement programs. A decline in patient volume or a shift in patient mix could greatly diminish net operating revenue. While the full faith and credit of the obligor is often pledged to whatever form debt service may take (bond payments or leases), the hospital must be viable if it is to continue to service its debt in a prompt and timely fashion. Generally, in order to qualify for a "high grade" rating, the obligor must demonstrate a very high degree of sophistication and level of service in the delivery of health care. This, in turn, is further evidenced by a strong market share and physician base in a characteristically dynamic service area.

Debt of counties may also be evaluated as high grade. Characteristically, counties have fewer capital demands and, therefore, lower per capita direct debt, than do states or smaller units of local government. Therefore, with a good economic background, a non-urban county's debt can more easily qualify as high grade than debt of many cities.

A bonds (good, or "strong" quality)—the issuer's ability to pay is strong, but may be more subject to adverse changes in economic conditions and circumstances than bonds with higher ratings.

Baa/BBB bonds (the issuer' credit is satisfactory). The issuer's ability to service it's debt is considered to be adequate, but the credit is much more susceptible to impairment than with higher rated bonds.

Bonds rated A or Baa are considered to be "medium grade." Together, medium and high grade bonds are considered to be "investment grade" bonds.

Bonds whose rating symbols are different from high or medium grade are deemed "speculative" at best, with assigned ratings varying from Ba/BB to D (defaulted).

Ba/BB rating. A Ba bond could be called a "good times" bond. Differentiation between a "good times" bond and an investment grade bond does not present particular problems, nor does identification of high grade credits (or, conversely, what is not high grade).

Speculative bonds have a great many shadings between gray and black. Either structurally or economically they have easily ascertained weaknesses. A weakly covered sales tax bond, for example, would have problems in a depression. A rating less than Ba would indicate at best a marginal chance of timely payment.

Among municipal bonds, almost all bonds that are not high grade are "good" or "satisfactory" quality. Perhaps the best definition of "satisfactory" is that the bond is a step better than a "good times bond," and that "good" is a step beyond that, but not high grade.

* Arthur J. Hausker

Chapter XVII

Overlooked Aspects of General Obligation Bonds

The economic viability of the issuer is the most important consideration, and cannot be determined solely from financial statements. The attractiveness of a community, county or state to people and to business enterprise will wane far in advance of the time that the effects show up definitively in annual reports or audits. Demographics of people and business enterprises are important aspects of economic viability.

Revenue debt for essential community-wide services must also be taken into account when looking at the financial structure behind a general obligation bond. For rating purposes, debt remains debt. As mentioned earlier, the so-called "double barreled" bond may not really be so.

The underlying debt of municipalities within a county can be a very significant factor in credit evaluation if the direct debt (including the above mentioned revenue debt) is high for all or most of the municipalities. This is not likely in a rural county. It is, however, an erroneous procedure to lump this aggregate debt together under overlapping debt.

The providers and costs of services essential to a community must be ascertained. In New York City counties exist in name only, and are not providers of services. St. Louis is not in a county. It is then, unfair, to make a value judgment about cost of services in New York or St. Louis as measured against the costs of services in a city where education is provided by a separate school district, and with a county providing the judicial system.

Politics can cause, or cure, a poor financial situation. If politics is the cause, the response by voters can be a key ingredient in the cure. The City of Cleveland is a good example of this cause and cure consideration, where the mayor was turned out of office and the voters authorized an increased local income tax to straighten out the finances.

Part III

CREDIT ANALYSIS WORKSHEETS

CASE I
SEAPORT REVENUE BONDS—
SPECIAL OR LIMITED TAX

NAME: $40,000,000 Puerto Rico Ports Authority

SELLING: 1/19/72

MATURITIES: 1973 thru 1991, Term Bonds 2002

PURPOSE: To finance a portion of a 5-year program of improvements to existing airports and seaport facilities.

CAPITALIZED: Maintenance Reserve Fd. $1,000,000
                 Bond Reserve: $ max d/s

SECURITY: Net revenues of the facilities together with proceeds of a 2 cent aviation gas tax (fuel flowage fee) authorized by the legislature.

DEBT:		
Prior Lien Bonds	$	0
Parity Lien		0
This issue		40,000,000
Total		$40,000,000

193

COVERAGE:	Historical (Years Ending ...)		Proforma or Projected**
	6/30/70	6/30/71	6/30/77
Operating Revenue	$11,082M	$12,618M	$28,967M
Operating Expense	6,830	7,198	16,770
Net Op. Rev.	4,252	5,420	12,197
Net Other Revenue*	2,798	2,695	3,420
Net Avail for d/s	7,050	8,115	15,617
Est Max d/s ($2.9M)	Cover 2.43x	2.79x	5.38***

   * Fuel flowage fee—directly to Bond Service Acct.
  ** After completion of 5-year program.
*** Coverage of est. max d/s on all bonds anticipated is 2.14x.

BOND RESERVE(S):
Parity Bonds—Single Reserve <u>Yes</u> special for each issue <u>No</u>
Required $ <u>max d/s</u> On Hand $ <u>capitalized</u>Pmts current <u>NA</u>
If depleted, balance to accrue from fixed pymts or surpluses over 5 yrs.

DEPRECIATION RESERVE: (Or Similar)   Available for d/s <u>Yes</u>
   Required $2.5MM   On Hand $1MM capitalized
   Balance to accumualte from fixed payments or surpluses over three years.

OTHER REQUIRED RESERVES:

   1.   Renewal and replacement fund—as recommended.
   2.   As needed—non ports operating fund, ferry assistance fund, general reserve and improvement.

ADDITIONAL PARITY BONDS TEST:
Funds available revenues in 12 of 15 months prior, as adjusted for rate and fees changes or contract cancellations etc., covers max d/s 1.50x.

COVENANTS:
Rates—to produce <u>net</u> revenues sufficient to cover <u>max.</u> d/s <u>1.25</u>times.
Insurance XXX   Audits and Books XXX   Proper Operation XXX
Prior Lien—no provision

FLOW OF FUNDS:	Operating Revenue	Fuel Flowage Fees
O and M	1	4
P and I (parity)	2	1
Bond Reserve	3	2
Depreciation	4	3
Other	5	
Surplus	6	1st $400,000 (balance locked in) to Commonwealth

CASE I—NOTES
SEAPORT REVENUE BONDS—
SPECIAL OR LIMITED TAX

These bonds were the first issue of debt by the authority and were to finance a portion of the 5-year improvements program for airports and seaports operated by the authority.

Of the $40.8 million for airports and $80.2 million for seaports, $112.3 million was anticipated to be funded by the authority, $8.5 million was expected from the federal government and $1.1 million from the Commonwealth. The authority provided $16.4 million, leaving $95.9 million to be funded—of which this $40 million was a part. Additional bonds issued had to be subject to an earnings test.

The Commonwealth Legislature enacted a 2 cent per gallon aviation fuel tax which, under the Act, could not be reduced as long as bonds were outstanding. The proceeds thereof were to flow directly to the Bond Service Account and Reserves therein before being available to the Revenue Fund. Receipts of this tax in the fiscal year ending 6/30/71 covered estimated maximum debt service on this issue ($2,900,000) 0.92 times and in the fiscal year ending 6/30/77 the projected amount ($3,420,000) covered maximum debt service on this issue 1.17 times and maximum debt service on all anticipated bonds ($7,264,000) 0.47 times.

Total funds available in the previous fiscal year covered maximum debt service for all anticipated bonds 1.11 times.

Projections of revenue and expenses are based on trend line extensions rather than specific seaport and airport operations. Except for certain contracts and leases the revenues were, by and large, based on growth of income from added use of facilities and fees and charges imposed therefor.

Historically, the seaport revenues provided in excess of 50 percent of gross revenues. Although the improvements program was 2/3 for seaports, the same portion was not expected for projected revenue increase. Airport revenues were primarily from San Juan International Airport.

The transportation consultants, Coverdale and Colpitts Inc. performed the projections for the Official Statement.

*　　*　　*

CASE II
UNIVERSITY HOUSING REVENUE BONDS

NAME: $4,925,000 California State University and Colleges Housing System Revenue Bonds, Series G

<u>SELLING:</u> 5/17/72

<u>MATURITIES:</u> 1975 thru 2002   <u>Callable:</u> 11/1/82 at prem.

<u>LEGAL OPINION:</u> Orrick, Herrington, Rowley and Sutcliffe (San Francisco)

<u>PURPOSE:</u> Additional housing and dining facilities at the Sacramento State College campus

<u>CAPITALIZED:</u> Interest—$295,500 for 12 months
Bond Reserve: $297,643

<u>SECURITY:</u> Parity lien on net revenues of the system together with proceeds of any debt service subsidy grants received

<u>DEBT:</u>

Prior Lien Bonds	$	0
Parity Lien		68,595,000
This issue		4,925,000
Total		$73,520,000

<u>COVERAGE:</u>

	Historical (Years Ending ...)		Proforma or Projected***
	6/30/70	6/30/71	6/30/74
Operating Revenue	$6,770,725	$7,816,960	$11,335,760
Operating Expense	4,243,389	4,351,103	7,090,760
Net Op. Rev.	2,527,336	3,465,858	4,245,000
Net Other Revenue*	329,431	459,246	555,000
Net Avail for d/s	2,856,767	3,925,104	4,800,000
Est Aver d/s** ($4,005,541)	Cover .71x	.98x	1.20x
Est Max d/s ($,076,613)	Cover .70x	.96x	1.18x

  * Excludes constr. fund interest income and d/s grants, which are estimated to average $401,400 thru 2002.
 ** 1973-2002
*** Probable first full year of operation of Series G financed facilities. Inclusion of d/s grants boosts coverage to 1.28x max d/s.

<u>BOND RESERVE(S):</u>
Parity Bonds—Single Reserve XXX
Required $ max d/s   On Hand $4,076,000*
* Includes amount capitalized from Series G bonds proceeds

<u>DEPRECIATION RESERVE:</u> (Or Similar)   Available for d/s XXX
Required—10 percent of construction and acquisition costs of facilities financed. On Hand $2,479,000
Balance to accumulate from payments of 25 percent of surpluses

ADDITIONAL PARITY BONDS TEST: The issues is limited by three tests. (see later herein)

COVENANTS:
Rates—to produce net operating revenues sufficient to cover annual d/s 1.25 times.
Audits and Books XXX   Proper Operation XXX
No Prior Lien XXX

FLOW OF FUNDS:
O and M	1	
P and I	2	
Bond Reserve	3	
R and R	4	
Surplus	5	(100 percent locked in)

CASE II—NOTES
UNIVERSITY HOUSING REVENUE BONDS

This system should not be mistaken for the University of California System (which is a branch campus system of the University of California operating under a separate Board of Regents). This system is composed of nineteen separate State Colleges operating under the control of the Board of Trustees of the California State Univesity and Colleges. At this time, each institution is identified as a State College. The State "University" syndrome has not yet affected the titling although criteria are being developed under which individual institutions may be designated as "University."

These bonds have the same elements of strength as found in the New York State Dormitory Authority's bonds issued for the New York State University system, namely the aggregate net revenues of the housing and dining facilities on all campus locations. Parietal rules for maximum occupancy are covenanted.

Upon completion of the project to be financed with proceeds from this bond sale, housing facilities will accommodate 16,036 students out of a total full-time equivalent enrollment of 264,300. It is estimated that approximately 25,000 additional students would avail themselves of campus housing if adequate facilities were available.

The present five-year capital budget of the California State University and Colleges calls for expenditure of over $30,000,000 for additional residence halls and dining facilities on the assumption that revenue bonds can be sold to finance dormitories. Actual outlays will be limited by earnings of the system, availability of debt service grants and interest costs incurred on bonds sold.

Combined board and room charges in residence halls for the 1971-72 academic year range from a high of $1,230 (single occupancy) at San Francisco State to a low of $938 (double occupancy) at Sacramento State. Room rates vary to some degree depending upon type of accommodation (single, double, suite) and the facility in which the room is located. The largest revenue variable, however, is the type of food service program offered and the cost of living at different locations throughout the state.

Rate increases are anticipated in 1973, 1975, and 1977. Under current policy these increases will be designed to meet the rate convenant while keeping charges as low as possible. These increases are based on the assumption that operating and maintenance costs will continue to increase as a result of inflation (assumed to be 6 percent annually), but in the event this does not occur, rate increases may not be necessary.

Additional Bonds. The issuance of additional parity revenue bonds is limited by three tests:

First, the Trustees must be in compliance with all provisions of the Resolution so that actual net operating revenues for the most recently completed fiscal year must have been 1.25 times actual debt service exclusive of amounts received as debt service subsidy grants;

Second, actual net operating revenues for the preceding fiscal year from only those facilities in operation during the entire year must have been equal to maximum annual debt service* on all outstanding bonds issued to finance said facilities; and

Third, the following must be equal to maximum annual debt service on all bonds to be outstanding following issuance of the proposed additional bonds: acutal net operating revenues for the preceding fiscal year from facilities in operation during the entire year, plus:

a. 90 percent of any additional net operating revenues estimated to be derived from any rate increase not in effect for the full fiscal year or from any rate increase to become effective during the next fiscal year, and

b. 75 percent of the net operating revenues estimated to be received from new facilities not in operation for the full twelve months of the preceding fiscal year and from those facilities to be acquired or constructed with proceeds of the bonds proposed to be issued.

* The Resolution defines maximum annual debt service as actual debt service less all receipts from debt service grants thus the wording "maximum annual debt service" is used in the resolution while, for the sake of clarity, the term "net" is used in the Official Statement.

* * *

CASE III
UTILITY REVENUE CERTIFICATES—
MIXED REVENUES PLEDGE

NAME: $12,950,000 Fort Pierce, Florida, Utilities Authority
Utilities Revenue Certificates
$8,160,000 Series 1973-A $4,790,000 Series 1973-B (refunding)

SELLING: 1/29/74

MATURITIES: 1975 thru 2003   Callable: 4/1/84 at prem.

LEGAL OPINION: Freeman, Richardson, Watson, Slade, McCarthy and Kelly (Jacksonville)

PURPOSE: Series 1973-A: Improvements to the electric and water systems
Series 1973-B: To advance refund a 1969 issue of water and electric bonds

CAPITALIZED: Bond Reserve $879,395

SECURITY: Surplus net revenues of the Utilities Systems, together with a junior lien on avails of the Utility Service Tax.

DEBT:

			Connections:	
Prior Lien Bonds	$22,509,000*		Electric	15,250
Parity Lien	0		Water	10,700
This issue	12,950,000		Sewer	10,000
Total	$35,459,000**		Nat. Gas	3,726
			TOTAL:	39,676

Total Debt Per Conn. $894

* Includes only the 1974-81 maturities of bonds
** Excludes bonds to be called

COVERAGE:

	Historical (Years Ending ...)		Proforma or Projected***
	9/30/72	9/30/73*	9/30/74
Operating Revenue**	$7,606,996	$9,053,267	$10,976,800
Operating Expense	4,586,977	5,418,527	6,222,000
Net Op. Rev.	3,020,019	3,634,740	4,754,800
Util. Service Tax	512,074	572,690	683,911
Net Avail for d/s	3,532,093	4,207,430	5,438,711
Est Max d/s ($2,491,770)	Cover 1.42x	1.69x	2.18x
Est aver d/s*** ($2,265,930)	Cover 1.56x	1.86x	2.40x

** Unaudited
** New water and sewer rates 4/1/73, new electric and gas rates 9/1/73
*** See d/s schedule

BOND RESERVE(S):
Prior Lien Required-see notes
Parity Bonds—Single Reserve XXX
Required $ max d/s   On Hand $879,395 (capitalized)
If not filled, balance to accrue from fixed pmts or surpluses over five years

ADDITIONAL BONDS: Funds available for d/s in prior fiscal year, or
any 12 consecutive months of prior 18, equal 1.25x max. d/s on all bonds
outstanding and to be issued. Adjustments may be made for rate changes
or connections to be acquired.

OTHER REQUIRED RESERVES: None

COVENANTS:
Rates—to produce net revenues sufficient to cover annual d/s 1.25 times.
Insurance XXX   Audits and Books XXX   Proper Operation XXX
No Free Service* XXX   No Competing Service XXX
No Prior Lien XXX
* Except amounts to the City.

FLOW OF FUNDS:

O and M	1
P and I (prior lien)	2
Bond Res (prior lien)	3
P and I (parity)	4
Bond Reserve (parity)	5
Excess Util. Service Tax	6
Surplus	7 (40 percent to City) (60 percent locked in)

(Retained Balance serves as Renewal & Replacement Fund, call bonds, etc.)

CASE III—NOTES
UTILITY REVENUE CERTIFICATES—
MIXED REVENUE PLEDGE

Purpose. The proceeds derived from the sale of the $8,160,000 Series-A
Utilities Revenue Certificates will be used to finance the next phase of the
Five-Year Planned Expansion Program for the combined electric, water,
sewer, and natural gas utility system operated by the Authority. The proceeds
derived from the sale of the 4,790,000 Series 1973-B Utilities Revenue
Certificates will be used for the advance refunding of a portion of the City's
Electric and Water System Revenue Certificates, Eleventh Series, dated
April 1, 1969.

Security. These bonds are secured by a junior (secondary) lien on the net operating revenues of each of the three systems and by a junior lien pledge of avails of a Utilities Service Tax imposed by the City, said tax also securing first lien sewer bonds.

Although the bond resolution pledges net revenues of the combined Utilities System to the Series 1973 bonds (subject to prior pledges), in reality the security lies in the pledge of the surplus net revenues of each of the systems until the prior lien bonds of each system are paid.

Operationally we have one system, financially we have three systems. Final maturities of the Gas, Sewer, and Electric and Water first lien bonds are, respectively 1991, 1996, and 2001. Each System bonds had Bond Reserve requirements and Renewal and Replacement Account requirements which, in the flow of funds, would come ahead of debt service on the 1973 bonds. These requirements are all funded with the exception of the Bond Reserve of the Electric and Water Bonds, for which the requirement is the succeeding two years debt service. On the basis of outstanding bonds this would amount to about $3,100,000, but the Series 1973-B bonds will advance refund the Eleventh Series Electric and Water Bonds on a junior lien basis, reducing the reserve requirement to about $2,200,000 on call date of the old bonds in 1981. On that basis all reserve and special accounts required under prior lien ordinances are filled.

Under Flow of Funds in the new Bond Ordinance, 60 percent of surplus revenues are retained within the combined system and are to be used for renewals, replacements, etc., allowing the R&R funds under the first lien ordinances to remain intact.

Series 1973-B, "Piggy Back" Refunding. This series will refund on call date (4/1/81) the then outstanding balance of the Eleventh Series Electric and Water System Revenue Certificates dated 4/1/69 (First Lien). These junior lien 1973 bonds will not move up to first lien status on defeasance of the 1969 Series. Interest to 4/1/81 on both Series 1973 bonds will be paid from the interest income of the escrow account established for the 1981 call, as well as surplus net revenues of the systems. (Double Indemnity?) The Authority's financial advisor informs us that the escrowed funds will be invested in Bank Certificates of Deposit (which will be collateralized by pledges of U.S. Treasury obligations or municipal bonds rated A or better by both Moody's and Standard & Poor's).

Net revenue of only the electric system in 1973 (unaudited, based on 10 months of operation) is more than adequate to cover maximum debt service, which was computed to reflect exclusions. Total funds available for debt service in 1973 covered max. d/s 1.69 times.

Subject to conditions shown later herein the lien on Utilities Tax Service, as pledged to these bonds, but not the Sewer Revenue bonds, will be released and is not subject to reinstatement.

Change of Management. A city charter election was held in Fort Pierce on May 30, 1972. The Fort Pierce Utilities Authority was established in accordance with the terms of the amended charter and management of the Electric and Water Utility, Sewer Utility and Natural Gas Utility passed from the city to the authority.

The authority consists of five members, one of whom is the Mayor-Commissioner of the City of Fort Pierce, who serves as long as such office is held. The other four members are appointed by the City Commission for four-year overlapping terms. The members of the Authority nominate and the City Commission elects all new members of the Authority. At the discretion of the City Commission, the City Manager may serve as an ex-officio member of the Authority without vote and whose term shall be set by the City Commission.

Financial management of the three utility systems had been separate, with each system issuing bonds, all of which were first lien bonds of the system.

Levy and Collection of the Utilities Services Taxes. The city is authorized to levy and collect a tax on all sales of electric, water and telephone services sold and rendered within the city limits of Fort Pierce. This tax is currently levied and collected at the maximum rate permitted by law of ten percentum (10 percent) of the charges made by the seller of each service. The City Commission agrees and consents to the pledge by the Authority of all of the proceeds of the utilities services taxes as additional security for these Certificates.

The authority covenants that it will not cause the repeal or cause the amendment of the ordinances now in effect levying the utilities services taxes in any manner so as to impair or adversely affect the pledge of such taxes or the power and obligation of the city to levy and collect such taxes. The city shall be unconditionally and irrevocably obligated, so long as any of the Certificates or the interest thereon are outstanding and unpaid, to levy and collect such taxes.

Release of Lien on Utilities Services Taxes. At the request of the city, the authority shall release the lien of the Certificates and any additional parity obligations on the utilities services taxes provided that the audited net revenues of the system, as defined in the Authorizing Resolution (excluding the proceeds of the utilities services taxes) for the two consecutive fiscal years immediately preceding the release of the lien on such utilities services taxes shall have been at least equal to 1.50 times the largest amount of principal, mandatory amortization installments (if any) and interest become due in any ensuing fiscal year upon all outstanding obligations, the Certificates, additional parity obligations and any other obligations intended to be paid from such net revenues after excluding from such principal, mandatory amortization installments and interest requirement, payments to be derived for the purpose from other sources. (The financial advisor to the Authority informs us that said release does not affect the pledge to prior lien sewer bonds.)

*　　*　　*

CASE IV
UTILITY TAX REVENUE BONDS—MIXED LIENS

NAME: $3,455,000 Riviera Beach, Fla. Utility Tax Revenue bonds Series 1973 (a Junior lien Bond)

SELLING: 9/19/73

MATURITIES: 1974 thru 1998   Callable: 4/1/83 at prem.

LEGAL OPINION: Freeman, Richardson, Watson, Slade, McCarthy and Kelly (Jacksonville)

PURPOSE: Storm drainage facilities

SECURITY: Junior lien on Utility tax receipts together with general fund receipts other than ad valorem taxes.

DEBT:		
	Prior Lien Bonds	$ 8,065,000*
	Parity Lien	219,000
	This Issue	3,455,000
	Total	$11,739,000

* Fully secured from other pledged funds.

COVERAGE:	Historical (Years Ending ...)	12 mos. ended 6/30/73
Avail. Pledge Funds	$370,391	$431,534
Est Max d/s ($281,850)	Cover 1.31x	1.53x
Est aver d/s ($278,400)	Cover 1.33x	1.55x

BOND RESERVE(S):
Parity Bonds—Single Reserve   1973 Bonds issue
Required $ max d/s   On Hand $—0—
If not filled, balance to accrue from fixed pymts over 5 years.

OTHER REQUIRED RESERVES: None

ADDITIONAL PARITY BONDS TEST: Pledged taxes in 12 consecutive months of prior 18, equal 1.50x max d/s on bonds outstanding and to be issued.

COVENANTS: To keep in force the ordinance levying the tax in the full amount permitted by law.
Audits and Books XXX
Additional prior lien—permitted (see notes)

FLOW OF FUNDS:
P and I	1
Bond Reserve	2
Street maintenance	3 (5 percent of pledged taxes, bal. avail. for d/s)
Surplus	4 (Any lawful purpose)

CASE IV—NOTES
UTILITY TAX REVENUE BONDS—MIXED LIENS

Introduction

The City of Riviera Beach (1973 estimated population, 23,000) is selling this 1973 issue of Utility Tax Bonds to finance the construction of street and storm drainage improvements within the City. The bonds are secured by a lien on and are payable from the City's Utilities Service Taxes. The bonds rank equally with $218,558 Utility Tax Bonds, Series 1972, and are subordinate to the lien on such Utilities Services Taxes enjoyed by $7,720,000 outstanding Water and Sewer Revenue Bonds and $345,000 Excise Tax Revenue Bonds of the City. WATER AND SEWER SYSTEM REVENUES AND OTHER REVENUES PLEDGED TO THE PRIOR LIEN BONDS HAVE BEEN MOST AMPLE TO MEET THE DEBT SERVICE REQUIREMENTS ON THOSE OUTSTANDING ISSUES AND NO UTILITIES SERVICES TAXES HAVE BEEN USED, OR IS IT ANTICIPATED THAT SUCH TAXES WILL BE USED THEREFOR.

The bonds herein offered are additionally secured by a covenant of the City to budget each year and use to the extent necessary its General Fund monies (other than monies derived from ad valorem taxation) to make the interest and principal payments and other payments required by the Bond Resolution.

Although the lien position of these bonds is technically in third place, and additional prior lien bonds may be issued, the full amount of collections of the pledged utility tax is, has been, and will, through security provisions in the bond ordinance, be available to service this issue and parity lien bonds (barring, of course, a catastrophe that impairs the self-serviceability of the prior lien issues).

The cross pledging of revenues, and pledge of general fund receipts other than ad valorem taxes, is institutionalized, so to speak, in Florida. These kinds of pledges are seldom seen in other states.

This is a strongly secured bond, with solid protective features to safeguard the full availability of the utility taxes.

Security

The Utilities Services Taxes. The principal, interest, reserve account payments and all other required payments for the Utility Tax Revenue Bonds, Series 1973, now being offered, are secured by and payable from the Utilities Services Taxes of the city, which is a tax in the amount of 10 percent on the gross sales of electricity, telephone and telegraph service, natural gas, and heating fuels sold within the city. This tax is collected by the sellers of such services and is remitted to the city on a monthly basis. The bonds now being offered rank equally with $218,558 principal amount of 4 percent Utility Tax Bonds of the city, Series 1972, due April 1, 1982, which are held by a local bank and are being retired through equal monthly payments of combined principal and interest. The lien of the 1972 bonds and the bonds now being offered on the Utilities Services Taxes is subject to a prior lien thereon of $7,720,000 outstanding Water and Sewer Revenue Bonds and $345,000 Excise Tax Revenue Bonds of the city. The net revenues of the water and sewer system and the pledged occupational license taxes have been ample to meet the debt service on those outstanding issues and no use of the pledged Utilities Services Taxes for such purpose is anticipated.

The General Fund Pledge. The principal and interest, and Reserve Account payments for the bonds are additionally secured by a General Fund pledge of the city, whereby the city covenants that if at any time the pledged revenues are insufficient to make the required payments into the Sinking Fund and Reserve Account, the city will budget and make such required payments or the necessary portion thereof, from legally available General Fund revenues, excluding ad valorem taxes. This covenant does not constitute a pledge of any specific General Fund revenues of the city.

The prior lien enjoyed by certain outstanding bonds upon the city's Utilities Services Taxes has minimal bearing on the security of the Utility Tax Revenue Bonds, Series 1973, now being offered. The combined water and sewer system provides annual net revenues in excess of two times the maximum annual debt service requirement on all outstasnding water and sewer bonds without reference to the Utilities Services Taxes, and furthermore, the city is obligated by the 1973 Resolution to charge water and sewer rates sufficient to provide for full operating costs and debt services requirements of the water and sewer system without use of any utilities tax money.

The city reserves the right to issue additional equally-ranking water and sewer revenue bonds provided that the average annual net revenues of the water and sewer system and the average annual pledged Utilities Services Taxes and the $70,000 of pledged cigarette taxes for the immediately preceding 24 months or 12 months, whichever is less, are at least equal to 1.35 times the maximum debt service due in any succeeding year on all parity bonds outstanding and those proposed. Certain adjustments may be made to the pledged revenues to reflect rate increases and net revenues of any water and sewer utilities being acquired.

Additionally, by the terms of the Subsection 15C of the 1973 Resolution authorizing the bonds being offered, the city is restricted in the issuance of any additional water and sewer bonds in that the net water and sewer revenues alone must provide a 1.00 times historical coverage of any proposed combined water and sewer maximum annual debt service requirement and a 1.15 times projected coverage of such debt service requirement.

Covenant as to Water and Sewer Rates. The 1973 Utility Tax Bond Resolution provides that the city will, as long as any obligations authorized by the Resolution remain outstanding and unpaid maintain such rates and collect such fees or other charges for the services and facilities of the city water system, and revised them from time to time to insure that the net revenues of the water and sewer system will be sufficient to pay 100 percent of the interest and principal on all water and sewer revenue bonds, including any pari passu additional bonds hereafter issued, maturing and becoming due in each year.

Pledged Revenues and Debt Service Coverage

Utilities Services Taxes collected during the 12 months ending June 30, 1973, totaled $431,534. The city's Utilities Services Taxes, for all practical purposes, is completely free to meet the debt service requirements on the bonds offered and the small outstanding parity issue of 1972. This historic 12-month figure of $431,534 then provides a 1.53 times coverage of the maximum feature annual debt service requirement of the bonds now being offered and the small outstanding 1972 issue.

*   *   *

CASE V
BUILDING REVENUE BONDS—HIDDEN LIEN

NAME: $6,000,000 University of Texas (Austin) Building Revenue Bonds
Series 1974-A

SELLING: 9/19/74

MATURITIES: 1976 thru 1998   Callable: 4/1/85 at prem.

LEGAL OPINION: Mcall, Parkhurst and Horton (Dallas)

PURPOSE: To finance various educational facilities to complete a
building program.

SECURITY: Third lien on Permanent University Funds appropriated
annually by the legislature, and as required, an unlimited student fee.

DEBT: Prior Lien Bonds $ 93,605,000*
        Parity Lien   53,000,000
        This issue   6,000,000
          Total $152,605,000
* Permanent Univ. Funds Bonds only, maturing through 1994

COVERAGE:

	Historical (Years Ending ...)		
	8/31/72	8/31/73	8/31/74— Prelim.
Funds Avail for d/s*	$19,874,085	$21,835,600	$24,717,000
Est Max d/s*** ($14,889,994)	Cover 1.33x	1.46x	1.65x
Est Aver d/s** ($9,742,080)***	2.04x	2.24x	2.54x

   * Total appropriation
  ** Includes prior lien, see d/s schedule
*** 1975-1988 (final maturity this series)

BOND RESERVE(S):
Prior lien Required   none
Parity Bonds—Single Reserve XXX
Required $ aver. d/s   On Hand $4,119,593*
* From prior parity bond proceeds

OTHER REQUIRED RESERVES: none

ADDITIONAL BONDS:
Prior lien—see notes
Parity lien—Pledged Revenues in prior fiscal, or any 12 consecutive months ending not more than 90 days prior, equal 1.25x aver. d/s on bonds outstanding and to be issued.

COVENANTS: Student Fee (if required), to produce revenues sufficient to cover all requirements.

FLOW OF FUNDS: Permanent University Fund monies
P and I (prior lien)   1
P and I (parity)   2
Bond Reserve   3
Surplus   4 (any lawful purpose) (—0— percent locked in)

CASE V—NOTES
BUILDING REVENUE BONDS—HIDDEN LIEN

The University of Texas at Austin has for several years been engaged in an extensive catch-up construction program to meet present and future plant and facility needs. The proceeds of these bonds will be used to finance the final phase of this construction program, involving the construction and equipping of a major addition to the existing chemistry building on the university's inner campus in Austin.

The bonds are secured by a first lien on "pledged revenues." It is the intent of the Board of Regents to pay debt service from available proceeds of the Permanent University Funds appropriated annually to the University of Texas System. The bonds are additionally secured by a convenant to impose, to the extent necessary, an unlimited student fee sufficient in amount for payments required under the bond resolution, together with indeterminate "additional revenues."

The funds appropriated to the University of Texas System are already encumbered by $93,605,000 Permanent University Fund (PUF) bonds, of which $22,860,000 are first lien and $70,745,000 second lien bonds. These liens are not closed out.

THE PUF MONIES CURRENTLY AVAILABLE TO ALL ISSUES ARE MORE THAN AMPLE, AS INDICATED BY THE FACT THAT MAXIMUM DEBT SERVICE, WHICH OCCURS IN 1975 IS COVERED 1.48 TIMES BY THE AVERAGE OF THE FUNDS AVAILABLE IN THE LAST THREE YEARS. (This can be watered down to a 1.25x cover by "pledged revenues" under the additional bonds clause.)

True, the pledge of a Special Fee, as required, is a priority pledge, but it is the intent of the Board to pay the bonds from the primary source, the unencumbered Permanent University Funds.

The par amount of bonds that may be secured by the PUF is limited to 20 percent of the value of the PUF at time of issuance. The University of Texas System is limited to 20 percent of its 2/3 share of the Fund. The outstanding first and second lien bonds approximately total that limit, thus the device of Building Revenue Bond secured by available surpluses and the Special fee.

We have seen an increasing tendency in new offerings of various kinds of bonds to disguise the junior lien nature of bond security by titling such as "available surplus," etc. The marketability (primary and secondary) of a junior lien bond of any kind is not enhanced by such obfuscatory procedures.

Pledged Revenues. The term "Pledged Revenues" shall mean collectively (a) any Pledged Available Fund Surplus, (b) the Special Fee, and (c) any additional revenues, income, receipts, or other resources, including, without limitation, any grants, donations, or income received or to be received from the U.S. Government, or any other public or private source, whether pursuant to an agreement or otherwise, which hereafter may be pledged to the payment of the bonds or the additional bonds.

"Pledged Available Fund Surplus" is the 2/3 allocation to the University of Texas System of the investment income of the Permanent University Fund (established under the Texas Constitution) after payment of pledges to prior lien bonds. The funds are subject to biennial appropriation by the state legislature.

Special Fee. The Board covenants and agrees to fix, levy, charge, and collect the Special Fee on a uniformly applied basis from each student in such amounts, without any limitation whatsoever, as will be at least sufficient at all times to provide, together with other Pledged Revenues, the money for making when due all deposits required to be made to the credit of the Interest and Sinking Fund and the Reserve Fund but it is specifically recognized that the Special Fee is to be fixed, levied, charged, and collected only if and when permitted or required and provided in this Resolution.

The Board may, at its option, deposit to the credit of the Interest and Sinking Fund and/or the Reserve Fund any Pledged Revenues hereafter pledged, and also any revenues derived from the ownership and/or operation of the Project, or funds available from any other source, and thus reduce, to the extent of any such deposits, the amounts that otherwise would be required to be deposited therein.

Use of Funds Appropriated. The allocation of investment income to the University of Texas System has been thus far utilized only by the University of Texas at Austin, although there are nine other enrolling institutions in the system. There is apparently nothing other than Board decisions that determine this. (The pledged fee would be charged to students enrolled at Austin.) The Board of Regents can issue bonds for the other schools as Permanent University Fund Bonds (prior lien) or as subordinate lien (on parity with this issue insofar as the pledge of PUF monies) but in either case the respective additional bonds clauses would govern additional issuance. This bond resolution does not close out prior lien financing. The only limit other than the restrictions of the additional bonds clause is the constitutional restriction that the amount of such PUF (prior lien) bond cannot exceed 20 percent of the value of the PUF (exclusive of real estate) at time of issuance.

The underlying PUF bond resolution also further restricts future bond issuance by requiring:

1. That there be held in the Permanent University Fund an amount of the U.S. Goverment direct or guaranteed obligations which (a) are at least equal in par value to the aggregate par value of all outstanding PUF bonds an the PUF bonds then proposed to be issued, and (b) are then yielding annual interest at least equal to the maximum annual interest requirements of all outstanding PUF bonds and the PUF bonds then proposed to be issued; and

2. That for the previous fiscal year the income from the Permanent University Fund was at least 1-1/2 times the maximum annual principal and interest on all outstanding PUF bonds and the installment of PUF bonds then proposed to be issued.

Such additional prior lien bonds will probably be issued within the framework of the restrictions set forth above.

*   *   *

CASE VI
UTILITY REVENUE BONDS—
COMBINED WATER, ELECTRIC, GAS

NAME: $2,900,000 Morgan City, Louisiana, Utility Revenue Bonds

SELLING: 1/11/72

MATURITIES: 1973 thru 1997   Callable: 3/1/77 or 3/1/82 at prem.

<u>LEGAL OPINION:</u>   Cox, Huppenbauer, Michaelis and Osborne (New Orleans)

<u>PURPOSE:</u>   First issue of $7,600,000 total for improvements to the electric system. Balance to be issued in 1973 or 1974.

<u>SECURITY:</u>   Parity first lien on net revenues of the systems.

<u>DEBT:</u>	Prior Lien Bonds	$ 0	Connections:	
	Parity Lien	10,210,000*	Elec.	7,900
	This issue	2,900,000	Water	4,350
	Total	$13,110,000	Gas	4,903
			TOTAL	17,153

Total debt per Connection: $764

* Excluding $1,984,000 for which sufficient funds are escrowed.

<u>COVERAGE:</u>	Historical (Years Ending ...)		Proforma or Projected
	12/31/70	12/31/71*	12/31/72
Operating Revenue	$3,412,926	$3,726,400	$4,146,100
Operating Expense	1,797,763	1,922,900	2,071,900
Net Op. Rev.	1,615,163	1,803,500	2,074,200
Net Other Revenue**	43,280	25,200	34,000
Net Avail for d/s	1,658,443	1,828,700	2,108,200
Est Max d/s ($984,411)	Cover 1.68x	1.85x	2.14x
Est Aver d/s ($924,625)	Cover 1.79x	1.97x	2.28x

   * 9 mos. actual, 3 mos. est.

** Interest income

<u>BOND RESERVE(S):</u>
Parity Bonds—Single Reserve XXX
Required $ max d/s   On Hand $810,000   Pmts current XXX
If not filled, balance to accrue from fixed pymts over 5 years.

<u>Capital Additions and Contingencies Fund:</u>   Available for d/s   yes
Required $10,000   On Hand $66,000   Pmts current XXX

<u>OTHER REQUIRED RESERVES:</u>   none

<u>ADDITIONAL PARITY BONDS TEST:</u>   Net revenues in each of 3 prior fiscal years is equal to 1.33x max d/s on all bonds outstanding and to be issued.

<u>COVENANTS:</u>
Rates—to provide net revenues sufficient to cover max. d/s 1.30 times.
Insurance XXX   Audits and Books XXX   Proper Operation XXX
No Prior Lien XXX

FLOW OF FUNDS:

O and M	1
P and I (parity)	2
Bond Reserve	3
Cap. add and Cont.	4 (payments of 5 percent gross revenue)
Surplus	5 Any lawful purpose (0 percent locked in)

CASE VI—NOTES
UTILITY REVENUE BONDS
—COMBINED WATER, ELECTRIC, GAS

Conversation with the engineer, Beard, Ellison and Davis, Inc. (Baton Rouge) discloses the following:

No additional utility financing, other than the balance of $7,600,000 authorized by the voters of the city for electric system improvements described herein, is anticipated for several years. Bids for steam boiler and turbo generating equipment were taken for 33,000 KW and 35,000 KW capability. The figures shown herein reflect the 35,000 KW numbers. The engineer is going to recommend increasing that capability to 37,000 KW. On the night of the bond sale, bids for an additional estimated $600,000 worth of equipment will be opened. Aggregate costs for the generating and boiler equipment are very close to estimate. A contingeny factor of $450,000 (7 percent of construction) is provided. The cost of electricity to the consumer is estimated at about 4 percent higher than if provided by an investor-owned utility. This is reflected in the fact that the coverage factor is high enough to produce surplus revenues that flow to the General Fund.

At present the water system is not providing sufficient revenues to cover its operational costs. R.W. Beck and Co. has been retained to do a rate study which will result in increased water system receipts, making the system fully self-supporting. This could bring electric rates down or eliminate an increase as additional bonds are sold.

Although the sewer system is not part of the utilities system, water and sewer are wedded for obvious reasons, and water customers generally are those who pay the sewer system costs. Therefore a discussion of the sewer system is appropriate.

The city at present has no sewage treatment facilities. Raw sewage is pumped into the Atchafayala River. It is anticipated that enforcement of anti-water pollution measures will catch up with the city in the near future. The engineer believes that bond financing will probably be done primarily from sales tax sources.

The city has never defaulted on any debt.

RATE STRUCTURE: Present Water Rates in Effect

First 200 cu. ft.—$17.75 per min.
Next 800 cu. ft.—$ .20 per 100
Next 1,000 cu. ft.—$ .16 per 100
Monthly 5M gal. or equiv. water $2.75 (3/4″ meter)
Provision for delinquent collections: 10 percent penalty after 30 days
                                                            Water and Elec. shut off

WATER SYSTEM CHARACTERISTICS:

Supply Surface—Atchafayala River and Lake Palourde
System Design Capacity—good for 10 years
Maximum Use/historical—6 million gpd
Average Use/historical—4 million gpd
Treatment Capacity—10,500,000 gpd
Storage Capacity—1,050,000 gal.
Pumping Capacity—10,500,000 gpd

*   *   *

CASE VII
REVENUE BONDS—
CORPORATE MUNICIPAL UTILITY

NAME: $10,000,000 Indianapolis, Indiana, Gas Utility Revenue Bonds

SELLING: 3/22/72

MATURITIES: 1975 thru 1992   Callable: 6/1/82 at prem.

LEGAL OPINION: Ice, Miller, Donadio and Ryan (Indianapolis)

PURPOSE: Improvements to the gas utility

SECURITY: Pledge of revenues of the utility

DEBT:

			Connections:	
Prior Lien Bonds	$	0		
Parity Lien	18,485,000		Gas—	198,215
This issue	10,000,000			
Total	$28,485,000		Total Debt per Connection:	$144

COVERAGE:	Historical (Years Ending ...)	
	12/31/70	12/31/71
Operating Revenue	$55,883,223	$60,506,261
Operating Expense	47,736,657	54,460,515
Net Op. Rev.	8,146,566	6,045,746
Net Other Revenue	1,416,409	1,110,367
Net Avail for d/s	9,562,975	7,156,113
Est Max d/s ($2,530,000)	Cover 3.78x	2.83x
Est Aver d/s ($2,125,050)	Cover 4.50x	3.37x

BOND RESERVE(S):   None

OTHER REQUIRED RESERVES: None

ADDITIONAL PARITY BONDS TEST: Net revenues in each of the two calendar years prior equal 1.50x average d/s on bonds and to be issued. Revenues shall be adjusted for rate increases or decreases.

COVENANTS:
Rates—to produce revenues sufficient to cover O&M, d/s, depreciation and other costs of the system.
Insurance XXX   Audits and Books XXX   No prior lien XXX

FLOW OF FUNDS: No priority of payment—Surplus funds (100 percent locked in)

SECURITY COMMENTARY:
   This utility, like Los Angeles DEWAP and Chicago Water, lacks in its contract with bondholders, some of the boilerplate covenants such as establishment of cash bond reserves and depreciation reserves. (In large systems these are niceties rather than necessities.) Like DEWAP, there is no priority of disbursement from gross revenues. From a viewpoint of technical deficiencies this system, in addition, is not free (under Indiana statutues) to fix its rates as it sees fit, but is subject (as are Wisconsin Municipal Utilities) to regulation by the State Public Service Commission.
   Section 54-609 Ch. 6, Burns Indiana Statutes, Vol. 10, Part 2—recites that charges must be sufficient to pay O&M, debt service, working capital, funds for extensions and improvement, taxes assessed, and provide reasonable profit. "Any rate too low to meet the foregoing requirements shall be unlawful."

CASE VII—NOTES
REVENUE BONDS—
CORPORATE MUNICIPAL UTILITY

This utility must be the only municipal conglomerate in the country. The next thing we may see is that it will make a donation to the Republican Party in exchange for a stay of divestiture order of its newly acquired oil wells.

The Official Statement reflects that the utility is d/b/a (doing business as) Citizens Gas and Coke Utility—presumably the name of the enterprise acquired in 1935 by the City when it issued $8,000,000 in revenue bonds (purchased by Halsey, Stuart and Co.) for the purpose.

If Citizens Gas and Coke runs afoul of the Justice Department under a new regime, it may also have its other identity referred to not in the business world term—d/b/a, but under the fugitive parlance—a/k/a (also known as), or "alias" Indianapolis Gas.

Who ever heard of a municipal utility buying metallurgical coal two states away, then processing it, in such volume as to account for 12 percent of foundry coke in the nation? Who ever heard of a city-owned enterprise selling 85 percent of its coke products in 5 states, or selling 50-60 percent of its output to General Motors, Chrysler, Ford, International Harvester and others in the automotive business? And who ever heard of a government-owned enterprise required by law to pay ad valorem taxes on the same basis as if the properties were privately owned? And you would think that the bond dating was on April Fools day when we are shown a history of sale of manufactured products generating as much, or in some years more, net revenue (after depreciation) than sales of natural gas. Revenues of the coke plant could pay the bonds.

* * *

CASE VIII
AIRPORT REVENUE BONDS

<u>NAME:</u> $10,600,000 State of Alaska International Airports

<u>SELLING:</u>   1/14/75

<u>MATURITIES:</u>   1976 thru 1992   <u>Callable:</u>   6/1/83 at prem.

<u>LEGAL OPINION:</u>   Orrick, Herrington, Rowlay and Sutcliffe (San Francisco)

PURPOSE: New terminal at the Anchorage Airport

CAPITALIZED: Bond reserve $1,089,560 (est. from avail. funds)

SECURITY: Parity lien on gross revenues of the Fairbanks and Anchorage International Airports

DEBT: Prior Lien Bonds $ 0
         Parity Lien   22,995,000
         This issue   10,600,000
             Total $33,595,000

COVERAGE:

	Years Ending ...		
	6/30/72	6/30/73	6/30/74
Operating Revenue	$9,687,562	$10,589,616	$12,131,048
Operating Expense	6,158,348	7,314,776	8,049,011
Net Op. Rev.	3,529,214	3,274,840	4,082,037
Net Other Revenue*	474,194	**	1,136,160
Net Avail for d/s	4,003,408	3,274,840	5,218,197
Est Max d/s ($3,279,520)	Cover 1.22x	0.99x	1.59x
Est Aver d/s ($2,768,620)	Cover 1.41x	1.18x	1.88x

 * Interest Income
** Amount unavailable at time of writing this report

BOND RESERVE(S):
Parity Bonds—Single Reserve XXX
Required $ max. d/s   On Hand $3,049,995*
If not filled, balance to accrue from first funds available
* Includes est. cap. amt.

DEPRECIATION RESERVE: (Or Similar)   Available for d/s XXX
Required $500,000
Balance to accumulate from fixed payments or surpluses of 1 percent of gross revenue

ADDITIONAL PARITY BONDS TEST: Net revenues in prior fiscal year or 12 months equal 1.30x max d/s on bonds outstanding and to be issued. Additional bonds must be authorized by the legislature.

COVENANTS:
Rates—To produce net revenues sufficient to cover annual d/s and Bond Res. 1.30 times.
Insurance* XXX   Audits and Books XXX   Proper Operation XXX
No Prior Lien   no provision

FLOW OF FUNDS:

P and I	1
Bond Reserve	2
R and R	3
Surplus	4 Any lawful airport purpose incl. O and M

CASE VIII—NOTES
AIRPORT REVENUE BONDS

Project Resources

Revenue Fund balance available for appropriation 6/70/74	$ 4,744,678
Bond Proceeds—Series E	10,600,000
Bond Proceeds prior bond issue	1,300,000
TOTAL RESOURCES	$16,644,678

Sources of Funds. The State Legislature has appropriated $7,000,000 from the bond proceeds for the project, but the Legislature has not yet appropriated the remaining $3,600,000 of those proceeds. That $3,600,000 cannot be expended until such an appropriation is made. The project cannot be completed unless sufficient appropriations are made therefor; however, the International Airports, without the project, have in the past produced revenues more than sufficient to pay the debt service on the bonds, including the bonds of Series E. The Legislature will be requested to appropriate the additional $3,600,000 of bond proceeds early in 1975. In addition, appropriations will be requested for the balance of the project from the Revenue Fund to finance the total project as outlined herein.

Alaska Aviation. Alaska is one of the most air-minded states in the Union, on a per-capita basis ranking first in number of airplanes, pilots, passengers and tonnage of cargo flown. Because of the great distances between principal cities, the limited surface transportation facilities available and waterways and rugged mountain ranges separating coastal areas and Interior Alaska, the airplane has long provided a major means of accessibility to and within the state. Since World War II, the number of passengers carried in Alaska by air each year has exceeded the total population of the state.

The state owns or has leasehold interests in approximately 400 aircraft bases and actively maintains an extensive system of 230 airports and seadromes to accommodate this vital tranportation mode. There are over 900 airfields or designated seaplane areas in Alaska, and scheduled air service is provided to nearly 300 locations throughout the state. To date, construction or improvements of state-owned airports have been financed from revenues and by revenue bonds, general obligation bonds and federal grant or matching-aid programs. A total of $15,725,000 in revenue bonds have been sold, $24,225,000 in general fund receipts have been expended, $31,275,000 par value of general obligation bonds have been issued and $63,027,000 in federal funds have been received or obligated since statehood for this purpose.

The two principal airports in the state, Anchorage and Fairbanks, are classified as international airports. Both were constructed by the federal government while Alaska was still a territory. Following Alaska's admission to statehood in 1959, the FAA continued to operate these two airfields until mid-1960 when personnel under the State Department of Public Works assumed responsibility for their management. In 1961, the Legislature authorized the issuance of $7,000,000 par value State of Alaska International Airports Revenue bonds, created the International Airports Revenue Fund, and dedicated the income generated by the Anchorage and Fairbanks airports exclusively to the operation, maintenance and improvement of these two airfields, including payment of debt service on the above bonds. Bond authorization increases to $34,825,000 and technical and clarifying amendments were made to this enabling legislation during the period 1968-1974. The initial offering of International Airport Revenue Bonds, designated Series A, was sold in the amount of $7,000,000 in May, 1968.

The volume of air carrier activity at the two International Airports during the year ended June 30, 1974, showed 41,495 landings, total in, out and through passengers of 2,255,693 and 163,244 tons of freight handled. The distance savings offered by polar routes between European capitals and the Orient, which exceed 4,000 miles compared to trans-Pacific routes, have resulted in increasing use of Anchorage as a fueling stop for these flights by scheduled, supplemental and charter carriers. Regularly scheduled service is presently operated by Air France, British Overseas Aircraft Corporation, Japan Air Lines, KLM Royal Dutch Airlines, Korean Air Lines, Lufthansa German Airlines, Sabena Airlines, Scandinavian Airlines System, Trans-Mediterranean Air Lines and Varig Airlines, among the foreign carriers. Alaska Airlines, Northwest Airlines, Pan American World Airways and Western Airlines offer regularly scheduled service to and from Anchorage or Fairbanks and points in the lower 48 states. Intra-Alaska carriers serving Anchorage or Fairbanks include Alaska International Air, Inc., Reeve Aleutian Airways and Wien Air Alaska.

*　　*　　*

CASE IX
ACQUISITION OF WATER AND SEWER

<u>NAME:</u>　$2,500,000 Scottsdale, Arizona, Water and Sewer Systems Revenue Bonds, Series A1973

<u>SELLING:</u>　7/17/73

<u>MATURITIES:</u>　1974 thru 1983　<u>Callable:</u>　non-callable

<u>LEGAL OPINION:</u>　Gust, Rosenfeld and Divelbess (Phoenix)

<u>PURPOSE:</u>　Acquisition of, and improvements to, a private water system

<u>SECURITY:</u>　Net revenues of the combined systems (subject to any deficiencies in escrowed funds for prior lien bonds)

<u>DEBT:</u>

Prior Lien Bonds	$4,870,000*	Connections:	
Parity Lien	3,910,000	Water	6,700
This issue	2,500,000	Sewer	18,886
Total	$6,410,000**		

Total Debt Per Conn.:　$250 (very low)

* Funds escrowed sufficient for Prin. and Int.
** $6,550,000 authorized unsold

<u>COVERAGE:</u>

	Historical (Years Ending ...)	
	6/30/72	6/30/73*
Operating Revenue	$1,299,247	$1,348,057
Operating Expense	409,815	388,780
Net Op. Rev.	889,432	959,277
Net Other Revenue*	174,344	238,487
Net Avail for d/s	$1,063,776	1,197,764
Est Max d/s ($726,751)	Cover 1.46x	1.65x
Est Aver d/s ($456,000)	Cover 2.33x	2.63x

* Unaudited
** Interest income and connection charges. Connection charges amount to $106,830 and $186,516 in 1972 and 1973 respectively. Interest income is believed to include monies from construction funds.

<u>BOND RESERVE(S):</u>
Parity Bonds—Single Reserve XXX
Required $ max. d/s　On Hand $278,839
If not filled, balance to accrue from fixed pymts over 5 years

REPLACEMENT AND EXTENSION FUND: Available for d/s XXX
Required 2 percent of tangible assets   On Hand $0
Balance to accumulate from fixed payments of 2 percent of gross revenue.

OTHER REQUIRED RESERVES: None

ADDITIONAL PARITY BONDS TEST: Net revenue in the prior fiscal
year equals 1.20x max. d/s on bonds outstanding and to be issued. Revenues
may be adjusted for acquired connections and rate increases.

COVENANTS:
Rates—to produce net revenues sufficient to cover annual d/s 1/29 times.
Insurance XXX   Audits and Books XXX
No Prior Lien XXX

FLOW OF FUNDS:
O and M	1
P and I (parity)	2
Bond Reserve	3
R and E	4
Surplus	5 Any lawful purpose

CASE IX—NOTES
ACQUISITION OF WATER AND SEWER

Maturities:

Year	Amount	Year	Amount
1974	$ 75,000	1979	$300,000
1975	150,000	1980	350,000
1976	175,000	1981	375,000
1977	225,000	1982	375,000
1978	250,000	1983	225,000

All bonds of this series are noncallable.

Purpose

The proceeds from the sale of the $2.5 million utility revenue bonds to
be sold July 17, 1973, will be used to expand the city's water service area
through the purchase of the Desert Springs Water Company. The Desert
Springs Water Company encompasses an area of approximately 36 square
miles and is located in the central section of the city's boundaries just north
of the McCormick Ranch. This acquisition will add more than 1400
accounts to the city's water system and with the continuing growth within

the area, it is anticipated this new service area will have 12,000 to 15,000 accounts by 1995. Distribution of water for the Desert Springs service area is through the use of 56 1/2 miles of main lines consisting of 3 1/2″ to 12″ pipe. These main lines are connected to and supplied by seven wells strategically located throughout the area. A more than adequate water supply is available within the Desert Springs service area as engineer's studies have indicated that there is sufficient ground water supply to satisfy demands through the year 2020.

Analysis of Bond Needs

	Reproduction Cost	Accrued Depreciation	Net Cost	Total Cost
Water Company	$2,077,035	199,984	1,877,051	
Improvements from Appraisal Date to City Acquisition			219,849	
Condemnation Judgment Premium			200,000	
Total Desert Springs Acquisition				$2,296,900
Immediate Improvements Necessary to Desert Springs per Appraisal Addendum:				
Feeder Mains			48,300	
Storage Tanks			66,500	114,800
Total for Desert Springs				$2,411,700
Contingencies				88,300
Total Necessary Bond Issue				$2,500,000

Water System

The properties presently serviced by the City of Scottsdale water system encompasses an area of 2,400 acres and are located in the central sector of the city. The major portion of the service area was acquired in 1971, through the purchase of the Indian Bend Water Company, while a smaller amount of service area was acquired in 1972, with the purchase of the Ocotillo Water Company. The area is largely comprised of medium and high valued residences complemented by commercial and industrial developments. At the present time the water system serves approximately 22,000 residents through 53,000 accounts. The 22,000 residents served by the city's water system represents approximately 25 percent of the city's population. The remainder of the city is served by Phoenix.

A major development that will greatly enhance and expand the service area of the Scottsdale water system has been the construction of a large scale residential community known as the McCormick Ranch. This planned community, located in the north sector of the city, when completed, will contain an estimated 7,500 units housing approximately 25,000 persons. In addition, the 4,200 acre development will contain schools, churches, recreational and commercial facilities. The impact of this development is of paramount importance in considering the future development of the water and sewer facilities.

All utilities for this important area are being provided by Kaiser-Aetna and given to the city upon completion of installation. These works include substantial expenditures for enhancement of the total water system, including wells, pumping and storage, and transmission facilities.

Presently the residences of the McCormick Ranch development obtain their water from the McCormick Ranch Water Company. But it is anticipated that the water company will be dedicated to the City of Scottsdale within the year 1973.

Available Water Supply

With the incorporation of the McCormick Properties into the city's water system, water will be supplied through ten wells strategically located throughout the system. A feasibility study conducted by A.E. Ferguson and Associates, Inc., in 1971, which related to the purchase of the Indian Bend Water Company, revealed that wells within the area were adequate to meet domestic supply to customers with a maximum one day's usage of 7 million gallons. With the expected growth within the water system, an estimated maximum of 10 million gallons for one day's use will be required. In order to meet the increased needs, it is anticipated that storage tanks and additional wells will need to be constructed in the future as water increases demand.

In 1967, a study was conducted to determine the ground water resources in the Scottsdale area by the Water Development Corporation. The report indicated that the water level decline in the southern areas of Paradise Valley (which includes the area to be served by the City of Scottsdale) was approximately 6 feet per year during the 1961-1966 period. The report further stated "that groundwater resources of Paradise Valley are more than adequate to sustain the additional water supply requirements for Scottsdale through the year 1990." Studies conducted by the consulting firm of A.E. Ferguson relating to the purchase of the Indian Bend Water Company indicated that two wells of the service area showed no appreciable drop in the water level in the last five years and that the conclusion drawn in the 1967 study of the adequate water supply for the City of Scottsdale through 1990 was very conservative.

Sanitary Sewer System

The City of Scottsdale initiated its first large scale sewer system construction in 1957 and since that time, has expanded its service area to accommodate approximately 90 percent of the residents of Scottsdale, plus residents located to the west of the city in the adjacent community of Paradise Valley. The sewer system contains trunk lines leading to the five city sewage treatment plants, which is jointly shared by the cities of Phoenix, Glendale, Tempe, Mesa and Scottsdale. The city's sewer system contained 18,866 connections as of April 1, 1973.

The City of Scottsdale

The City of Scottsdale which is located in central Maricopa County, Arizona, adjoins the City of Pheonix, the State Capital, on the west and the City of Tempe to the south. Scottsdale, together with Phoenix, Tempe and the neighboring City of Mesa form the heart of the Phoenix metropolitan area which is the hub of economic and political activities in the state.

Within the last two decades, the city has exhibited an exceptional rate of growth, partially due to annexations, but mainly due to increased development in indusry and residential properties. Today, Scottsdale is the third largest city in the state with a population of 80,000.

*   *   *

CASE X
UNIVERSITY STUDENT FEE REVENUE BONDS

NAME: $5,000,000 California State Universities and Colleges (system) Auxiliary Facilities Revenue Bonds Series A

SELLING: 6/28/72

MATURITIES: 1977 thru 2001 Callable: 43/1/82 at Prem.

LEGAL OPINION: Orrick, Herrington, Rowley and Sutcliffe (San Francisco)

PURPOSE: Construction of student health centers on four campus sites.

CAPITALIZED: Bond Reserve $269,636

SECURITY: Proceeds of a student fee charged to enrollees at all system locations

DEBT:
Prior Lien Bonds	$	0
Parity Lien		0
This issue		5,000,000
Total		$5,000,000*

* Est. $23,500,000 add'l to be sold through 1975

COVERAGE:	Historical (Years Ending ...) 6/30/71	Projected 6/30/74
Fee Revenue	$1,517,123	$1,843,604
D/S Grant		133,864
Net Avail for d/s		1,977,468
Est Max d/s ($403,500)	Cover 3.76x	4.90x
Est Aver d/s ($377,448)	Cover 4.02x	5.24x

BOND RESERVE(S):
Parity Bonds—Single Reserve XXX
Required $ net max. d/s   On Hand $ capitalized

ADDITIONAL PARITY BONDS TEST:

1. Actual revenues during the most prior fiscal year, or 12 months ending not more than 60 prior, equal 1.20x annual net d/s on all bonds outstanding and to be issued during each of the next three ensuing fiscal years following issuance of the additional bonds;
2. Actual revenues during prior fiscal year, or 12 month ending not more than 60 days prior, equal maximum annual net debt service on all bonds to be outstanding following issuance of the additional bonds;
3. Estimated revenues, based on the most recent official enrollment projects, must equal 1.20x annual net debt service on all bonds in any future year.

COVENANTS:
Rates—To produce fee revenues sufficient to cover net annual d/s 1.20 times (d/s less d/s grant).
Insurance XXX   Audits and Books XXX   Proper operation XXX
No Prior Lien   no provision

FLOW OF FUNDS:

P and I (parity)	1
Bond Reserve	2
Surplus	3 (100 percent locked in)

PLEDGED FUNDS:

FY Ending June 30	Fee Collections	Investment Income	Total
1970	$ 274,602	—	$ 274,602
1971	1,517,123	—**	1,517,123
1972*	1,621,776	137,012	1,758,788
1973	1,716,724	362,506	2,079,230
1974	1,843,604	289,086	2,132,690
1975	1,962,400	201,906	2,164,306
1976	2,047,100	198,743	2,245,843
1977	2,133,876	150,000	2,830,876
1978	2,209,942	100,000	2,309,942
1979	2,275,610	100,000	2,375,610
1980	2,327,356	100,000	2,427,356

* Estimated. Previous two years are actual
** Included in fee collections

DEBT SERVICE:

The interest rate of the bonds of Series A has been assumed to be 6 percent for the purpose of estimating future debt service. Under this assumption maximum annual gross debt service is $403,500 occurring in fiscal 1984. Debt service grants awarded on the first four projects are estimated to be $133,864 thereby resulting in maximum annual net debt service of $269,639. This figure will be further reduced by $86,320 when the grants for San Diego and Sonoma are received thereby resulting in next maximum annual debt service of $183,319 for the first six construction projects.

*   *   *

CASE XI
CIGARETTE TAX REVENUE BONDS (FIFTH LIEN)

NAME: $2,000,000 Alabama State Industrial Development Authority, Special Tax Bonds (Junior Lien)

SELLING: 11/20/73

MATURITIES: 1965 thru 1987 Callable: 12/1/83 at coupon rate

LEGAL OPINION: Chapman and Cutler (Chicago)

PURPOSE: To finance industrial site surveys for local municipalities

SECURITY: Closed Junior (fifth) lien on gross receipts of a 1 cent allocation of cigarette taxes amounting to 6 cents per 20-pack.

DEBT:
Prior Lien Bonds	$10,735,000	
Parity Lien	0	
This issue	2,000,000	
Total	$12,735,000	

COVERAGE:

	Historical (Years Ending ...)		
	9/30/70	9/30/71	9/30/72
Funds Avail for d/s	$3,082,286	$3,203,821	$3,323,334
Est Max d/s ($1,327,982)	Cover 2.32x	2.41x	2.50x
Est Aver d/s ($1,262,790)	Cover 2.44x	2.54x	2.63x

REQUIRED RESERVE(S): None

ADDITIONAL BONDS: No provision—all prior liens are also closed.

COVENANTS: To continue to impose the tax so long as any bonds are outstanding

FLOW OF FUNDS:
P and I (prior lien)	1
P and I (parity)	2
Surplus	3 (Presume any lawful purpose)

CASE XI—NOTES
CIGARETTE TAX REVENUE BONDS—FIFTH LIEN

Purpose. The bond proceeds will be used as a source of grants to counties, municipalities and public local industrial development boards, for the making of surveys to promote the attraction of industry to the localities and for the preparation of industrial sites.

The 1965 Cigarette Tax. The state levies the 1965 cigarette tax on every person in the state who sells, stores, or receives for distribution cigarettes for any use. The rate of the tax is 1 cent on each package of cigarettes containing twenty cigarettes or less, 2 cents on each package of cigarettes containing twenty-one to forty cigarettes and 3 cents on each package of cigarettes containing more than forty cigarettes.

The state has levied cigarette taxes at varying rates since 1935. On October 1, 1959, the cigarette taxes in effect in the state totaled 6 cents for each package of twenty cigarettes. The levy of the 1965 cigarette tax increased cigarette taxes in effect in the state by 1 cent for each package of twenty cigarettes. Since 1965, additional cigarette taxes other than the 1965 cigarette tax have been appropriated for purposes unrelated to the 1973 bonds.

Since the 1965 cigarette tax became effective, the receipts from the tax have been kept in a special fund separate from all other funds and have not been commingled with the receipts from other cigarette taxes.

The bonds are payable from the residue of the revenues from this excise tax remaining after provision is made for payment of the principal and interest that will mature during the then current fiscal year on the outstanding Special Tax Bonds of the State Industrial Development Authority, dated May 1, 1966, December 1, 1967, November 1, 1969, and March 1, 1972.

*   *   *

CASE XII
STATE GASOLINE TAX ANTICIPATION BONDS

NAME: $5,050,000 Birmingham, Alabama State Gasoline Tax Anticipation Bonds

SELLING: 1/30/73

MATURITIES: 1973 thru 1988   Callable: 7/1/72 at prem.

LEGAL OPINION: Bradley, Arrant, Rose and White (Birmingham)

PURPOSE: Final emission of $15,750,000 authorized (by vote) for street improvements

SECURITY: Pledge of so much as is necessary of state gasoline taxes distributed to the city

DEBT:

Prior Lien Bonds	$	0
Parity Lien		8,400,000
This issue		5,050,000
Total		$13,450,000

COVERAGE: Historical (Years Ending ...)

	9/30/70	9/30/71	9/30/72
Pledged Funds	$2,841,827	$2,971,825	$2,752,721*
Est Max d/s ($1,411,750)	Cover 2.01x	2.11x	1.95x
Est Aver d/s ($1,275,343)	Cover 2.23x	2.33x	2.16x

* Effective October 1, 1971, the amounts distributed to the city decreased approximately $375,000 per year as a result of the 1970 census which showed a decline in the population of the city.

BOND RESERVE(S):   none

OTHER REQUIRED RESERVES: none

ADDITIONAL PARITY BONDS TEST: Average of pledged funds in the two prior years equal 2.0x max. d/s on bonds outstanding and to be issued (no additional bonds are voted).

FLOW OF FUNDS: not available at time of this writing.

CASE XII—NOTES
STATE GASOLINE TAX ANTICIPATION BONDS

State Gasoline Tax.   The term "state gasoline tax," refers to the excise tax of the State of Alabama, levied on the sale, use, distribution, storage or withdrawal from storage of gasoline, naphtha, and other liquid motor fuels commonly used in internal combustion engines, exclusive of those portions used to propel aircraft or to propel vessels on inland and coastal waterways of the state. The term "city's share of the gasoline tax," as hereinafter used, means that portion of the net proceeds from the state gasoline tax that may be apportioned by law to the city and received by it (the said net proceeds being the entire proceeds less costs of collection and refunds). The state gasoline tax is required by law to be distributed in varying proportions among the State of Alabama and the counties and municipalities therein.

Since 1923, the state has levied an excise tax on the sale of gasoline. The present rate of seven cents per gallon has been in effect since 1955. Effective October 1, 1967, a significant amount of such revenue was required to be distributed to the larger municipalities in the state, including the City of Birmingham. Prior to that date, the city's share of the state gasoline tax was less than $15,000 per year.

Allocation of the State Gasoline Tax.   Of the state's net receipts of approximately $120 million per year, 45 percent is allocated to the state and the remaining 55 percent is allocated to the counties and municipalities, the distribution to counties and municipalities being subject to a contingent appropriation for the payment of outstanding highway bonds, Series 1966, of the Alabama Highway Finance Corporation. These bonds mature through June 1, 1976, with an average debt service requirement of approximately $3.1 million. The contingent appropriation is not expected to become effective.

* * *

CASE XIII
SECOND LIEN ELECTRIC REVENUE BONDS

<u>NAME:</u> $100,000,000 South Carolina Public Service Authority, Second Lien Electric Revenue Bonds

<u>SELLING:</u> 11/8/73

<u>MATURITIES:</u> 1980 thru 1993 (Term Bonds 2013) <u>Callable:</u> 1/1/84 at Prem.

<u>LEGAL OPINION:</u>   Wood, Dawson, Love and Sabatine (New York)

<u>PURPOSE:</u>   To finance 1/3 ownership in a nuclear generating plant.

<u>CAPITALIZED:</u> $28,020,000 for 60 months—Bond Reserve $6,746,000

<u>SECURITY:</u>   Second lien on net revenues of the system

<u>DEBT:</u>

Prior Lien Bonds	$ 75,720,000
Prior Lien Contract	4,303,827
Parity Lien	100,000,000
This issue	100,000,000
Total	$280,023,827

<u>COVERAGE:</u>

	Historical Year Ending ... 6/30/73	Proforma or Projected* 6/30/76
Operating Revenue	$41,130,958	$61,978,000
Operating Expense	27,082,274	40,323,000
Net Op. Rev.	14,048,684	21,655,000
Net Other Revenue	1,079,604	1,858,000
Net Avail for d/s	15,128,288	23,513,000
Est Max d/s ($18,465,000)	Cover 0.82x	1.27x

* First year that net revenue covers d/s on all bonds. Interest on this issue capitalized until 1978. D/S until then is $12 million (excluding capitalized interest).

BOND RESERVE(S):
Prior Lien—Required ensuing 2 yr. d/s   On Hand—Required amount
Jr. Lien bonds—Required max d/s   On Hand—Required amount*
* Includes capitalized funds

DEPRECIATION RESERVE: (Or Similar)
Required $1,152,000   On Hand $ in excess of requirement

OTHER REQUIRED RESERVES: See flow of funds

ADDITIONAL PARITY BONDS TEST: Net revenues in 12 of 18 months
prior, as adjusted by engineer for additional earnings, etc., and projected
for 6 years must equal total d/s plus lease payments plus 8 percent of gross
revenue. Bond reserves must be filled or capitalized. D/S payments on
additional bonds must be level.

CONVENANTS:
Rates—To produce revenues sufficient to cover payments required under
the bond resolution. Audits and Books XXX
Prior Lien—no provisions

FLOW OF FUNDS:
O and M (less lease payment)   1
P and I (prior lien)   2
Bond Res (prior lien)   3 (amt. equal to 24 mos. ensuing d/s)
P and I (Jr. lien)   4
Bond Reserve (Jr. lien)   5
Lease Fund   6
Contingency Fund   7
Capital Improvement Fund   8 (generally 8 percent gross revenues)
Special Reserve   (from 50 percent of surplus, balance to
                                       State of South Carolina)

EFFECT OF THE RESOLUTION: After all priority obligations have
been retired, the Expansion Bonds will become gross revenue bonds. Monies
shall then be disbursed by the Authority from the Revenue Fund in the
following order: (1) Expansion Bond Fund; (2) Lease Fund; (3) Operating
Expenses; (4) Capital Improvement Fund.

*   *   *

CASE XIV
MOTOR FUEL TAX REVENUE BONDS

NAME: $5,000,000 Clark County, Nevada, Highway Improvement
Revenue Bonds

SELLING: 12/20/72

MATURITIES: 1973 thru 1992   Callable: 1/1/83 at prem.

LEGAL OPINION: Dawson, Nagel, Sherman and Howard (Denver)

PURPOSE: Street and Highway Construction

SECURITY: Proceeds of a 2 cent motor fuel tax levied by the county and its allocation of 1 1/2 cent tax levied by the state, less administrative expenses

DEBT:

Prior Lien Bonds	$	0
Parity Lien		8,850,000
This issue		5,000,000
Total		$13,850,000

COVERAGE:

	Historical (Years Ending ...)		
	6/30/70	6/30/71	6/30/72
County 2 percent tax	$2,293,980	$2,990,752	$3,238,023
State 1 1/2 cent tax	1,363,976	1,577,400	2,091,450
Tax proceeds	3,657,956	4,568,152	5,329,473
Deductions	50,613	70,037	74,505
Net Avail for d/s	3,607,343	4,498,115	5,254,968
Est Max d/s ($1,161,832)	Cover 3.10x	3.87x	4.52x
Est Aver d/s ($1,110,090)	Cover 3.25x	4.05x	4.73x

BOND RESERVE(S):
Prior Bond issues reserves—required at max d/s on each issue. All payments are current
Required $ max. d/s—this issue   On Hand $—0—
If not filled, balance to accrue from fixed pymts over 5 years

OTHER REQUIRED RESERVES: None

ADDITIONAL PARITY BONDS TEST: Net pledged revenues in prior fiscal year equal 2.0x max. d/s on bonds outstanding and to be issued.

COVENANTS: Maintenance of rates—The 1966 Act requires that the Board of County Commissioners must determine that the funds collected pursuant to the County Motor Vehicle Fuel Tax Law (presently two cents per gallon) are sufficient to pay all bonds and securities including any proposed issues before it may secure payment of any bonds by creation of a lien upon other motor vehicle fuel taxes authorized at the time of issuance of such securities. It is the intent of the law as well as of the Board of County Commissioners of Clark County and its Regional Street and Highway Commission that at no time shall revenue bonds be outstanding in an amount which cannot be fully serviced as to both principal and interest by the proceeds of the motor vehicle fuel tax specifically imposed for the purpose of securing revenue bonds. These bonds are secured by a pledged of three and one-half cents per gallon of motor vehicle fuel taxes, revenues should always widely cover debt service costs even without growth and no additional parity securities can be issued unless the pledged revenues for the prior fiscal year meet maximum debt service requirements on the outstanding and proposed issues by at least 200 percent.

FLOW OF FUNDS: from gross receipts

Adm. Exp.	1
P and I (parity)	2
Bond Reserve	3
Surplus	4 (any lawful purpose—0 percent locked in)

*   *   *

CASE XV
STATE PARK REVENUE BONDS

NAME: $3,500,000 Department of Parks and Tourism of the State of Arkansas, State Park System Revenue Bonds, Series 1973

SELLING: 1/26/73

MATURITIES: 1974 thru 1993   Callable: 10/1/81 at prem.

LEGAL OPINION: Smith, Williams, Friday, Eldredge and Clark (Little Rock, Arkansas)

PURPOSE: Improvements to various parks in the State Park System

SECURITY: Parity lien on gross revenues of the State Parks System

DEBT:

	Prior Lien Bonds	$ 0
	Parity Lien	3,860,000
	This issue	3,500,000
	Total	$7,360,000

COVERAGE:

	Historical (Years Ending …)		Proforma or Projected
	6/30/71	6/30/72	6/30/74
Operating Revenue	$827,610	$799,124	$2,425,669
Est Aver d/s ($562,280)*	Cover 1.47x	1.42x	4.31x

* Through 1993, final maturity this issue

BOND RESERVE(S):
Parity Bonds—Single Reserve XXX
Required $ 2x aver. d/s
If not filled, balance to accrue from fixed pymts over 10 years

DEPRECIATION RESERVE: None

OTHER REQUIRED RESERVES: None

ADDITIONAL PARITY BONDS TEST: Gross revenues for the prior fiscal year must equal 2 times the average d/s on outstanding bonds combined with average d/s on bonds to be issued.

COVENANTS:
Rates—To produce gross revenues sufficient to cover annual d/s and reserve payment 1.0 times.
Proper operation XXX
Prior Lien—no provision

FLOW OF FUNDS:
P and I (parity)	1
Bond Reserve	2
O and M	3
Surplus	4 (any lawful purpose)

CASE XV—NOTES
STATE PARK REVENUE BONDS

The bonds are issued for the purpose of financing a portion of the cost of the construction of improvements to various parks in the State Parks System and paying expenses incidental thereto and to the issuance of the bonds.

Note: Bond Counsel advises that no appropriated funds are pledged for payment of the bonds, but appropriated funds not specificallly designated for other uses (such as specific capital improvements) may, at the discretion of the Department, be used as necessary for the payment of debt service.

*   *   *

CASE XVI
FOURTH LIEN LIGHT AND POWER
REVENUE AND REFUNDING BONDS

NAME: $24,000,000 Seattle, Washington, Municipal Light and Power Revenue and Refunding Bonds, 1972

SELLING: 1/25/72

MATURITIES: 1975 thru 2000

LEGAL OPINION: Preston, Thorgrimson, Starin, Ellis and Holman (Seattle)

PURPOSE: Portion of financing for 1971-76 improvement program, including refunding of short term notes.

SECURITY: Junior (apparently 4th) lien on net revenues of the facility

DEBT:
Prior Lien Bonds	$ 79,959,000	Connections:	252,351
Parity Lien	115,675,000	Total Debt Per Conn.: $870	
This issue	24,000,000		
Total	$219,634,000		

COVERAGE:

	Historical (Year Ending ...) 12/31/70	Proforma* 12/31/71
Operating Revenue	$53,425,387	$56,664,000**
Operating Expense	32,117,339	33,367,000
Net Op. Rev.	21,308,048	23,277,000
Net Other Revenue	1,584,056	1,085,000
Net Avail for d/s	22,892,104	24,362,000
Est Max d/s ($15,145,000)	Cover 1.51x	1.60x
Est Aver d/s ($11,242,000)	Cover 2.03x	2.16x

* 9 mos. actual, 3 mos. est.
** Reflects 7 percent rate increase effective 8/3/71

BOND RESERVE(S): There appears to be a single reserve for all bonds. Required $ max. d/s   On Hand $ prior requirements
Pmts. current XXX   If not filled, balance to accrue from fixed surpluses over 5 yrs

DEPRECIATION RESERVE: None

OTHER REQUIRED RESERVES: None

ADDITIONAL PARITY BONDS TEST: Average net revenues for 2 year period ending not more than 120 days prior, as adjusted for rate increases, are equal to 1.25x future max. d/s on bonds outstanding and to be issued.

COVENANTS:
Rates—To produce revenues sufficient to cover O and M, d/s and all other obligations.
Insurance no requirement* Audits and Books not required*
Proper operation XXX No Prior Lien XXX
* Although not required in the resolution these are provided

FLOW OF FUNDS:

O and M	1	
P and I (prior lien)	2	
P and I (parity)	3	
Bond Reserve	4	
Surplus	5	(8 percent of gross to ciy provided d/s, O and M, etc., are provided for. Further transfers are not precluded.) (0 percent locked in.)

CASE XVI—NOTES
FOURTH LIEN POWER AND LIGHT
REVENUE AND REFUNDING BONDS

Lien Position. Neither the fiscal agent nor the bond counsel could give us an iron clad answer, but this issue and those parity bonds issued in 1958 and subsequently are at least Fourth Lien and possibly Eight Lien. Bond counsel was unsure if each issue prior to 1958 closed out a lien position. *Moody's Municipal Manual* says "Priority, in opinion of counsel, is determined by the order of authorization and not necessarily the order of issuance."

Prior Lien bonds outstanding as of 11/30/71 were as follows:

$ 1,331M	Series	LL	1 (1948)	Final Maturity			1973
1,043M	"	LL	2 (1948)	"	"		1973
2,480M	"	LL	3 (1949)	"	"		1974
5,880M	"	LL	4 (1950)	"	"		1975
18,275M	"	LM	(1951)	"	"		1980
27,100M	"	LN	1 (1952)	"	"		1983
23,850M	"	LN	2 (1952)	"	"		1987
$79,959M							

The letter series seems to indicate an authorization and that being the case, and if Moody's is right, this issue enjoys a parity Fourth Lien on net revenues.

It is interesting to note that although Boeing is still the largest customer of the system (in 12 accounts), and with its revenue down nearly 1/3 from 1969 peak, total revenue increased slightly in 1970 and apparently would have held even in the 12 months ending 11/30/71 even had there not been a 7 percent increase effective 8/3/71. Total industrial revenue under 1970 rates accounted for only 12.7 percent of total while residential and commercial accounted for 46.1 percent and 32.8 percent respectively.

The total picture for Seattle is that of overcoming the effects of the Boeing setback. Its role as a finance, trade, commerce and manufacturing center is very little (if any) diminished.

Even after the 7 percent increase, the city's residential rates are the lowest of major systems in the Pacific Northwest and 1/2 to 1/3 of the U.S. average.

* * *

CASE XVII
STUDENT FEES AND CHARGES REVENUE BONDS

NAME: $6,485,000 Iowa State University (Ames)

SELLING: 4/13/72

MATURITIES: 1973 thru 1992   Callable: 7/1/84 at prem.

LEGAL OPINION: Chapman and Cutler (Chicago)

PURPOSE: Various capital improvements

SECURITY: All unencumbered student fees and charges and, to the extent required, the institutional income received

DEBT:

Prior Lien Bonds	$	0
Parity Lien		3,610,000
This issue		6,485,000
Total		$10,095,000

COVERAGE:

	Historical (Years Ending ...)		
	6/30/69	6/30/70	6/30/71
Pledged Fees Avail for d/s**	$7,663,820	$11,974,685*	$12,342,709
Est Max d/s ($1,088,827)	Cover 7.04x	11.00x	11.33x
Est Aver d/s ($734,741)	Cover 10.43x	16.30x	16.80x

 * Fees raised

** Does not include institutional income, which is a back-up pledge only

BOND RESERVE(S):
Required $ max. d/s
If not filled, balance to accrue from fixed pymts of 12 percent of annual d/s

OTHER REQUIRED RESERVES: None

ADDITIONAL PARITY BONDS TEST: Fees and charges in the prior fiscal year, adjusted for any changes equal 1.25x max. d/s on bonds outstanding and to be issued.

COVENANTS:
Fees and charges—To produce revenues sufficient to cover annual d/s and reserve fund payments 1.0 times.
Audits and Books XXX
Prior Lien—no provision

FLOW OF FUNDS:

P and I (parity)	1
Bond Reserve	2
Surplus	3 (University General Fund) (0 percent locked in)

APPLICATION OF BOND PROCEEDS:

Veterinary Medicine Bldg. and Equip.	$3,435,000
Steam Generating Equip.	2,300,000
General Utilities and Remodeling	400,000
Physical Education Equipment (Women)	100,000
Class Room No. 3—Equip.	250,000
BOND ISSUE	$6,485,000

CASE XVII—NOTES
STUDENT FEES AND CHARGES REVENUE BONDS

For 63 years Iowa State University of Science and Technology was called Iowa State College of Agriculture and Mechanic Arts, with its current name bestowed in 1959. This school is Iowa's Land Grant College.

It seems that A&M colleges collectively had reputations as "Cow Colleges," and as such were not prestigious enough for the Eastern Establishment. Even "college" does not have the connotation of "university," and the number of "state colleges" across the country is certainly declining.

The present coverage factor is high at 11.33x max. d/s, but can be diluted to 1.25, and is even programmed down to 2.0x, based on the past year's fee income and 10-year building program. Fortunately this being a state supported school, fee income is not an unduly large portion of total receipts.

Computation Assumptions. (Computations below are based on these):

1. That future legislatures will not make direct appropriations for any part of the construction programs.
2. That all of the construction programs will be funded with Academic Building Revenue Bonds.
3. That each issue of bonds will mature with level principal payments over a period of twenty years.
4. That all bonds will bear interest at 5 percent per annum.
5. That the entire funding for each biennium will occur on the July 1 in the middle of the biennium.
6. Without consideration for changes in rates of student fees and charges or increased enrollment.
7. Without calculation of other institutional income pledged to these bonds, if needed, and which amounted to $2,191,098 in fiscal year 1970-1971.

Maximum Principal Outstanding
    July 1, 1980 .... $53,415,000
Interest on Maximum Outstanding 2,670,750
Available Student Fees, FY 70-71 12,342,709
Max. Ann. Principal
    Due 7/1/83 .... $3,705,000   Coverage
Interest on Outstanding
    $49,329,000 7/1/83 2,466,450   6,171,450   2.00x
Avg. Principal Maturity 2,383,000
Interest on Average Principal
    Outstanding ($25,637,900) 1,281,895   3,664,895   3.36x

Supreme Court Decision

In accordance with the enactment of the General Assembly, the Board of Regents authorized the issuance and sale of an initial $1,165,000 Academic Building Revenue Bond issue for the Iowa State University of Science and Technology, which bonds were sold March 11, 1971. A test case had been brought to establish the constitutionality of the legislation and the bond issue in the District Court of Polk County, Iowa. The bond resolutions to date, as well as the resolution authorizing these bonds, provide for the pledge of all student fees and charges, including all tuition and other fees and charges collected from students attending the university as defined in the bond resolution but excluding those rentals and charges imposed and collected for revenue projects as defined in the bond resolution and pledged under the provisions of previously existing law.

The decision of the Supreme Court was broad and emphatic including, among others, the assertion that student fees and charges for the various projects may be charged even though a particular student does not use the project. In other words, the Board was affirmed in its pledge of all student fees and charges to the extent necessary to meet principal and interest and reserves. The court also affirmed the provision of the Act that such bonds would not be a charge against the state and that the student fees, tuitions, and institutional income could not be construed as state funds.

In accordance with this Act, the board has authorized and to date has sold the following bonds now outstanding:

> $11,670,000 State University of Iowa
> 3,610,000 Iowa State University
> 3,330,000 University of Northern Iowa

*   *   *

CASE XVIII
NUCLEAR POWER BONDS

NAME: $155,685,000 City of Eugene, Oregon, Trojan Nuclear Project Revenue Bonds, Series 1977

PURPOSE: To advance refund $74,145,000 Series 1971 bonds and $58,470,000 Series 1975 bonds, and to fund $10,000,000 Bond Anticipation Notes due 2/1/78.

SECURITY: Junior (second) lien on net revenues of the project. The lien is subordinate to that of the outstanding bonds of the City's Electric System.

PROJECT REVENUES: Revenues are derived from sale of power to the city's electric system and to 13 other participants through the Bonneville Power Administration Net Billing Agreement. These payments and credits began on January 1, 1974.

PROJECT OPERATIONS: The project is in commercial operation. Power generation first commenced in late December 1975, and Portland General declared May 20, 1976 as the date of Commercial Operation. Because of favorable hydro conditions in the Pacific Northwest and the availability of lower cost secondary hydro energy for purchase, it was economically prudent to postpone commercial operation until early September 1976.

During the period from September through mid-November, operation of the project was occasionally interrupted for the examination and repair of equipment, which is a common experience of new generating facilities during the early months of service. Since mid-November 1976, the project has produced dependable power within 95 percent of design capability, with a project availability exceeding 95 percent.

BOND RESERVE(S):   An amount equal to future maximum annual debt service is required to be in the account by 9/1/80. Of the required amount, 67 percent is currently on hand.

ADDITIONAL PARITY BONDS:

    a. Completion bonds may be issued without restriction. None are anticipated.

    b. Other additional bonds for purposes associated with the project may be issued without any particular tests, but with corroborating opinion of the Consulting Engineer that adequate revenues for all project purposes will be produced.

ADDITIONAL PRIOR LIEN BONDS: May be issued under earnings tests which include average of all bonds payable from the system.

OTHER ADDITIONAL BONDS: May be issued to finance generating systems other than the Trojan Projects. These bonds would be junior lien bonds in a fashion similar to the Trojan Project Bonds.

COVENANTS: The city has covenanted to fix rates and charges sufficient to pay all costs in connection with its Electric System, including debt service on Electric System Bonds, so that all Project Revenues will be available to pay project costs including debt service on the 1977 bonds. The city has also covenanted to fix rates and charges for the city's share of power from the project, which shall be sufficient to pay its share of the Operating Expenses of the project, and debt service and reserve requirements on the 1977 bonds.

CASE XVIII—NOTES
NUCLEAR POWER BONDS

Purpose. This bond issue will complete the financing of the construction and related costs of the city's share (30 percent) of the 1,130,000 Kilowatt Trojan Nuclear Electric Generating Project. The project is owned jointly with Portland General Electric Company (67 1/2 percent) and Pacific Power and Light Company (2 1/2 percent).

Withdrawal of Project Capability by the City. The city may give notice to BPA and the Project Participants that it elects to withdraw and use in its own system all or any portion of the city's or any participant's share of project capability, provided certain conditions have been met. The Net Billing Agreements provide that any notice of withdrawal by the city shall be given on or before July 1, 1977, but the Board and BPA have agreed in principle to extend the notice date to July 1, 1978, subject to the concurrence of the participants, the requirements, if any, of the National Environmental Protection Act, and the negotiation of a formal agreement satisfactory to the parties. Any such withdrawal shall take effect not earlier than July 1, 1984.

In the event of such withdrawal, the city, rather than BPA or the participants, is obligated to pay for the project capability withdrawn upon the same basis and terms as BPA or the participants under the Net Billing Arrangements. To the extent of any such withdrawal, the 1977 bonds will become payable from the revenues of the Distribution Division resulting from the sale of utility or other services by that Division, subject to the prior charge for the payment of the city's Electric System Revenue Bonds.

The city and the Consulting Engineer have concluded that the city will be able to satisfy the conditions for withdrawal, but the city has not determined whether or when or to what extent any such withdrawal shall be effected.

Commentary. Bond analysis, like economics, is a "dismal" science. A bond credit should be looked at from the perspective of what the picture looks like with the most attractive subject removed. In this case, the most attractive subject would be the Net Billing Agreement with Bonneville Power.

Assume that the city will withdraw its project capability from sale to Bonneville and the participants. As indicated earlier the source of funds will then be the net revenues of the Electric Distribution Division of the Electric System, after payment of charges for prior lien bonds.

The Electric System would have to pay the full operating and debt service costs from operation of its Electric Distribution System rather than from sales to participants (including itself) through Bonneville. This would more than likely result in a loss of surplus revenues of the Trojan Project (after O and M and debt service).

*   *   *

CASE XIX
WATER, ELECTRIC, GAS REVENUE BONDS

<u>NAME:</u> $6,500,000 Norwich, Connecticut Utility System Revenue Bonds

<u>SELLING:</u>   4/13/72

MATURITIES: 1973 thru 2000 Callable: 1/1/82 at prem.

LEGAL OPINION: Mudge, Rose, Guthrie and Alexander (New York)

PURPOSE: Improvements to the water and electric system

CAPITALIZED INTEREST: $330,200 for est. 10 months

SECURITY: Net revenues for the city's water, electric and gas system

DEBT:				Connections:	
	Prior Lien Bonds	$	0		
	Parity Lien		0	Water	8,322
	This issue	6,500,000		Elec.	15,338
	Total	$6,500,000		Gas	7,591
				Total Debt per Connection:	$208

COVERAGE:	Historical (Years Ending ...)		Proforma or Projected
	6/30/70	6/30/71	6/30/72
Operating Revenue	$5,562,835	$6,139,614	$8,370,900
Operating Expense	4,461,609	5,090,165	6,040,700
Net Op. Rev.	1,101,226	1,049,449	2,330,200
Net Other Revenue	93,193	132,161	112,900
Net Avail for d/s	1,194,419	1,181,610	2,443,100
Est Max d/s* ($660,000)	Cover 1.80x	1.79x	3.70x
Est Aver d/s ($461,550)	Cover 2.59x	2.56x	5.29x
* 1972			

BOND RESERVE(S):
Required $ max. d/s
If not filled, balance to accrue from fixed pmts over 5 years

RENEWAL AND REPLACEMENT FUND: Available for d/s XXX
Required $300,000 On Hand $—0—
Balance to accumulate from fixed payments of 5 percent of gross revenues.

OTHER REQUIRED RESERVES: None

ADDITIONAL PARITY BONDS TEST: Half of total net revenues for 24 consecutive months out of prior 30 equals 1.35x d/s on bonds outstanding and to be issued. Revenues may be adjusted for rate increases placed in effect during said period.

COVENANTS:
Rates—To produce revenues sufficient to cover O and M, d/s and other required payments at 1.0 times.

Insurance XXX   Audits and Books XXX
Proper Operation XXX
No Prior Lien XXX

FLOW OF FUNDS:
O and M	1	
P and I (parity)	2	
Bond Reserve	3	
R and R	4	
Other	5	Payments of up to 10 percent of gross revenues to General Fund
Surplus	6	(100 percent locked in)

CASE XIX—NOTES
WATER, ELECTRIC, GAS REVENUE BONDS

Other than the fact that the quality of this bond is excellent, the outstanding feature of it is the fact that it is a utility revenue bond from New England, the first of its nature we've seen.

Three other aspects stand out:

1. Capitalized interest during construction with at least 2 years history of high coverage of maximum debt service.
2. Federal participation to the tune of over 33 percent for a utility with a pro forma 1972 coverage of 3.70 times.
3. The Debt per Connection is very low for a combined water, electric and gas system.

The Official Statement does not disclose what is perceivable, the water and gas systems serve only a portion of the city. Other information is lacking about the systems, which ordinarily would be important if the cosmetics of the bond were not so admirable.

The federal grants, particularly the EDA grant, were based on an unemployment situation a few years ago. Eligibility is based on "substantial unemployment," meaning over 6 percent. (Theoretically, 6.1 percent would qualify.) It is unkonwn at this time what the unemployment level is.

Like a great portion of New England, this city lost a considerable textile industry in the 1950s. Norwich has had an influx of new industries to take up most of the slack. Among the newer industries of those listed later herein are King Seely-Thermos, Dahl Enterprises, Wakefield Industries, Atlantic Carton Corp., and, most recently, the Ohio Rubber Co.

Gas rates were increased in December 1971, reflecting an increase from the supplier, and water rates were increased on 1/1/72 to pay d/s on the portion of this issue attributable to the water system. It is the policy of the city to make all portions of the utility system self-supporting. These increases reflect in the very high pro forma coverage for 1972. Electric system revenues can pay the debt service.

The population gain between 1950 and 1960 was due to annexation. Those annexed areas apparently already were being served with water and gas.

Part IV

APPENDICES

New York State Constitutional and Statutory Provisions:
Regarding The Contracting of Debt
(Current as of 1978)

THE CONSTITUTION

State Debt

In general, but with three exceptions, voters of the state must approve debt issued by the state. The main constitutional provisions, as found in Article VII, are as follows:

Except for short term debt contracted for in anticipation of taxes and revenues, anticipation of the proceeds of authorized bonds; or debt contracted to repel invasion, suppress insurrection, defend the state in war or to suppress forest fires, no debt may be incurred unless approved by a majority vote in a general election.

Tax Anticipation Notes (TANs) and Revenue Anticipation Notes (RANs) must be repaid within one year from date of issue, from such taxes and revenue. Bond Anticipation Notes (BANs) must be paid from the proceeds of bonds within two years from date of issue, except notes issued for housing under Article 18 which shall be paid from sale of bonds within five years.

Money derived from note or bond debt may be applied only to the purpose specified in the act authorizing the debt, and no debt shall be contracted for a period longer than the probable life of the work or purpose for which it is contracted.

Except for notes and debt incurred for insurrection, etc., debt contracted by the state must be paid in equal annual installments, the first due in no longer than a year and the last no longer than 40 years. The legislature is required to annually provide appropriations for interest and principal.

First Revenues Received—Section 16. Article VII provides in part "if at any time the Legislature shall fail to make any such appropriation, the Comptroller shall set apart from the first revenues thereafter received applicable to the General Fund of the State, a sum sufficient to pay such interest and installments of principal, and shall so apply the monies thus set apart. In such circumstances, the Comptroller may be required to set aside and apply such revenues as aforesaid, at the suit of any holder of such bonds."

The following appeared in an Official Statement for an issue of bonds by the State of New York:

> The State Constitution does not provide for the contingency where such an appropriation has been made but monies are unavailable on the payment date. If the above described Constitutional provision were inapplicable in such situation, the holder of any bond could recover judgment against the State in the State Court of Claims for principal and interest due and the State Comptroller would be required to pay the judgment, after audit, and upon presentation to him of a certified copy of the judgment. Judgments against the State may not be enforced by levy and execution against property of the State and such enforcement is limited to the amount of monies appropriated by the Legislature and legally available for such purposes.

Exceptions To Voter Approval. Article VII, Section 14-provides that debt in the amount of $300,000,000 may be incurred without a referendum for elimination of railroad crossings at grade. Of this total authorization, $60 million may be for construction of state highways and parkways.

Article VII, Section 19-provides that debt in the amount of $250,000,000 may be incurred without a referendum for expansion of the state university system.

Article XVIII, Section 3-provides that debt in the amount of $300,000,000 may be incurred to make loans for low rent housing. The debt shall be called "Housing Bonds," except where issued in connection with municipal urban renewal projects, in which event the bonds are known as "Urban Renewal Bonds." Combined payments may be made nearly equal and the first installment may be as long as three years from the date of issue. The final payment may be made as long as 50 years from date of issue. Debt in excess of $300,000,000 may be authorized by a referendum.

The Constitution is silent on limits for state debt, except as outlined above.

Local Debt

In general no county, city, town, village or school district may contract debt except for its respective purposes. The debt, like that of the state, may not run longer than the probable usefulness of the object or purpose of the debt, and in no event can it run longer than 40 years. No debt can be incurred unless the faith and credit of the subdivision are pledged. (Provision is made for deductions from debt computation for self supporting bonds, or a given bond issue to the defined extent that it is self supporting).

Bond debt must be paid in annual installments, the first of which must be paid not more than 18 months after date of contraction, and no installment shall be more than 50 percent larger than the smallest prior installment. Where BANs have been issued, the first installment may be two years after contraction. Exceptions from time limits are made for water supply debt for the City of New York, and for debt incurred for rapid transit railroads and construction of docks, including land acquisition. Time periods for the foregoing purposes are 50 years and 40 years, respectively.

A new constitution in 1938 restricted the legislature from creating any new form of municipal or other corporation with power to contract debt or levy taxes or assessments. Counties or towns may, however, create improvement districts and pledge the faith and credit of the county or town on debt contracted for the purposes of the district. A recent example of this type of loan is the Suffolk County G.O. bond issues for its Southwest Sewer District.

Limitations on Local Debt. Except as especially provided elsewhere, Section 4 of Article VIII imposes the limits on local debt, expressed as a percentage of the average full valuation (generally current year and four prior years) of taxable real estate. Debt Limits:

a. the county of Nassau, 10 percent;
b. any county, other than the county of Nassau, 7 percent;
c. the city of New York, 10 percent;
d. any city, other than the city of New York, having 125,000* or more inhabitants, 9 percent;
e. any city having less than 125,000* inhabitants, excluding education purposes, 7 percent;
f. any town, 7 percent;
g. any village, 7 percent;
h. any school district which is coterminous with, or partly within or wholly within, a city having less than 125,000 (according the latest federal census) inhabitants for education purposes, 5 percent; provided, however, that such limitation may be increased in relation to indebtedness for specified objects or purposes with
   (1) the approving vote of 60 percent or more of the duly qualified voters of such school district voting on a proposition therefor submitted at a general or special election

(2) the consent of The Regents of the University of the State of New York and

(3) the consent of the state comptroller.

*In ascertaining the power of any city having less than 125,000 inhabitants to contract indebtedness, indebtedness contracted by such city for education purposes if any shall be excluded. Such indebtedness so excluded shall be included in ascertaining the power of a school district which is coterminous with, or partly within, or wholly within, such city of contract indebtedness.

The following are excluded from computation of debt:

1. Debt incurred for purposes other than financing capital improvements which matures in one of two fiscal years immediately after the year of issue, and tax and revenue anticipation notes. Notes and their renewals which are not retired within five years of date of original issue are not excluded.
2. Debt for water supply purposes.
3. Self-supporting debt, to the extent self-supporting, provided that net revenues of the improvement or service are at least 25 percent of debt service.
4. Bonds issued for pension fund payments where the pension system is not current on an actuarial basis.
5. Bonds issued between 1962 and 1983 for sanitary sewage treatment if approved by the state comptroller.

Special exclusions from debt computation are made for debt contracted for improvements to be paid from special assessments (to the extent paid) for the cities of Buffalo, Rochester and Syracuse. The amounts of exclusion are $10,000,000 for Buffalo and Rochester and $5,000,000 for Syracuse.

The City of New York is also afforded some special exclusions from debt computation:

1. Debt incurred before 1910 for dock purposes, to the extent self-supporting.
2. Debt in an amount not exceeding $300,000,000 and incurred in 1928 or later for new rapid transit railroads.
3. Debt in an amount not exceeding $150,000,000 and incurred in 1950 or later for City hospitals.
4. Debt in an amount not exceeding $500,000,000 and incurred in 1952 or later for new rapid transit railroads, including extensions and interconnections between existing systems and for reconstruction and equipment of existing systems.

5. Debt for schools to the extent that debt service can be paid from $2,500,000 annually in state aid for common schools.
6. Debt in an amount not to exceed $315,000,000 for acquisition of railroads and railroad facilities, or to acquire the securities of such railroads. The city is authorized to deliver its obligations to the corporations owning the railroads or to holders of the securities of the corporations owning the railroads.*
7. Debt incurred for transit purposes to the extent self-supporting.
   * This would amount to an exchange of bonds for ownership of railroads rather than issuance of debt through the bond market-explanation supplied.

In general, where exclusions from debt are conditional, i.e., based on formulae, etc., the legislature is required to prescribe the method and terms and conditions by which the computations are made. In some cases the determination is conclusive if made or approved by the state comptroller. Section 12 of Article VII recites as follows:

> It shall be the duty of the legislature, subject to the provisions of this constitution, to restrict the power of taxation, assessment, borrowing money, contracting indebtedness, and loaning the credit of counties, cities, towns and villages so as to prevent abuses in taxation and assessments and in contracting of indebtedness by them. Nothing in this article shall be construed to prevent the legislature from further restricting the powers herein specified of any county, city, town, village or school district to contract indebtedness or to levy taxes on real estate. *The legislature shall not, however, restrict the power to levy taxes on real estate for the payment of interest on or principal of indebtedness theretofore contracted* (emphasis added).

STATE AND LOCAL FINANCE LAWS

State Finance

The State Finance Law is by and large repetitive of the constitution insofar as dealing with debt. It does in addition, though, provide sharper definition of some of the the the constitutional provisions.

An important aspect of note financing is provided in Article V, Section 55, relative to state short term debt, which states that "so much of the anticipated taxes and revenues from which the debt is to be paid are *pledged* for that purpose" (emphasis added).

Section 58 provides that bonds for the state university shall be payable within 30 years. Section 59 limits grade crossing bonds to 40 years. Section 61 takes up the problem of "probable life" of a work or purpose and defines such probable life by categories. Examples are: road or street improvements have a probable life of five years, certain classes of buildings—15 to 30 years, land acquisition—30 years and public housing—50 years.

Most of the other content of the State Finance Law that does not repeat the constitution deals with the mechanics of contracting debt and sale of bonds.

Local Finance

The Local Finance Law, like the State Finance Law, repeats a great deal of the constitution.

Article I, Section 2 deals with definitions, including, political subdivisions and valuations of taxable real property (real estate). The following definitions are listed for subdivisions:

1. The term "municipality" shall mean a county, city, town or village.
2. The term "school district" shall mean any school district except the school districts of the cities of New York, Buffalo, Rochester, Syracuse and Yonkers.

2-a. The term "city school district" shall mean the city school district of a city having less than 125,000 inhabitants according to the latest federal census.

2-b. The term "school district in a city" shall mean any school district which is coterminous with, or partly within, or wholly within, a city having less than 125,000 inhabitants, according to the latest federal census.

3. The term "district corporation" shall mean
    (a) A fire district
    (b) A river improvement, river regulating or drainage district established by or under the supervision of the department of conservation, or
    (c) Any other territorial division of the state, other than a municipality or a school district, which as of December 31, 1938,* possessed the power to:
        (1) Contract indebtedness in its own name, and
        (2) Levy taxes or benefit assessments upon real estate or require the levy of such taxes or assessments.

* Note—as indicated earlier the 1938 constitution forbids the creation of any new form of municipal or other corporation with the power to contract debt and levy taxes.

Section 20 defines evidences of indebtedness which may be issued. The types are denominated as follows:

1. Serial bonds.
2. Sinking fund bonds or corporate stock.
3. Bond anticipation notes.
4. Tax anticipation notes.
5. Revenue anticipation notes.
6. Capital notes.
7. Budget notes.
8. Urban renewal notes.

Serial bonds must mature in annual installments. The first installment must mature not later than 18 months after the date of such bonds, or two years after the date of the first BANs issued in anticipation of the bonds. This first installment may be delayed up to five years if systematic payment on the BANs is made from a source other than bond proceeds, or up to six years for housing and urban renewal bonds.

An exception is made in the case of BANs issued to finance assessable improvements (curbs, gutters, sidewalks, etc.). There is no limit as to the number of note renewals, but the maturity of the last renewal must be no longer than the period of probable usefulness of the project, computed from the date of completion.

Sinking Fund Bonds—The authorization for municipalities to issue sinking fund bonds is limited to the City of New York and such bonds may be called "corporate stock."

Provision For Payment of Notes. Bond Anticipation Notes (BANs). These notes may be issued whenever bonds are authorized, and the proceeds can be expended only for the same purpose as bonds. The notes must mature within one year from date of issue, and may be renewed or "rolled over" for up to an additional year, but not to exceed two years from date of issue of the original notes. As indicated above when certain conditions are met the renewals may extend to five years.

BANs cannot be issued in an amount exceeding the par value of the bonds they anticipate.

BANs must be paid from the proceeds of the sale of the anticipated bonds. If such bonds are not sold the notes must be paid from any unencumbered balance in any fund which may be applied thereto, or, by a budgetary appropriation. BANs may be paid prior to the sale of bonds from any monies which are lawfully available.

Tax Anticipation Notes (TANs). These notes may be issued by any municipality, school district, or district corporation other than a fire district. TANs may be issued during, and within, ten days prior to commencement of a fiscal year in anticipation of collections of taxes or assessments levied, or in any fiscal year in anticipation of the collection of taxes or assessments levied for any of the four preceding fiscal years.

In anticipation of taxes or assessments to be levied TANs cannot be levied, prior to adoption of an annual budget, in an amount in excess of the combination of (a) debt service on any debt which comes due in the first four months of the current fiscal year, and (b) 35 percent of the difference between the amount of its annual budget for the preceding fiscal year and the amount provided therein for debt service. Taxes and assessments cannot be reduced to an amount less than the amount of outstanding notes issued against taxes to be levied.

Otherwise, in the case of notes issued against taxes and assessments levied, the notes cannot be issued in an amount greater than the uncollected taxes at the time of borrowing less (a) the amount of outstanding notes against such taxes, and (b) the amount offset for anticipated deficiencies in collections.

TANs must mature within one year from date of issue but may be renewed for one year periods which in total cannot exceed five years after the close of the fiscal year for which the taxes and assessments were anticipated.

Note: A serious structural defect is found in paragraph (e), Section 24.00 of the Local Finance Law, regarding TANs. If a municipality, (or district) does not make a budgetary appropriation for redemption of the notes it is required to set the collections of the anticipated taxes or assessments into a special bank account to be used only for the payment of the notes. If an appropriation is made, payment into a special account is not required, and the collections may be used in the manner provided by law. In the absence of any provision of law the proceeds shall be treated as surplus monies for the fiscal year.

Under the State Finance Law, the collections of anticipated taxes and revenues are pledged to the respective notes issued by the state.

A renewal of a TAN cannot be made in an amount in excess of the remaining uncollected amount of taxes or assessments at the time of renewal, nor can a renewal be in an amount in excess of the original amount.

TANs may be issued in anticipation of special assessments to pay the cost of capital improvements. The assessments may be in one installment or in several annual installments.

Revenue Anticipation Notes (RANs). TAN and RAN provisions are, as seen, very similar, including the structural weakness mentioned under TANs. In general we shall use "revenue" to mean all sources of receipts except real estate taxes, although in the RAN section of the Law "taxes" is defined as taxes other than on real estate.

RANs may be issued in anticipation of collection of revenue, provided that each note shall be issued only against a specific type of revenue, or for renewal of a note. RANs may be issued during any fiscal year in which the revenue is anticipated, except that a school district may issue notes during the two weeks prior to such fiscal year. An exception is New York City, which may issue notes against aggregate revenues.

The proceeds of RANs must be used for meeting expenditures payable from the anticipated revenue, or for redemption of notes to be renewed. Maturity and renewal provisions are the same as for TANs, except that final maturity can be no longer than the end of the second fiscal year after the year of issue.

A single RAN issue may combine all or some revenues but the note resolution must specify the amount chargeable against each specific type of revenue.

Capital Notes. These are seldom, if ever, seen in the market, and are more than likely placed with a local bank. These notes must be paid from taxes or assessments levied or to be levied in the fiscal year in which they mature. The notes may be issued to finance purposes for which bonds may be issued. They may be renewed from time to time but final maturity generally must be no later than the last day of the second fiscal year succeeding the year of issue.

At least half of the amount of the notes must mature in the first fiscal year after the year of issuance, unless they are authorized in a fiscal year at a time subsequent to the date of adoption of the next year's budget.

The capital notes are not described as being related to a specific source of funds, thus they do not enjoy the distinction of being identified as CANs.

Budget Notes. These like capital notes, are seldom, if ever, seen in the market. Also like capital notes they do not anticipate any specific source of funds, otherwise they might be identified as BUDGANs. Budget notes may be issued by a municipality or district (which adopts a budget) during any fiscal year for expenditures for which no provision (or insufficient provision) is made in the budget. Budget notes are also authorized to be issued for any unforeseeable emergency during a fiscal year for which no provision, or insufficient provision, was made in the budget. The amount of notes that can be issued is tied to the size of the budget, except that a county may issue notes in an unlimited amount for apprehension and prosecution of persons charged with commissions of a crime.

Budget notes may be paid from taxes or assessments levied for the fiscal year in which they mature and may be renewed but with final maturity no later than the end of the fiscal year after the year of issuance.

Urban Renewal Notes. These notes are basically the same as RANs. Initially the notes have a seven year maximum maturity, but they can be renewed indefinitely, usually a year at a turn, by a special act of the legislature. Approval by the state comptroller and the Division of Housing and Urban Renewal is required.

Referenda. The local finance law deals with a mandatory referendum or a permissive referendum. A mandatory referendum is one in which purpose and amount of a debt issue must be approved by a majority of voters at a general or special election. A permissive referendum is one where a referendum may be petitioned for if a required number of qualified voters sign the petition. The question in the referendum would be to approve a resolution passed by the governing body to authorize debt.

The local finance law deals with each type of municipality separately insofar as referenda on debt is concerned.

Counties—except for Westchester County, no referendum is required although a resolution for a housing bond issue could be subject to a permissive referendum. In Westchester County an amount of debt exceeding $5,000,000 must be approved at a general or special election, except bonds issued for sanitary sewers, solid waste disposal or hospitals.

Cities—bond or note resolutions are not subject to referendum. A city may pass a local law requiring referendum.

Towns—except as noted, towns generally must submit a bond resolution to a permissive referendum. Exceptions are road bonds with final maturity no longer than five years, street or highway improvements through a town with part of the cost paid by the county or state, and for payment of judgments.

Villages—may pass bond resolutions subject to a permissive referendum with the same exception as towns. Additional exceptions are granted where the cost is payable primarily from special assessments against benefited property, and where sewage treatment facilities are required by the state commissioner of health.

School District—a vote at a regular or special election is required in a non-city school district. Included in the proposal must be a tax to be collected in installments. In certain city school districts specific exceptions are granted.

Fire District and Other Districts—in general voter approval is required of the bond resolution.

Bonds for Pensions. The purpose of such bonds is "to place such pension or retirement system or fund on a solvent basis." A municipality must submit certain data to the state insurance superintendent and request a certificate ascertaining the amount of bonds which may be issued. Presumably the law anticipated a one shot borrowing.

Many observers are of the opinion that debt incurred under this section is a very significant part of the burgeoning debt, and its cost, that rose to be such a large portion of budget expenditures for the City of New York.

Whether or not New York City was financing all of its annual contribution requirements in this fashion may be difficult to ascertain. To whatever extent, there were short term benefits to be derived in addition to the fact that the bonds are excludable from debt computation. The annual tax required to provide current requirements might fall under tax rate limits, but bonds secured by the faith and credit of the municipality are backed by unlimited taxes.

Debt Limits. The Local Finance Law repeats the constitution almost verbatim. In addition it defined the debt limit for school districts not in a city (see section of definitions) and fire districts.

Non-city school district debt is limited to 10 percent of full valuation. Fire districts are limited to 3 percent of full valuation except that a five percent limit may be approved by a two-thirds vote at a referendum.

Exclusions From Debt. The Law generally describes the same exclusions as the constitution, and appears to add some which presumably are not in conflict with the senior document. Obvious offsets are sinking fund assets, cash on hand for debts and appropriations for debts.

The Albany Mall G.O. debt of Albany County is excludable because the bonds are payable in the first instance from appropriations made by the State for such purpose.

Probable Usefulness. As described in the Local Finance Law, with definite maximum time periods for categories of purpose. "A vehicle propelled by any power other than muscular power" has a probable usefulness of five years, whereas the usefulness of a muscular powered vehicle is not defined. A tax map is good for ten years. Planning for future capital improvements is good for three years; OTB equipment is good for ten years; electric power plants—30 years; rapid transit new facilities—40 years.

School Bond Protection. Section 99-b of the State Finance Law provides that if a city, city school district or school district defaults on its debt issued for school purposes, the state comptroller shall, subject to certain procedures and verification, withhold the default amount from state aid for schools to the issuer and remit the amount direct to the pay agent. If the state aid payment is insufficient he shall withhold from succeeding aid payments.

The state covenants that it will not repeal this section nor amend it so as to impair bondholder rights, although the continuance of state aid to any city, city school district or school district is not required under this section.

State Guarantee of Authority Obligation. The State Constitution provides that the State is generally prohibited from becoming liable on the obligations of public corporations (including Authorities) or loaning its credit to public corporations. However pursuant to Constitutional amendments, the Legislature has provided for a guarantee by the State of certain bonds of the Thruway Authority, the Job Development Authority and the Port Authority of New York and New Jersey. An aggregate of $526 million of guaranteed bonds of these Authorities was outstanding as of March 31, 1976.

The State will be called upon to make payments to the holders of such guaranteed bonds and notes of the Authorities if the revenues derived by such Authorities from their operations are inadequate to meet debt service requirements on any guaranteed notes or bonds. There has been no indication that such Authorities will be unable to meet debt service requirements with respect to the guaranteed bonds and notes.

CONSTITUTION AND FINANCE LAWS: WEAKNESSES AND STRENGTHS

Constitution

State Debt

Weaknesses

1. But for the three exceptions listed there is no limitation on debt amount.
2. Under those three exceptions a substantial amount of debt may be contracted.
3. There are no protections against escape devices which circumvent the requirements of voter approval (e.g., agencies, authorities, leases).

Strengths

1. Referring to (1) above, although there is no constitutional limit on the amount of debt that may be contracted, the fact that voter approval is required puts brakes on incurring debt for which the faith and credit, and General Fund, may be pledged and obligated.

2. Debt cannot be contracted for a period of time in excess of that probable life of a project or purpose.
3. Debt must be paid in equal annual installments, the first due within a year. This tends to retire total debt quicker than in patterns usually seen, and total annual principal and interest payments always are on a declining schedule over the life of the debt. No "balloon payments."
4. Bond proceeds cannot be frittered away for current expenses (New York City avoided this restriction).
5. First monies received if funds are not appropriated. (This assumes that there is no contest between providers of "essential" state services (i.e., state employees) and bondholders if funds are not adequate.
6. There is no provision for renewal of short term debt contracted by TANs or RANs.
7. BANs, except for housing, must be repaid from bond sale proceeds within two-years, with no renewal provision.

Local Debt

Weaknesses

1. There is no requirement that unlimited taxes be pledged to pay debt. This may be, and usually is, provided in a bond resolution, or other document relative to the particular debt, and has probably been imposed by the market.
2. There are exclusions from debt limit computations.
3. Provision for pension fund borrowing could lead to (and may have already led to) abuse of privilege.
4. Counties, Cities, villages and towns can contract for debt without a mandatory referendum.

Strengths

1. The faith and credit of municipalities must be pledged.
2. Debt limits are established.
3. Borrowing that is excluded from debt limits, even though the faith and credit are pledged, must by and large be demonstrably fully, or partly, self-supporting from special revenues.
4. Debt cannot extend past the probable life of the project or purpose.
5. Debt must be paid in annual installments. Though not equal, as with state debt, the installments are limited as to disparity in size, thus no "balloon" payments.
6. Huge amounts of overlapping debt are precluded by the 1938 constitution which forbids the creation of new forms of municipal corporations.

State and Local Finance Laws

State Finance Law

Weaknesses

1. There are no sections of the State Finance Law that establish any particular weaknesses. Weaknesses arise from the creation of certain kinds of agencies under other laws.

Strengths

1. In the case of short term debt the anticipated revenues are pledged.
2. "Probable" lives are defined.

Local Finance Law

Weaknesses

1. Limits for BANs are set so that for smaller communities the limits are inordinately high.
2. TANs-final maturity of these notes can be extended to five years.
3. Anticipated taxes or other revenues are not specifically pledged to the TANs or RANs issued.
4. TANs and RANs generally should be paid in the budget year of issuance and should be limited to a fixed ratio, less than 100 percent, of the anticipated receipts in that budget year.
5. Debt for counties, cities, towns and villages generally is not subject to voter approval at a mandatory referendum.
6. No provision required of pledge of unlimited taxes.

Strengths

1. "Probable Life" is defined.
2. Short term debt in the form of TANs and RANs cannot exceed the total amount of anticipated receipts.
3. Renewals of TANs and RANs are limited to the uncollected portion of anticipated receipts.
4. Withholding of state aid for school purposes upon default of school bonds.

THE CREDIT OF THE STATE OF NEW YORK AND POLITICAL SUBDIVISIONS

Without taking sides in the argument of whether or not the State should have come to the aid of the City of New York, a number of facts must be taken into consideration regarding the relationship between the City and state.

1. New York City though not the seat of government of the State, is the capitol city, and the capital city of the State.
2. The City, though not a creation of the State (antedating it by many years), except perhaps in the consolidation of the five boroughs, is however, an instrumentality of the State, and by and large has only those powers granted to it by the State.
3. The economic well being of the State itself, and of a great many other political subdivisions is dependent on the well being of the City.
4. Nearly half the population of the State lives in the City.

Within the confines of its constitution and the federal constitution, New York state, like any other state, is a "sovereign" government. It may do just about anything not specifically prohibited in either of the two Magna Chartas to which it is subject. Through actions of its elected representatives the State took whatever action it deemed (wisely or unwisely) necessary in 1975 to prevent New York City from defaulting and/or being forced into bankruptcy.

The state provides a large portion of the revenues of all its political subdivisions. The disbursement of funds to these subdivisions does not always match the calendar as to time of receipt of taxes and other monies by the State. Part of the monumental effort of the State for the City consisted of advance payment of formula aid funds under already existing municipal aid programs. This action resulted in a drastic change in the normal pattern of cash flow of the State. In order to maintain the flow of aids funds to counties, cities, towns, school districts, etc., the State sought to borrow in the marketplace money which under the constitution and statutes has to be repaid from anticipated taxes or other receipts.

Market psychology nearly up-ended this cash flow, causing at the very least a great deal of pecuniary embarrassment.

Investors were at no time advised that payment of principal and interest on bonds of the State was in jeopardy and there is no publicly known evidence that such was the case. The apprehension concerning the solvency of the State was primarily a derivative of the calculus of a market scare caused by UDC and New York City.

The ebb of the tide of fear was demonstrated in the fact that two of the largest banks in the midwest and on the west coast were part of the management group of the syndicate that recently bought over $3 billion in state tax and revenue anticipation notes. It must be repeated that the State is relatively sovereign in the manner in which it may raise funds to meet its obligations.

True, the State has lost population work force, industry, jobs and revenue generated by an economy which has perhaps "topped out." True, it must bring its budget into alignment with the realities of socio-economics, but a slowdown, or even a decline in economic activity is not in itself a disaster.

POLITICAL SUBDIVISIONS

Counties are the basic subdivisions of the State, and are in any state the instrument which brings state law to the local level. In New York, most counties are of some consequence in size, and because of size will have a diversity of tax base and economy. Except in metropolitan areas most counties will have a most important element of strength of tax base-agriculture. Those heavily forested counties may have lumber or other forest products in place of agriculture. The 20 million people in the New York Metropolitan area are availing themselves, more and more, of outdoor recreation. The facilities to accommodate those 20 million people are located in counties away from the metropolis.

Towns, (or Townships) are not the six mile square areas on the map, located by number east or west of a principal meridian (longitude line) and north of another line. (This geographical grid arose from the Northwest Ordinance.) In states from Pennsylvania and North they are the subdivisions of pre-1776 counties, and the boundaries generally follow hills and ridges, or stream beds.

Like a county, away from a metropolitan area, they may be large enough to include agricultural or other natural resources as part of the tax and economic base. The most important thing to remember about a town borrower is that like a school district they receive 100 percent of their tax levies through the county, except in Westchester County.

Cities and villages are difficult to categorize. Needless to say, the larger they are, the more diverse they are likely to be. They may have yet undeveloped land within their boundaries and could still appear frequently in the market. The smaller units are mature, and may even be on decline. Like senior citizens they are not likely to be borrowers, and because of constitutional requirements on repayment of debt they probably have only a small debt that is being retired in orderly fashion.

A County seat city will almost always have a reason for continued existence. This city being a seat of government will have a certain stability of employment for that reason and is likely to attract and hold commercial enterprises.

Until recent years, when we've seen a proliferation of bond purposes we never thought of 25 years ago, the largest single purpose of debt issued by political subdivisions throughout the nation was that of education. New York School Districts were the most frequently seen borrowers in the market among local governments.

Population growth in urban areas, and consolidation of school systems in rural areas, necessitated large scale construction of new schools and issuance of school bonds. School districts, other than city school districts or in Westchester County, receive 100 percent of their tax levies from their respective counties. The reason for this is that school districts lack enforcement powers on tax liens.

Many states stand four-square behind their systems and New York is one of the strongest supporters. State aids are paid to districts for operating expenses-and-to help retire debt. An outstanding feature of New York state bonds is that if a borrower defaults the State comptroller is required, under certain conditions to withhold the required amount from the next state payments and remit directly to the pay agent.

As mentioned in discussing the State, a large portion of the total receipts of local subdivisions, except villages comes from the State. Over half of state general fund disbursements were for local assistance in fiscal 1976. In a given year, such as the last two, it may be debated as to whether this source of funds is a strength or a weakness for local subdivisions. If it is a strength a school is a best buy—if a weakness a village bond may be the best.

But remember, behind a general obligation bond is the faith and credit of a local subdivision, including its own taxing power. A categorical rejection of any kind of local unit is baseless. New disclosure rules for municipal borrowers make credit appraisal more tedious, but at the same time more accurate. When in doubt, buy schools. A medium grade school bond may be located in a high grade county. As a matter of policy, Standard and Poors rates any New York School Bond as an "A" credit.

NEW YORK STATE AND LOCAL DEBT: STRENGTHS AND WEAKNESSES OF ISSUERS

I. State Credit

    Weaknesses

    1. Comparatively high per capita direct and indirect debt
    2. High amount of potential liability thru "moral obligation"
    3. High amount of lease and guaranteed debt
    4. Wealth of state leveling off

Strengths

1. Still wealthy
2. Diverse economy
3. N.Y.C. still one of the financial capitals of the world—many benefits to state
4. Direct debt—rapid retirement
5. Direct debt—needs voter approval
6. No renewals of short term debt

II. Local Credits

A. Counties

Weaknesses

1. Can issue bonds without mandatory referendum
2. Can contract direct G.O. debt for districts
3. Must absorb tax delinquencies of towns and school districts

Strengths

1. Usually diverse economic and tax base
2. Limited purposes for debt
3. Limited amounts of debt
4. Orderly retirement of debt
5. Not frequent borrowers
6. Considerable amount of "outside money coming in," i.e., state and federal aids

B. Cities

Weaknesses

1. Can issue debt without mandatory referendum
2. Old small city can easily lose population and industry to suburban areas
3. Small cities may have single or few industries

Strengths

1. Still are overall business hubs
2. Limited purposes of debt
3. Limited amounts for debt
4. Orderly retirement of debt
5. Many cities are county seats of government, economic stability

    6.   Large number of taxpayers in given area

    7.   Because of compactness of population may be served by investor owned utilities thus minimizing debt purposes.

C. Towns

Weaknesses

No mandatory referendum for some debt

Strengths

    1.   Permissive referendum for most debt, (better than no referendum)

    2.   Limited purposes of debt

    3.   Limited amounts of debt

    4.   Orderly retirement of debt

    5.   Away from large urban areas, towns may be the recipient of industries and population moving from cities

    6.   100 percent tax collection through county

    7.   May have agricultural as well as residential and commercial tax and economic base

D. Villages

Weaknesses

    1.   Responsible for its own tax collections

    2.   Limited size (five square miles) limits growth of tax and economic base

    3.   Small state aids—(could be blessing—not dependent on outside sources)

    4.   No mandatory referendum

Strengths

    1.   Bond resolution subject to petition and permissive referendum

    2.   Limited purposes of debt

    3.   Limited amounts of debt

    4.   Orderly retirement of debt

Villages—note: Although categorically there are no meaningful strengths vis-à-vis weaknesses for villages it must be said that this does not put them way down on a rung of the ladder.

An analyst or investor appraises the bonds of a village on more than anything else, the basis of the community profile, and the usual financial statement. The Village of Scarsdale, for instance, ranks as a triple A credit by Moody's.

    E.   School Districts—Weaknesses

        School districts as such do not have weak characteristics

        Strengths

1. Mandatory referendum for debt
2. Purpose limit for debt
3. Orderly retirement of debt
4. 100 percent tax collections in most districts
5. Back up by witholding, and payment from, state aids
6. Constitution requires state support
7. Direct aid for capital construction

Analytical Checklist:

Hospital Revenue Bonds
(to be used in conjunction with the revenue bond checklist)

Issuer: _____

Hospital: _____

Amount: _____

Maturities—Serials: _____ Terms: _____

Purpose:

    New Construction: _____ Addition: _____

    Replacement: _____ Remodeling: _____

    General Description: _____

Construction Period: _____

Security: _____

Underwriter: _____

Feasibility Consultant: _____ Study Date: _____

Management Consultants: _____

Loan Proceeds

    Amounts $ _____

    Construction and Related $ _____

    Capitalized Interest $ _____ Months _____

    Capitalized Bond Reserve $ _____

    Retire Existing Debt $ _____

    Legal and Printing $ _____

    Bond Discount $ _____

    Other: _____

Hospital Equity: Existing Facility Funded By

    G.O. Bonds: _____

    Federal and State Grants: _____

    Earnings Accumulations: _____

Prior Lien Bonds: _____

Parity Lien Bonds: _____

Tax Levies: _____

Donations: _____

Other: _____

New Building Program Financing

Federal: _____

State: _____

G.O./Revenue Bonds: _____

Funds to be Generated*: _____

Other Money: _____

Local Fund Drive:

Amount to be Raised: _____

Time Period: _____

Cash on Hand: _____

Pledged on Hand: _____

Pledged Acceptable as Bank Loan Callteral? _____

Bed and Service Information

Number Now: _____ No. to be Added: _____

Number to be Replaced: _____ New Additions: _____

Total Beds: _____ Debt/Bed: _____

Bed Need Determined by Whom: _____

Currently Available: _____ Currently Needed: _____

Total "Approved": _____

"Approved" After Construction: _____

Present Service Area Bed Need: _____

Projected Bed Need in Projected Service Area: _____

Competition

Name	Distance	No. of Beds	Occupancy	Rate	Market Share
____	____	____	____	____	____
____	____	____	____	____	____
____	____	____	____	____	____

State Licensing and/or Regional Planning

State License to Operate: _____

Certificate of Need State: _____

Certificate Issued? _____

Financial Factors (000's omitted as appropriate)

	Historical			Projected		
	19__	19__	19__	19__	19__	19__
Bed Available	__	__	__	__	__	__
Patient Days	__	__	__	__	__	__
Pecent Occupancy	__	__	__	__	__	__
Gross Revenue	$ __	__	__	__	__	__
Revenue less Allowance, etc.	$ __	__	__	__	__	__
Operating expense	$ __	__	__	__	__	__
Net Operations Revenue	$ __	__	__	__	__	__
Depreciation and Interest	__	__	__	__	__	__
Per Patient Day						
Gross Revenue	__	__	__	__	__	__
Less Allowance	__	__	__	__	__	__
Operating Expense	__	__	__	__	__	__
Net Revenue	__	__	__	__	__	__
Maximum d/s	$ __	__	__	__	__	__
Maximum d/s P.P.D.	__	__	__			

Revenue Source

Medicare: _____ Medicaid: _____

Blue Cross: _____ Private Ins.: _____

Private Pay: _____ Other: _____

Hospital Organization and Management

Owner: _____ Proprietory/Non-Profit: _____

Operator: _____

  "Municipal" Hospital Board: _____

  Non-Profit Organization: _____

  Further Description: _____

Board:

  Who Names Members: _____

  Terms of Office: _____

Accreditation

Joint Commission: _____ A.H.A. _____

A.M.A. _____ Amer. College Surgeons: _____

Other: _____

Associations

_____
_____
_____
_____

Medical Staff

No. of Doctors: _____ Average Age: _____ Beds/Doctor _____
Active Doctors: _____ Average Age: _____ Percent Adms. _____
Diversity of Specialities/Services: _____
Recruitment Program: _____ Goal: _____
Certification of Doctors: _____
_____

Nursing Staff: _____ Nurses/Bed: _____
_____

Labor-Management-Organization/Relations: _____
_____

Other Comments: _____
_____
_____

Other Services Information

_____
_____
_____
_____

Primary Service Area

Type: Rural _____ County Seat/Capital _____
       Urban _____ Blue Collar _____
       Suburban _____ White Collar _____
       Agriculture _____ Manufac. _____ Mixed _____

Location and General Description

Distribution of Employment
   Manufacturing _____ % Percent Service _____ %
   Retail/Wholesale _____ % Government _____ %
   Unemployment _____ % U.S. _____ %
   Per Capita Income $ _____
   Median Family Income $ _____

Major Employers:

Name	Type	No. Employees
_____	_____	_____
_____	_____	_____
_____	_____	_____
_____	_____	_____
_____	_____	_____
_____	_____	_____
_____	_____	_____
_____	_____	_____

Community Profile

Type: Rural _____ County Seat/Capital _____
      Urban _____ Blue Collar _____
      Suburban _____ White Collar_____
      Agriculture _____ Manuf. _____ Other _____

Distribution of Employment
  Manufacturing _____ % Percent Service _____ %
  Retail/Wholesale _____ % Government _____ %
  Unemployment _____ % U.S. _____ %

Per Capital Income:
  Median Family Income $ _____ state _____
  Median Home Value $ _____
  Percent Owner Occupied _____ %

Distribution of Taxable Property:
  Residential _____ % Industrial _____ %
  Commercial _____ % RR/Utility _____ %

Appendix III

Documents and Other Requirements for Tax-Exempt Lease* Obligations**

1. The credit of municipal lessee must be reviewed.
2. Lease payments should not pass through any intermediary but should be made directly to Paying Agent or Trustee bank.
3. Lease payments must be unconditional and not subject to counterclaims or set-off.
4. Equipment to be financed must be determined by document to be necessary and competitive in price.
5. A purchase contract providing for immediate passage of title is preferred over a lease.
6. A Lease should provide passage of title on final payment.
7. The term of the agreement should be shorter in term than the useful life of financed equipment.
8. A no substitution clause is preferred.
9. Statutory authorization for entering into a lease or contract must be documented.
10. The agreement should provide for timely payment of rental, preferably at beginning of lessee's fiscal year.
11. The lessee must agree to maintain equipment and provide full insurance coverage during lease term.
12. The lessee must covenant to exercise maximum effort to obtain necessary appropriations, and to include provision for necessary payments in its budget.

13. A legal opinion on authorization of lease and bond counsel's opinion on tax status of obligations are necessary.
14. Retention of title by the purchaser under a contract must be conditioned on meeting the terms of the agreement.
15. A security interest in the equipment should be established for holders of participation certificates.

* "Lease" also means Installment Purchase Contract
** To be used in conjunction with General Obligation Check List

Appendix IV

City of Chicago
Water Revenue Certificates:
Candidate for Upgrade Aaa Quality?*

There has been a water system operating in Chicago since 1842, and since 1909 the system has been serving a growing community of suburbs. Chicago's water system boasts the largest and second largest water filtration plants in the world, eleven water pumping stations, and a distribution network comprised of 72.6 miles of water supply tunnels and over 4,150 miles of water mains. Chicago's water system can meet an hourly load equal to nearly 2.5 billion gallons per day. The 1973 average load for the water system was 1.04 billion gallons per day or approximately 34 percent of system pumping capacity. Maximum daily load in 1973 was 1.75 billion gallons, 58 percent of pumping capacity.

In conformity with the provisions of the Sanitary District Act of 1889, the City of Chicago is required to furnish water to any incorporated suburban community located within the Metropolitan Sanitary District of Greater Chicago requesting service, at a price no greater than the amount charged to the consumers within the City.

The City of Chicago currently supplies water to the residents of Chicago and also to residents of 74 suburban communities, two of which were added in 1974. Another 45 suburbs are in various stages of negotiation.

The Chicago Metropolitan Area is growing, especially the former fringe suburban areas (25 to 35 miles from the city limits). With some modifications to the existing plant, the City of Chicago could supply water at the city limits to meet the needs of most of this area at a price which would be mutually advantageous to the City and the suburban users.

In 1957 the Illinois State Legislature passed an amendment to the 1889 Sanitary District ordinance which enables Chicago to provide water service 35 miles from the city limits. In support of this, a planning study entitled "Report upon Adequate Water Supply for the Chicago Metropolitan Area 1969 to 2000," by Alvord, Burdick & Howson was prepared. The plan evaluated the Water System and its adequacy was reviewed as to Lake Intake Tunnels, Filtration Plants, Clear Water Storage, Pumping Stations, Land Tunnel System, and Distribution System. In general, it was determined that the Chicago Water System with relatively minor modification has sufficient capacity to serve the growing area outside of the City.

The Chicago Water System's great capacity, unlike most water systems, does not rely on reservoirs. By the addition of finished water reservoirs, the System would be capable of minimizing the effect of peak pumpage hours by drawing from these reservoirs during the peak hours. Perhaps the most important factor increasing the desirability of Chicago water is that many suburban areas are faced with an increasing water problem as the ground water table drops and well water becomes more expensive to obtain. A further expense for the consumer in many suburban areas is the purchase of chemical softeners and additives. The realities of the situation indicate that Chicago's Water System will provide the most economical source for tomorrow's water user.

The Chicago Water System currently serves over 4,500,000 people. Population estimates for the year 2000 indicate there will be over 9.16 million people in this area of which the majority could be furnished water from the Chicago Water System.

A key factor in evaluating the Chicago Water System is not only the quantity but also the quality of the water supplied. The results of a two month study released July 9, 1973, by the U.S. Environmental Protection Agency and the National Sanitation Foundation of Ann Arbor, Michigan, stated that Chicago Metropolitan Area citizens receive consistently highest quality water.

While Chicago's water is of consistently high quality, it remains low in cost. In a study made by the consulting firm of Alvord, Burdick & Howson in April, 1973, the metered rate charged in Chicago was found to be the second lowest in the twelve large cities surveyed: New York, Los Angeles, Philadelphia, Detroit, Baltimore, Louisville, Kansas City, New Orleans, Milwaukee, Dallas, Indianapolis and Chicago. Even after the rate increase in late 1973, Chicago remained the second lowest of these cities. Measured against a survey of 39 suburbs not served by the Chicago Water System but in the Chicago area, Chicago has the lowest water and sewer charges. The annual cost for 150,000 gallons of water in Chicago is $56, compared to $100-220 for communities now served, or that could be served.

Table 1. Rate Schedule Large City Water Works

Moody Rating	City	Effective Date	Rate (5/8' Meter 1,000 C.F.)
Aa	Atlanta	Na	$3.09
—	Baltimore*	6/1/72	3.60
A	CHICAGO	10/24/73	2.83
Aa	Dallas	2/1/69	5.33
Aa	Detroit	11/1/72	1.72
Aa	Kansas City	5/1/73	5.20
Aa	Los Angeles	6/2/72	4.67
Aa	Louisville	5/1/71	3.50
Aaa	Milwaukee	12/29.72	3.86
Aa	New Orleans	1/1/72	3.08
—	New York*	8/1/70	5.25
A	Philadelphia	7/1/70	2.90

* No water revenue bonds
Study by Alvord, Burdick & Howson, 10/23/74

The outstanding bonds of the City are rated A. A review of the strengths of the system, and its weaknesses reveals a potentially higher grade bond than the rating indicates. Comparisons will be drawn between the system and the Los Angeles System, because its closest comparable size and rated Aa, and the Milwaukee System, because it is on Lake Michigan and rated Aaa.

Pluses

The necessary basic ingredients for Aaa quality are prevalent in the Chicago Water System.

1. Large system—many users.
2. Low rates.
3. Low debt per connection.
4. Growth system.
5. Existing treatment facilities adequate (as improved from time to time) for well into the future.
6. Expansion primarily at the expense of additional users, i.e., extensions past city limits.
7. Half of $150 million in additions to plant in the last 10 years was financed from retained earnings.
8. Capital improvements for the next 5 years amount to an estimated $50 million, of which part could be financed from revenues.

Minuses

1. Under the current bond ordinance there are no provisions for a Bond Reserve nor for funded Depreciation.
2. Rates are not required to be set so as to provide net revenues sufficient to meet debt service on an annual basis.
3. Rates must be approved by the City Council.
4. There is no mechanism under the bond ordinance to provide surplus net revenues for small ticket improvements.
5. Failure to provide annual net revenues sufficient for debt service has resulted in a net reduction of equity (after depreciation charges) in some years.
6. Under the existing ordinance it is conceivable that surplus revenues could be transferred out of the system after retirement of the last bonds issued under the ordinance (1991-final maturity).
7. Free service amounting over $3.8 million is provided to city agencies, churches, schools, hospitals, etc., and state and county agencies.
8. The Water Department incurs the operating expenses of the sanitary sewer system, nearly $11 million in 1971. (There are no sewer service charges. Sewage treatment is afforded by the Metropolitan Sanitary District and financed by ad valorem taxes.)

We have recommended to the Water Department in the appendix attached hereto the features for the security provisions of the ordinance under which the next bond issue could be authorized.

SUMMARY

Appraisal of the underlying strengths of the Chicago Water System can be done from three viewpoints.

1. Observation of large capacity, minimal cost of expansion and abundant supply very close.
2. Comparisons of statistics with a large Aa system and a Lake Michigan Aaa system.
3. Comparison of existing Bond Ordinance security provisions.

Reviewing the debt service picture, it should be noted that the Chicago Water System has never refinanced nor missed a payment of interest on a Water Bond.

Chicago is deficient in only the Bond Ordinance. If a new Bond Ordinance is written incorporating, in substance, the recommendations in the appendix hereto attached the comparisons have to show that bonds secured under such new ordinance are much closer to Aaa quality than Aa. Many Aa bonds and some currently rated Aaa, or just upward revised to Aaa, are not as secure in all respects.

CITY OF CHICAGO WATER REVENUE CERTIFICATES CREDIT RESEARCH REPORT: RECOMMENDED BOND ORDINANCE SECURITY PROVISIONS

Flow of Funds

All monies received from sale of water and other income derived from operation of the waterworks shall be credited to the Revenue Fund and disbursed in the following order of priority:

1. To the Operating Fund to pay expenses related to operation and maintenance of the system as they become payable.
2. To the Debt Service Fund to pay bond principal and interest as they become due. Starting at the beginning of each fiscal year monthly payments of 1/5 of the next interest payment and 1/10 of the next principal payment.
3. To the Bond Reserve Fund to pay principal and interest if required payments to the Debt Service Fund have not been met. Monthly payments of 1/12 of 10 percent of [maximum debt service] [average debt service] on outstanding bonds until the balance therein is equal to [maximum debt service] [average debt service] on bonds outstanding. Interest income on invested funds in this fund shall be credited to the fund until the fund is at its required amount and thereafter may be credited to the Revenue Fund. If payments are made from the fund it shall be replenished in same fashion.
4. To the Depreciation Fund—to pay for extraordinary expenses or to pay for replacement of obsolete equipment. Monthly payments of 5 percent of gross revenues shall be made to this fund. In the event that the Debt Service Fund and the Bond Reserve do not have balances adequate to pay principal and interest as they become due monies in the Depreciation Fund shall be transferred to those funds in the amount of the deficiency.

5. To the Surplus Fund, monies in this fund may be used for improvements and extensions to the system, to call or purchase in the market, bonds or to make transfers to any of the above funds.

Additional Bond Clause (parity bonds)

1. All required payments must be current.
2. Net revenue in the last fiscal year [or as adjusted for rates currently in effect or for additional net revenue from new connections added since end of fiscal year or to be added from the projects to be financed, as estimated by consulting engineer] equal maximum debt service on bonds outstanding and to be issued together with estimated amount to be paid into Depreciation Reserve in succeeding year and prior year's reserve payment, if any.

Additional bonds may be issued to finance extensions and improvements to the system, or to refund any outstanding issues providing debt service in any future year is not increased as a result of such refunding. Junior lien bonds may be issued.

Rate Covenant

To fix rates and charges and to adjust from time to time as necessary to provide in each fiscal year operating revenues sufficient to pay O&M, debt service, and required payments into Depreciation and Bond Reserves.

Other Covenants

Proper operation of system, books and audits (audited reports to bondholders which describe earnings reports, balance sheet, number of connections, etc.), insurance as carried by similar enterprises.

* Halsey, Stuart & Co., Inc. Research Memo No. 35, April 1975.

Table 2. Comparative Statistics

City	Chicago	Los Angeles	Milwaukee
Moody Rating	A	Aa	Aaa
Water Supply	Lake Michigan (back door)	86 percent piped from 233 or more miles	Lake Michigan (back door)
Water Rates	Subject to approval of City Council	Subject to approval of City Council	Subject to aproval of State P.S.C.
Service Area	City and 74 Suburbs	City only	City and 9 Suburbs
Population	4,500,000	2,817,300	1,100,000
Residential*	1,285,714	804,940	314,285
Equivalent Connections Approx.			
Debt (incl. forthcoming sales)	$196,200,000	$288,890,000	$44,900,000
Debt per Connection	$153	$358	$143
Gross Plant	$568MM	$784MM	$147MM
Net Plant	$438MM	$547MM	$119MM
Debt—Percent of Gross Plant	34	37	30
Debt—Percent of Net Plant	44	53	37
Future Finance	$250-300MM	$250-300MM	—0—

* Estimates, based on population with 3.5 persons per household.

(*continued*)

Table 2. (continued)

BOND ORDINANCE SECURITY PROVISIONS

	Chicago (as recommended)	Los Angeles	Milwaukee
Bond Reserve	Max. d/s or Aver. d/s	none	Max. d/s
Deprec. Reserve (Federal)	Payments of 5 percent of of Gross over life of bonds	none	Payments of 2 percent of Gross over life of bonds
Flow of Funds	O & M D/S Bond Res Deprec. Res. Surplus (locked in)	O & M − D/S no priority — — Surplus—limited transfers out	O & M 73 percent D/S 25 percent* Inc. above 2 percent
Rate Covenant	100 percent of required amounts for all these cities**	?	none
Free Service	Only to City agencies in return for specified services		
Additional Bonds Test	Historical or pro forma future net rev. covers max. d/s plus add'l Deprec. pymt.	Historical 1/25x max. d/s plus 2.00x max. int.	Historical or pro forma 1.30x max. d/s

* This will be adjusted as necessary to ensure sufficient funds for debt service.
** See Note 1 and Minuses p. 4 #2.

Note 1. The Water Department has the biblical Egyptian Syndrome of fat years—lean years as a guide to cash for servicing debt. Under State law rates cannot be reduced while bonds are outstanding. Therefore if debt service were to continue till the final bond issue on a pattern of declining debt service (see schedule) it is felt that the surpluses would be unconscionable.

State of New Jersey*:

Notes to Financial Statements

Fund Accounting

The Governmental Accounting Standards Board in its Statement 1 entitled Authoritative Status of NCGA Pronouncements and AICPA Industry Audit Guide continued in force the National Council on Governmental Accounting's (NCGA) Statement 1. NCGA Statement 1 defines a fund as a fiscal and accounting entry with a self-balancing set of accounts recording cash and other financial resources together with all related liabilities and residual equities or balances, and changes therein, which are segregated for the purpose of carrying on specific activities or attaining certain objectives in accordance with special regulations, restrictions, or limitations. These statements reflect financial reporting practices in accordance with that definition.

Governmental Funds

General Fund. The General Fund is the fund into which all state revenues, not otherwise restricted by statute, are deposited and from which appropriations are made. The largest part of the total financial operations of the State is accounted for in the General Fund. Most revenues received from taxes and Federal sources and certain miscellaneous revenue items are recorded in the General Fund. The appropriations act enacted by the Legislature provides the basic frame work for the operation of the General Fund.

Special Revenue Funds. Special Revenue Funds are used to account for the proceeds of specific revenue sources (other than special assessments, expendable trusts, or for major capital projects) that are legally restricted to expenditure for specified purposes.

Debt Service Fund. The Debt Service Fund accounts for the accumulation of resources for, and the payment of, general long-term debt principal and interest. Amounts provided by the General Fund are deposited with banks that serve as paying agents.

Capital Projects Funds. The Capital Projects Funds are used to account for financial resources to be used for the acquisition or construction of major capital facilities for state use. Funds granted to other units of government for facilities are not classified as Capital Projects Funds and are included as expenditures of Special Revenue Funds. The state Land Acquisition and Development Fund, state Recreation and Conservation Land Acquisition Fund (1971), and state Recreation and Conservation Land Acquisition and Development Fund (1974) which have been classified as Special Revenue Funds, and the Transportation Rehabilitation and Improvement Fund, which is classified as a Capital Projects Fund, include funds both for capital facilities for state use and for grants to other units of government.

Basis of Accounting

Basis of accounting refers to when revenues and expenditures or expenses are recognized in the accounts and reported in the financial statements. Basis of accounting relates to the timing of the measurements made regardless of the measurement focus applied.

The General Fund, Special Revenue Funds, Debt Service Funds, Capital Projects Funds, Expendable Trust Funds, and Agency Funds are accounted for using the modified accrual basis of accounting. Under this basis, revenues are recognized in the accounting period in which they become susceptible to accrual—that is, when they become both measurable and available to finance expenditures of the fiscal period. Available means collectible within the current period or soon enough thereafter to be used to pay liabilities of the current period. Those revenues which are considered to be susceptible to accrual include amounts received by the Treasury during the month of July that were earned as of June 30 and in the hands of receiving agents. In addition, accruals include amounts earned as of June 30 for Investment Earnings, Federal Revenues, and items billed as of June 30 but received subsequent to July 31.

Pension and non-expendable Trust Funds are accounted for on an accrual basis of accounting.

Revenues that are determined not to be susceptible to accrual because they either are not available soon enough to pay liabilities of the current period or are not objectively measurable include various fees and self-assessed taxes.

Refunds of revenue applicable to June 30 but anticipated to be paid subsequently are recorded as liabilities and reductions of revenue when they are measurable and their validity seems certain.

Appropriations are authorized by an act of the Legislature for expenditure during the fiscal year and for a period of one month thereafter. Expenditures are recorded on an accrual basis when the related liability is incurred. Modifications to the accrual basis of accounting include:

a. Disbursements for prepaid expenses, inventory items, and fixed assets are recorded as expenditures when incurred.
b. Accumulated unpaid vacation and sick pay are not accrued. Expenditures for principal and interest on general obligation long-term debt are recognized as expenditures when due.

Encumbrances represented by purchase orders and contracts are recorded and reported as reservations of fund balance since they do not constitute expenditures or liabilities.

The General Long-Term Obligations Account Group is not a fund. An account group is concerned only with the measurement of financial position and does not involve measurement of results of operations.

STATE OF NEW JERSEY
COMBINED BALANCE SHEET
JUNE 30, 1986

	Governmental Fund Types			
	General Fund	Special Revenue Fund	Debt Service Fund	Capital Projects Funds
Assets				
Cash and cash equivalents	$ 18,158,884	$ 3,601,338	$6,801,122	$180,781
Investments	52,793,252	163,207,008	—	—
Receivables, net of allowances for uncollectibles				
Federal government	340,880,225	114,361	—	37,136,396
Departmental accounts	649,382,598	136,848,582	—	23,820,903
Loans	1,500,000	74,044,798	—	—
Mortgages	—	—	—	—
Other	—	34,430,617	—	1,437,194
Fixed Assets, Net				
Other Assets				
Due from other funds	1,724,904,270	508,172,278	—	185,937,817
Due from intergovernmental agencies	—	—	—	—
Advances to other funds	4,376,736	—	—	—
Deferred charges	2,940,000	846,894	—	—

(continued)

State of New Jersey Combined Balance Sheet *(continued)*

	Governmental Fund Types			
	General Fund	Special Revenue Fund	Debt Service Fund	Capital Projects Funds
Assets (cont'd)				
Amount to be provided for:				
Retirement of bonds	$ —	$ —	$ —	$ —
Payment of capital leases	—	—	—	—
Other	—	10,796	—	—
Total assets	$2,794,935,965	$921,276,672	$6,801,122	$248,513,091
Liabilities and Fund Balances				
Liabilities				
Accounts payable and accured expenses	$ 782,211,655	$200,455,705	$ —	$ 48,101,091
Deferred revenue	43,009,445	9,993	—	6,400,717
Due to other funds	186,089,602	118,179,023	—	—
Due to intergovernmental agencies	—	—	—	—
Advances from other funds	4,006,199	3,520,453	—	—
Other	59,781,263	11,576,873	—	—
Matured interest payable	—	—	3,822,122	—
Matured bonds payable	—	—	2,979,000	—
Deferred compensation payable	—	—	—	—
General obligation bonds payable	—	—	—	—
Revenue bonds payable	—	—	—	—
Notes payable	—	—	—	—
Capital leases payable	—	—	—	—
Total liabilities	1,075,098,164	333,742,047	6,801,122	116,254,018
Fund Balances				
Cost of investment in facilities	—	—	—	—
Reserved for:				
Encumbrances	391,418,930	156,439,670	—	141,474,808
Higher education programs	—	—	—	—
Pension benefits	—	—	—	—
Other	62,895,920	83,005,944	—	—
Unreserved:				
Designated for continuing appropriations	821,020,636	622,032,368	—	191,840,505
Undesignated	444,502,315	(273,943,357)	—	(201,056,240)
Total fund balances	1,719,837,801	587,534,625	—	132,259,073
Total liabilities and fund balances	$2,794,935,965	$921,276,672	$6,801,122	$248,513,091

STATE OF NEW JERSEY
COMBINED STATEMENT OF REVENUES, EXPENDITURES AND CHANGES IN FUND BALANCES
ALL GOVERNMENT FUND TYPES
FOR THE FISCAL YEAR ENDED JUNE 30, 1986

| | *Governmental Fund Types* | | | |
	General Fund	*Special Revenue Fund*	*Debt Service Fund*	*Capital Projects Funds*
Revenues				
Taxes	$5,730,443,915	$2,255,148,090	$ —	$ —
Federal and other grants	2,248,377,849	7,885,214	—	206,034,346
Licenses and fees	440,824,130	37,900,429	—	133,899,000
Services and assessments	648,954,570	33,689,074	—	14,018,336
Investment earnings	52,013,394	44,181,763	—	14,018,336
Contributions	—	—	—	—
Other	66,548,912	1,009,816,235	—	886,559
Total revenues	9,187,162,770	3,388,621,768	—	354,838,259
Other Increases				
Transfers from other funds	539,627,270	27,307,880	295,832,584	—
Proceeds from sale of bonds	—	53,600,000	—	119,000,000
Other	31,544	14,994,373	—	824,706
Total other increases	539,658,814	95,902,253	295,832,584	119,824,706
Total revenues and other increases	9,726,821,584	3,484,524,021	295,832,584	474,662,965
Expenditures				
Public safety and criminal justice	661,151,429	40,721,814	—	43,661,680
Physical and mental health	1,527,504,936	4,410,208	—	710,303
Educational, cultural and intellectual development	2,577,729,243	1,658,090,678	—	942,434
Community development and environmental management	342,755,266	86,574,285	—	17,178,374
Economic planning, development and security	1,390,577,617	72,306,235	—	—
Trasnportation programs	621,341,320	3,255,965	—	391,227,232
Government direction, management and control	1,826,551,982	455,960,320	—	—
Special government services	80,608,242	585,047,659	—	—
Debt service:				
Principal	—	—	136,705,000	—
Interest	—	—	159,127,584	—
Total expenditures	9,028,220,035	2,948,367,164	295,832,584	453,720,023

(continued)

State of New Jersey Combined Statement of
Revenues, Expenditures and Changes in Fund Balances *(continued)*

	Governmental Fund Types			
	General Fund	Special Revenue Fund	Debt Service Fund	Capital Projects Funds
Other Decreases				
Transfers to other funds	$ 440,166,782	$ 483,128,895	$ —	$ 14,537,337
Other	829,047	8,508,135	—	607,948
Total other decreases	440,995,829	491,637,030	—	15,145,285
Total expenditures and other decreases	9,469,215,864	3,440,004,194	295,832,584	468,865,308
Net increase (decrease) in fund balances for the year	257,605,720	44,529,827	—	5,797,657
Fund balances—July 1, 1985	1,462,232,081	543,014,798	—	126,461,416
Fund balances—June 30, 1986	$1,719,837,801	$ 587,524,625	$ —	$132,259,073

The accompanying notes (not shown) are an integral part of the financial statements.

REVENUES AND EXPENDITURES—CASH BASIS

The following table sets forth the composition of revenues for the General Fund, the Property Tax Relief Fund, the Gubernatorial Elections Fund, the Casino Control Fund, and the Casino Revenue Fund for fiscal years 1983 through 1986, inclusive.

Revenues (Millions)

	Fiscal Year Ended December 31			
	1983	1984	1985	1986
General Fund:				
Sales tax	$1,582.3	$1,974.4	$2,260.8	$2,529.1
Motor fuels tax	282.3	294.1	296.2	318.2
Corporation taxes	737.3	891.1	976.3	996.1
Motor vehicle fees	280.3	288.8	317.9	333.4
Cigarette tax	214.5	217.2	216.6	214.2
Other major taxes	617.2	659.6	693.4	748.0
Miscellaneous taxes, fees and revenues	578.3	568.2	658.0	724.4
Lottery fund	295.0	359.8	390.6	419.4
Other transfers	97.2	100.1	69.3	76.0
Total general fund	4,684.4	5,353.3	5,879.1	6,358.8

(continued)

Revenues (Millions) *(continued)*

	Fiscal Year Ended December 31			
	1983	*1984*	*1985*	*1986*
Property Tax Relief Fund:				
Gross income tax	$1,391.6	$1,732.2	$1,935.2	$2,052.6
Gubernatorial Elections fund	1.5	1.4	1.7	1.7
Casino control fund	34.9	40.5	48.4	34.8
Casino revenue fund	130.6	152.8	166.6	185.6
Total	$6,243.0	$7,280.2	$8,031.0	$8,633.5

Source: State of New Jersey Department of Treasury, Division of Budget and Accounting.

Expenditures (Millions)

	Fiscal Year Ended June 30			
	1983	*1984*	*1985*	*1986*
General Fund:				
Legislative branch	$ 21.3	$ 24.5	$ 29.4	$ 45.6
Chief Executive's office	2.9	4.0	4.5	4.2
Department of:				
Agriculture	20.7	20.4	21.4	21.7
Banking	4.2	4.3	4.6	4.9
Civil service	12.7	13./6	16.6	16.8
Commerce and economic				
development	8.1	10.0	22.8	43.2
Community affairs	186.1	202.3	207.6	262.3
Corrections	217.9	246.7	293.5	338.2
Defense	12.1	14.2	15.4	16.8
Education	1,218.1	1,182.8	1,136.2	1,352.6
Energy (Public Utilities)	21.9	24.6	31.1	27.3
Environmental protection	169.1	199.8	224.6	279.6
Health	96.7	112.5	116.4	134.2
Higher education	671.1	714.5	794.1	887.0
Human services	2,273.8	2,435.6	2,638.9	2,877.0
Insurance	5.8	6.4	9.0	11.7
Labor	189.8	244.7	273.2	326.1
Law and public safety	200.8	225.4	259.6	290.9
Public advocate	29.2	34.4	36.9	39.6
State	14.3	18.2	24.6	32.6
Transportation	491.5	581.3	769.7	649.7
Treasury	944.3	1,029.7	1,160.5	1,246.5
Miscellaneous executive commission	2.8	2.6	3.0	3.8
Inter-department accounts	422.8	506.9	566.2	617.4
Judicial branch	58.2	64.6	80.6	95.0
Total general fund	$7,296.2	$7,924.0	$ 8,740.0	$ 9,624.7

(continued)

Expenditures (Millions) *(continued)*

	Fiscal Year Ended June 30			
	1983	*1984*	*1985*	*1986*
Property Tax Relief Fund:				
Education	$1,048.4	$1,268.7	$ 1,552.5	$ 1,648.7
Treasury	373.6	371.2	380.3	422.7
Total property relief fund	$1,422.0	$1,639.9	$ 1,932.8	$ 2,071.4
Gubernatorial Elections Fund	$ —	$ —	$ 3.7	$ 2.8
Casino Control Fund:				
Law and public safety	$ 20.2	$ 21.9	$ 24.8	$ 26.4
Treasury	13.6	14.9	17.1	18.8
Total casino control fund	$ 33.8	$ 36.8	$ 41.9	$ 45.2
Casino Revenue Fund:				
Community affairs	$ —	$ 1.3	$ 1.6	$ 6.1
Human services	71.1	84.7	100.3	129.5
Transportation	—	3.0	10.0	11.4
Treasury	45.2	50.9	50.7	17.9
Total casino revenue fund	$ 116.3	$ 139.9	$ 162.6	$ 164.9
Total expenditures	$8,868.3	$9,740.6	$10,881.4	$11,909.0

* *Source:* State of New Jersey Department of Treasury, Division of Budget and Accounting.

Index